CHICAGO LIVES

MEN AND WOMEN WHO SHAPED OUR CITY

Chicago Tribune

EDITED BY **JAMES JANEGA**

TRIUMPH
BOOKS
CHICAGO

Library of Congress Cataloging-in-Publication Data

Chicago lives : men and women who shaped our city / James Janega [editor].
        p. cm.
    ISBN-13: 978-1-57243-821-7 (pbk.)
    ISBN-10: 1-57243-821-5 (pbk.)
    1. Chicago (Ill.)—Biography. I. Janega, James.

F548.25.C558 2005
977.3'11—dc22

                                                                    2005052937

This book is available in quantity at special discounts for your group or organization. For further information, contact:

Triumph Books
542 S. Dearborn St.
Suite 750
Chicago, IL 60605
(312) 939-3330
Fax (312) 663-3557

Printed in U.S.A.
ISBN-13: 978-1-57243-821-7
ISBN-10: 1-57243-821-5
Design by Chris Mulligan
Cover design by Tony Majeri, Chuck Burke
All photographs courtesy of the Chicago Tribune

Contents

Introduction

Had it not been for a serendipitous letter passed between her neighbors, Zofia Kuklo might have been dismissed as just another fading, elderly widow, and it would have been a crime.

She died on the Northwest Side as the twentieth century drew to a close, a quiet, churchgoing woman who'd become part of the Chicago landscape. Almost as secretive as she'd been in Poland during World War II, she blended into the immigrant neighborhood she lived in so completely that nobody in Chicago knew she'd once rescued more than a dozen Jews from the Holocaust.

For years, she hid them in her barn. Perhaps from the long habit of keeping silent among Nazis, Mrs. Kuklo said little after the war, and even less after immigrating to the United States twenty years before her death in January 2001.

Word reached her Chicago neighbors after a letter from one of the Holocaust survivors helped get Kuklo's name memorialized in Israel's Yad Vashem Holocaust Memorial in 1994.

When she was recognized, her exploits were a staggering revelation for local Polish and Jewish groups, for whom Kuklo became an instant icon. Her story was also one of those obituary-section discoveries for readers that shows the fine line that sometimes separates a touching account from total obscurity.

On street corners and in office towers, in barrooms and in back rooms, the history of Chicago in the twentieth century was played out in the lives of its residents. As is often the case with history, the full impact of those lives wasn't known until they were gone.

At the *Chicago Tribune*'s obituary desk, the chances to tell the stories came by the dozens each day. Possibilities were circled in death notices and waited behind the blinking red lights of telephone messages. By the next day, readers with their morning coffee would learn about neighbors they'd long been fascinated with or who'd slipped their attention. The obituaries are one of the best-read sections of the paper.

Failing to remember Kuklo clearly would have been a grievous omission, but her clandestine accomplishments made hers an exceptional case. Imagine the stirring tales, the fascinating events and accomplishments in ordinary lives that go untold because nobody thinks to present them as noteworthy.

We don't even have to imagine.

A paid death notice appeared in the *Chicago Tribune* on August 8, 2000, as follows:

Margaret M. Mullane, née Hopkins, beloved wife of the late John P. Mullane; loving mother of

Jack (Gerry), James (Mary), Philip (Susan), and Robert Mullane; cherished grandmother of Sean, Steve, Tricia, Chrissy, Jack, Kiley, and Lucy; fond great-grandmother of Joseph and Colson. Visitation Wednesday, 4:00 to 9:00 PM. Funeral Thursday, 9:45 AM. From Andrew J. McGann & Son Funeral Home, 10727 South Pulaski Road, to St. Germaine Church for Mass at 10:30 AM. Interment St. Mary Cemetery. In lieu of flowers, donations to the American Cancer Society would be appreciated.

The pen that would have circled that death notice and made it a news obituary assignment passed by. There are a lot of "beloved wives" in the world. But Mullane's family was lying. Her son James later explained why: "We didn't lie because we were ashamed of my mother's profession. It was simply that we were advised, 'Unless she is a doctor or a lawyer or teacher, etc., most put down "housewife."' Being in the fog of grief, we went along."

As it turned out, Mullane—better known as Peggy—was a waitress, working for the past twenty years at Sonny's Inn, where the Illinois Central tracks begin in the South Chicago neighborhood. She opened the restaurant every morning at 5:30 for regular commuters, even though the place wasn't supposed to open until 6:00. For countless people each working day for twenty years, she provided the first smile and first cup of coffee of the day. With the change they left her, Mullane put her four sons through college.

Titans used to dominate the obituary page just as much as they did society columns and news sections. Women, to a large extent, are recent appearances. And more and more often, room is being made for "regular" people.

As it turns out, their stories are not so ordinary, and a lot of the best ones are in this book.

What makes a good obituary?

The best ones tell charming stories that lend a little magic, a little wonder to everyday life. One needn't be a titan to qualify.

Take Donald Luchene, a Blue Island man who worked as a technician at St. Francis Hospital and Health Center and, incidentally, collected more than three thousand flamingo knickknacks, dressed in flamingo motifs, kept a flock of plastic flamingos in his front yard, and opened his mail with a flamingo letter opener.

He gathered flamingos fashioned from glass, wood, papier-mâché, concrete, and plastic. He wore a flamingo earring and hung a flamingo from his rearview mirror. Lots of folks in Blue Island knew who the "Flamingo Man" was when the topic came up in conversation.

In a world that embraces the rational first, his hobby was a pleasant reminder that not everything has to make perfect sense. In a way, his obituary made us happy to know that somebody, somewhere in the world, did what Luchene did—because if he could do that, anything is possible, no matter what the rational world says.

Luchene's whimsy aside, the obituaries also offer sober reflection, a degree of comfort that comes from encouraging the longer view.

How else to take the obituary of Carl P. Miller Sr., 100, who spent his estimable lifetime discrediting modern medical advice against eating red meat, drinking booze, or working backbreaking days of physical labor?

Other centenarians attribute their longevity to temperance and moderation, but Miller ate and drank what he wanted. His mother was a good cook, he told his family, and he ate a lot of red meat and potatoes over 100 years.

He also had a soft spot for Scotch old-fashioneds and drank them without fail every Saturday until the week before his death in April 2000.

He saw Chicago move from kerosene to gas lighting to electricity, remembered when indoor running water became widespread, and experienced the invention of such things as radio and television.

As in Kuklo's instance, the obituary section can remind us of terrible truths that the world would rather forget and the costs they exacted on people. (Kuklo, for instance, could not discuss her encounters with the Nazis without trembling. Her family said she would sometimes cry for days afterward.)

Very often, we newspaper writers highlight how badly society can behave. If we focus on individual lives at all, we celebrate only the people who amass the grandest of grand achievements.

Most people don't fit into either category. The majority of everyday life falls somewhere in between.

Will all the people in the obituary section—the nontitans—be remembered by historians at the end of the twenty-first century? Ten years from now?

Probably not, beyond the memories of their families. But no neighborhood, no industry, no county fairground, no skyline, no coffee shop would have been complete without them, and likely, quite a few lives wouldn't have been either.

There will always be room for giants on the obituary pages.

But some of the best stories are the small ones. Enjoy.

—James Janega
Chicago Tribune obituary reporter

SECTION

I

Who We Thought We Knew

There are people we see every day and think we know well enough, or names we tie to achievements, assuming we are familiar with all that matters. But a thrill comes from moving beyond our assumptions.

If we can reconsider the parking lot attendant we thought we had pegged, we can revisit the lawyers and labor leaders for the same sense of surprise. We can look at a city skyline and see the silhouette of its creators. We can look at a warm and inviting neighborhood street and recognize not a play of light, but the far more subtle work of the person who designed it.

SUNDAY, MARCH 4, 2001

Earnest Harris, Forty-Eight;
Beloved Valet Exuded Joy, Toted a Secret
By Kirsten Scharnberg, *Tribune* Staff Reporter

In two grubby, bulging shopping bags Ernie Harris carried a mystery.

For more than thirty years, the parking garage attendant lugged the bags from his humble house in the south suburbs to the bus stop to the succession of city buses that transported him five days a week to the North Lake Shore Drive high-rise where he parked Mercedes-Benzes and Jaguars and Volkswagen Passats as happily as if he owned them himself.

The bags would be from Marshall Field's or Filene's Basement or any number of little stores without household names, and Harris would carry them until the plastic wore out before transferring the bulky contents—though it seems nobody in the building knew what those contents were—into two new bags that would be toted until they, too, started to fall apart.

Up until February 23, the day Harris was murdered and the first day he ever failed to show up for work as scheduled, the gaunt, disheveled man always arrived at the Hawthorne House apartment building early, up to three hours before his 3:00 to 11:00 PM shift. He almost always stayed late, sometimes sleeping in the garage overnight, hunched in a padded old chair next to his plastic bags.

"He was this building's unofficial ambassador," said Hawthorne House owner Scott Ross, "and that was something he took upon himself and took more seriously than you can even imagine."

In an impersonal high-rise in an intimidating city where people can go for weeks without bumping into someone they know on the streets, there was something comforting and familial about walking out to the garage each day to be greeted by a boisterous parking attendant who remembered not only your name, but your husband's name and your children's names and your visitors' names. Ask any of the thousands of people who have lived in the 400-apartment high-rise over the years, and they'll tell you Harris considered chitchatting with them as much a part of his job as parking their cars.

"Beautiful day, beautiful day," he would mutter, day in and day out, sometimes to no one in particular, like a broken record completely oblivious to skin-stinging sleet or ten inches of snow or bitter Chicago cold.

"One more day," he reminded residents every Thursday as they got into their cars and headed off to work. "One more day till your weekend."

And on Fridays, without fail: "TGIF, folks, TGIF."

Make no mistake, forty-eight-year-old Earnest H. Harris was an eccentric. Even after a shower was installed for his use, he didn't often take advantage of it and usually left a strong reminder of his presence in any car he had just parked or retrieved. Unlike the rest of the parking attendants, his white shirt was never crisply starched or tucked in, his black bow tie was always slightly askew, and his hair was a fright of unruly curls.

The Pine Bluff, Arkansas, native seemed to have a near-photographic memory and a keen interest in other people's business, and it wasn't uncommon for him to raise an eyebrow in knowing disapproval if a resident pulled into the garage with someone who wasn't that person's spouse or steady sweetheart.

"He was the kindest, goofiest, most happy-go-lucky person I've ever met," said Caryl Dillon, who has lived in the building at 3450 North Lake Shore Drive for more than a year. "He knew everyone by name, and I mean everyone. The first day I parked in that garage just to look at an apartment here, he immediately said, 'Hi. I'm Ernie. What's your name?' I told him my name and said I was only considering renting an apartment here, and he said, 'Well, we sure would love to have you join us.' And then, when I moved in almost a month later, he walked right up to me and said, 'Hi Caryl. You took the apartment.'"

So because Harris treated them differently, the residents treated him differently right back. When they went out to eat, they brought him either their leftovers or a carry-out dinner they'd ordered just for him.

They tipped him at least a couple times a week, even though they only contributed to a holiday-tip fund for the rest of the guys who worked in the garage. If people saw Harris shopping with his family somewhere in Chicago, they'd shout, "Hey, Ernie," across the department store.

When Lidia Wolin's son moved into the building during college, the overprotective mother pulled Harris aside and asked him to watch out for her boy and to call her if anything seemed amiss.

"Don't worry, Miss Lidia," he'd say when he saw her. "Everything's going just fine."

Knowing all this, understanding just who Ernie Harris was and how a whole apartment building came to love him, will explain why everyone noticed when he didn't show up for work February 23. He was scheduled for 3:00 PM, but since Harris usually came early, the guys in the garage were starting to worry by about 1:30.

"Where's Ernie?" countless people asked when they got home from work in the afternoon. By then it was nearly 5:30, and Francisco Lerma, another parking attendant who had come to think of Harris as a brother, didn't know what to tell them; he felt sick to his stomach.

About 5:35, the phone in the garage rang, and Lerma answered it.

"Ernie won't be coming in," Harris' wife, Barbara, told him.

"Why not?" Lerma asked.

"He's dead."

Still too shocked to even cry while telling the story, Barbara Harris relayed to the Hawthorne House parking garage what the Chicago police officers had just told her:

Harris, who just a month before had purchased a 1987 Hyundai for about $600 so he didn't have to take the nearly two-hour bus ride to work, had been at a stop sign in the 2000 block of West Sixty-fifth Street.

He was headed to work after dropping off a nephew he had been babysitting when two young men approached his car, threw open both front doors, and shot him once in the face. The young men ran away, not even bothering to take Harris' wallet or steal the car, after a bunch of children outside a nearby public school started screaming for help. Harris died immediately, his face on the street's bloody pavement, his feet still in the car. Fewer than two blocks away in the high-crime neighborhood, a hand-painted sign tacked to a tree beseeched, "Stop the black-on-black violence. It's got to stop."

Last week, two fifteen-year-olds, Rasson Davis and Gregory Brown, were charged as adults with first-degree murder and aggravated vehicular hijacking on Wednesday morning. Judge Neil Linehan set bond at $500,000 for Brown, who is accused of being the gunman, and $400,000 for Davis after Assistant State's Attorney Maureen Lynch told the judge that one of the two told police they wanted Harris' car for a planned drive-by shooting.

After word of the killing made its way to the high-rise, the guys in the parking garage handed a printed announcement to residents as they pulled into the garage that night. "It is with deep regret and extraordinary sadness," the one-paragraph statement began. "Earnest was murdered Friday afternoon . . ."

The garage manager, Steve Barakat, removed Harris' Polaroid picture from the center of a bulletin board introducing all the parking attendants. He blew the picture up—in it, Harris' shirt is wrinkled and untucked, his hair is jutting in a dozen directions, his bow tie is hopelessly crooked. Barakat posted the photo near the garage entrance next to a sign that reads, "Take a minute to ponder the silence of our garage." On the garage's work schedule, which hung nearby, five words were typed into the five days Harris was supposed to work the following week: "He will not be forgotten."

Within hours, the building's residents had created a makeshift memorial of flowers and cards in Hawthorne House's lobby. "Thank you, God, for sharing Ernie with us," one card read.

Two days later, on Sunday night, Barbara Harris and the couple's son, Earnest Jr., drove from their Markham home to the forty-story building where Harris had parked cars all those years. Wife and son had simply planned on cleaning out Harris' locker—it turned out he kept next to nothing in it, choosing instead to keep his two bags near the sturdy, wooden chair where he always sat between parking cars—but they ended up staying at Hawthorne House apartments for hours. Hundreds of residents lined up in the building's comfortable lobby, wanting to offer their condolences and kind words.

Since then, the building's residents have established a trust fund they hope will pay the remainder of Earnest Jr.'s college education. The twenty-year-old is a freshman at Kishwaukee College in DeKalb.

Harris also has a second son, Robert Jackson, who is twenty-seven and lives in Chicago.

It was while the residents chatted with Harris' wife and youngest son on Sunday night that someone finally asked the question. What about those bags? What had been in them all these years?

Everyone had their guesses: maybe Harris was rich, and the bags were filled with money. Maybe he really had been homeless and they were filled with his only possessions.

Barbara Harris, a quiet woman who calls Ernie "the best husband and father a woman could ask for," and Earnest Jr., an effusive young man who has his father's quick smile, got a kick out of the questions.

Those plastic bags—and several more just like them out in the family's garage—had never been a mystery to this family who knew how much Earnest Harris loved his job and the people he met there.

The bags were filled with cards and letters from the hundreds of Hawthorne House residents who had taken time over the years to jot down a heartfelt thank-you to the bedraggled little man who parked their cars and never failed to remind them to have a "beautiful day, beautiful day."

SECTION

II

Coming to Chicago

In a city of immigrants, in a country of immigrants, new-comers to Chicago have forged not only an American metropolis, but have reached over oceans to change the lands they left.

Chicago owes its soul to Poles, and to Mexicans, to African American migrants from the American South, to the Swedes and Puerto Ricans and Czechs, and waves still arriving to chart its future.

TUESDAY, JANUARY 25, 2000

Wanda Szygowski, Eighty-Nine; Welcomed Poles

By James Janega, *Tribune* Staff Reporter

Once a month for more than forty years, Wanda Szygowski would open her house to Poles who had recently arrived in Chicago.

Szygowski, a consummate entertainer, was as versed in Polish politics and culture as she was in the traditional Polish dishes she served.

So formally did Szygowski, eighty-nine, practice the customs of her homeland that it was easy to forget she and her husband, a World War II–era Polish diplomat, were no longer officials. They were stranded here when communists took over their country in 1945.

Szygowski, who spent the next twenty-five years working for Montgomery Ward & Co. but never relinquished her social position as the wife of Poland's former consul general to Chicago, died Sunday, January 23, in Northwestern Memorial Hospital of complications from a stroke.

For years, she traveled with her husband, Julius, on diplomatic trips to Warsaw, New York, Winnipeg, and Chicago, often hosting visiting Eastern European royalty on their tours of the West.

But when her husband was forced to relinquish the Chicago consulate to Poland's communist regime, Szygowski maintained her connections with expatriate Poles here, even as she became an American citizen and wrote the index for the Montgomery Ward catalog.

She and her husband moved to a house in Rogers Park, holding a prominent position among the Polish nationals in the city, which is said to have the largest concentration of Poles outside Poland.

Szygowski discussed Polish and national politics over card games with friends and listened to chamber music written by Polish composers. She hung Polish tapestries on her walls.

"It was such a strong part of her," said her granddaughter, Margaret Newell. "In Chicago, she could keep her Polishness very much alive."

Even after her husband became a banker and assumed a role in Poland's government-in-exile, Szygowski zealously maintained their cultural traditions, such as the monthly receptions she and her husband hosted for new Polish immigrants, a form of hospitality said to have been started by Polish royalty.

And she was among the thousands of Polish citizens living in the Midwest who stood under cloudy Chicago skies in 1989 to vote in the Polish election that returned a noncommunist government to their homeland.

"They were thrilled. I think they felt like they had come full circle," Newell said.

In addition to her granddaughter and husband, Szygowski is survived by a son, Mathew; four other granddaughters; four grandsons; nine great-grandsons; and nine great-granddaughters.

WEDNESDAY, DECEMBER 6, 2000

Nora E. Olivares, Fifty-Two; Activist for Latinos

By James Janega, *Tribune* Staff Reporter

Nora Elia Villarreal de Olivares, fifty-two, a volunteer at Queen of Angels Parish in the Lincoln Square neighborhood, sought to build bridges between white and Latino cultures, to strengthen families, and to help Latino immigrants become American citizens.

"She was a leader to both language communities," said Rev. William O'Brien, pastor of the Catholic church. "She was an extremely dedicated person, a person who was concerned about blending people."

Olivares died of a heart attack Sunday, December 3, in Ravenswood Hospital.

She was a common sight at parish activities, from school board meetings— she was the first Hispanic member—to mass, for which she coordinated bilingual liturgies.

During parish dinners, she headed food preparation and ensured that the kitchen workers were as multicultural as the hot dogs and tortillas they dished out.

When young couples wanted to get married in the parish, many first met with Olivares and her husband, Juan, for advice on how to stay married.

Born Nora Villarreal in Nueva Rosita, Coahuila, Mexico, she moved to Chicago as a young girl.

She attended the former Loop College, now Harold Washington College, where she founded several Hispanic organizations, and later went to work as a counselor at a private school. She left the job when her health deteriorated in 1986.

"She looked so meek, so frail, and yet she could probably go up to Mayor Daley and say this is what we need and not be shy about it," said her friend Cristina Ruiz, who added that Olivares was a powerhouse when it came to making connections work.

She and her husband joined Queen of Angels in the late 1970s as the parish was adapting to the changing neighborhood around it.

Olivares was the first director of immigration and citizenship efforts at Queen of Angels, and she also served on the parish school board committee that gives financial aid to pupils.

And as she worked in the church and its school to make them more inclusive, she opened her home for parish meetings and people in need. "She was like the answer to everyone's prayer in a new place. They knew that she would help; she would receive them with open arms and go totally out of her way to make things easier for them," her friend said. "She knew what it was like to struggle, and she wanted to do everything in her power to help the underprivileged."

Olivares is survived by her husband, Juan; a daughter, Nely; her mother, Minerva Villarreal; a brother, Emigdio Villarreal; and two sisters, Ruth Lara and Gloria Villarreal.

SATURDAY, DECEMBER 23, 2000

Selma Jacobson, Ninety-Four; Swedish Booster

By James Janega, *Tribune* Staff Reporter

Selma Jacobson, the ninety-four-year-old grande dame of Chicago's Swedish American community, once the largest Swedish population in the world outside Stockholm, died Thursday, December 14, of natural causes in Our Lady of the Resurrection Medical Center.

Jacobson was instrumental in establishing the Swedish American Museum Center on North Clark Street and preserving writings on Swedish American life in the Swedish American Archives of Greater Chicago at North Park University.

"[The fact] that much of what Swedish America was, in its 'capital' city of Chicago, has not perished or been destroyed . . . can be attributed in no small measure to the diligent efforts and achievements of this remarkable woman," the *Swedish American Historical Quarterly* wrote in 1991.

For decades Jacobson gathered diaries and letters to early settlers, yellowed Swedish newspapers, and memorabilia of Chicago's Swedish pioneers.

"It's the most exciting thing I could ever do," she told the *Tribune* in 1965. "My desk is always full of papers, and my typewriter is always going."

Jacobson was the daughter of a Lutheran minister and a past president of the American Daughters of Sweden.

A home economics teacher in the Chicago public schools, Jacobson left her position at Bridge School for a sabbatical in Sweden in 1950.

After a year of study, she stayed in Sweden for two more years, teaching traditional crafts at an elementary school in Södertälje.

When she returned to Chicago, her home movies and craft demonstrations made her a popular figure at exhibits and lectures, while the antique dresses she kept in the attic of her Northwest Side home eventually became a periodic exhibit of their own.

She returned to Sweden to teach for another year in 1956 and was asked by Mayor Richard J. Daley to prepare a history of the Swedish in Chicago for a holiday folk fair.

Frustrated by a lack of material, she led the Swedish American Historical Society to establish its archives in 1968. She also lobbied for the creation of a Swedish American museum, which was established in 1976 through collaboration with the late Kurt Mathiasson and others.

That year, she also was instrumental in rededicating a statue of Carl von Linne, an eighteenth-century Swedish botanist, at its current site on the Midway in Hyde Park.

"At a very critical point in time, Selma had the foresight to collect materials and make sure they would be preserved and made accessible to the public and researchers," said Philip Anderson, president of the Swedish American Historical Society. "Without Selma, [none] of those things would have happened. It's the end of an era, I think."

Jacobson graduated from Chicago Normal Teachers College in 1926 and earned a master's degree from Northwestern University in 1943. She retired in the 1960s.

In the 1970s, she was named Swedish American of the year, an award given in Sweden by the Vasa Order, and received the Swedish American Historical Society's Carl Sandburg medal and the Commander of the North Star medal from the king of Sweden, among other awards.

Survivors include a sister, Hannah.

WEDNESDAY, JANUARY 10, 2001

Zofia Kuklo, Ninety-Four; Saved Polish Jews in World War II

By James Janega, *Tribune* Staff Reporter

Nothing about the woman who lived in a tiny Northwest Side bungalow indicated she was the heroine that Jewish and Polish organizations in Chicago believed her to be.

Zofia Kuklo was unassuming, walked to her nearby church as often as twice a day when she could walk, and preferred visiting with family members in her home to going out.

It wasn't until the last decade or so that she was recognized for harboring Jews on her farm in Poland during the Holocaust at great risk to herself and her family. But even after the accolades, she talked rarely about her experiences.

In the past few years, Kuklo, ninety-four, who died of kidney failure Sunday, January 7, in Our Lady of the Resurrection Medical Center, became a symbol for Polish and Jewish organizations in Chicago, while keeping a low public profile.

As Jews being used as slave labor were rounded up for extermination camps during World War II, Kuklo hid those who worked on her farm, once swearing at gunpoint that she was sheltering no one.

A dozen refugees were huddled in her barn at the time, as they would be for years, said Brian Abrahams, a volunteer at the Jewish United Fund of Metropolitan Chicago, who knew Kuklo.

"To be in her presence was an incredible thing," he said. "You had this sense of being in the presence of someone angelic, with inner peace and inner power."

Karen Popowski, executive director of the Polish American Association, called Kuklo a model of moral courage.

"She was a quiet, humble woman, as was her response" during the war, Popowski said. "Just to know that somebody living in a little bungalow on the Northwest Side was such a hero, it just was extraordinary."

To Kuklo, however, heroism was never involved. She said she still had

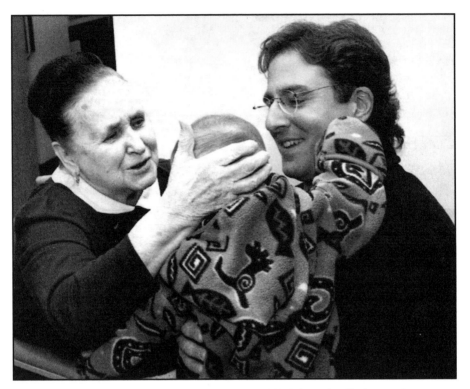

Zofia Kuklo (left) greets five-month-old Jacob Abrahams and his father, Brian Abrahams, at her Chicago home.

nightmares about the people she could not save, particularly about the few who died of disease while in her care.

"What I did, I did only because I couldn't live with the thought that someone else's death could be on my hands," Kuklo told the *Tribune* in 1995.

"They still come to me in the night, the people I couldn't save."

Her grandson, Andrzej Dajnowski, said her hands shook when she could be persuaded to talk about her experiences. Sometimes, he said, she would cry for days afterward.

Born Zofia Debkowska and raised in a small village in northeastern Poland, she was young when she married Franciszek Kuklo. They had a dairy farm when the Nazis invaded Poland, and the first Jews they took in were people they knew from town. Later, others came as the Kuklos risked being revealed by neighbors.

They continued farming after the war, and after the death of her husband in 1970, Kuklo frequently visited her daughter in the United States.

She moved to Chicago in the late 1980s, around the time one of her former Jewish charges, then living in Israel, nominated her for recognition in the Yad Vashem Holocaust Memorial.

Her contributions during the war were certified in Israel in 1994.

Since then, Kuklo has been honored by the Chicago-area branch of the Avenue of the Righteous, the Interfaith Coalition to Honor Polish Rescuers, and the New York–based Jewish Foundation for the Righteous, among others.

In addition to her grandson, she is survived by four daughters, Irena Srzedzinska, Halina Jasiak, Zdzislawa Dajnowska, and Henryka Gogolkiewicz; eleven grandchildren; and eight great-grandchildren.

WEDNESDAY, MAY 23, 2001

Rev. Vojtech Vit, Seventy-Eight; Priest Ran Newspaper, Helped Czech Immigrants

By James Janega, *Tribune* Staff Reporter

Rev. Vojtech Vit, seventy-eight, editor of the Chicago Czech-language religious newspaper *Hlas Naroda* and a Catholic priest who served the city's Czech immigrants, died Saturday, May 19, after collapsing in the rectory of Our Lady of the Mount Catholic Church in Cicero.

Hlas Naroda—which means "voice of the nation"—helped keep the Czech language alive in the city as it reported news from the communist country at a time when authorities there kept tight control of its press. The newspaper's audience was a community for which Father Vit had found jobs, schools, and apartments since arriving in Chicago in 1961.

"It was very important," said Rev. Dusan Hladik, a priest at Our Lady of the Mount. "Most of them didn't know English, but they came here and found somebody who spoke their language. They could feel some piece of their homeland in his person."

Father Vit also founded a Saturday-morning Czech-language school at the Czech Heritage Center in the Little Village neighborhood and prodded people to attend anticommunist rallies. For his work at *Hlas Naroda*, he recently received the Order of Merit from Czech president Vaclav Havel.

After finishing his secondary education in Prague, the Czech native entered the city's Brevnov monastery in 1944 and left two years later to study theology in Belgium. He remained there after the 1948 communist takeover in Czechoslovakia and was ordained a priest in 1951.

He taught in French as a missionary to the then-Belgian Congo in Africa from 1956 to 1961 and then came to Chicago. He initially was at St. Procopius Parish on the Southwest Side and worked extensively through the Czech Heritage Center from 1975 to 1983, focusing on helping Czech immigrants adjust.

"He was doing whatever he could to accommodate them very quickly," said Karel Chrobak, a former language teacher at the Czech Heritage Center. "He tried to be everything for everybody."

Vit started *Hlas Naroda* in 1975

and lived most recently at Our Lady of the Mount.

He is survived by two brothers, Antonin and Stanislav.

FRIDAY, MAY 25, 2001

Ibrahim Abu-Lughod, Seventy-Two; Key Voice in America for Palestinians
By James Janega, *Tribune* Staff Reporter

Ibrahim Abu-Lughod, seventy-two, was chairman of the political science department at Northwestern University in the 1980s and a key American voice in articulating the plight of Palestinians in the Middle East.

Abu-Lughod died in his home in Ramallah on the West Bank on Wednesday, May 23. He had been undergoing treatment for lung disease.

An urbane and dynamic man, Abu-Lughod was one of a small group of Palestinian academics in the United States to articulate the Palestinian cause in the 1960s, 1970s, and 1980s.

For years he was an American member of the PLO's Palestinian National Council. After the Oslo Peace Accords in 1993, he received broad acclaim for establishing a new curriculum for Palestinian schoolchildren once control of the schools was handed over to the Palestinian Authority.

"He was one of the two or three most important Palestinian voices in the United States for decades and was one of the first Arab American scholars to have a really serious effect on the way the Middle East is portrayed in political science and America," said Rashid Khalidi, director of the Center for International Studies at the University of Chicago.

"He helped to legitimize the idea that Arabs had something important to say."

Born in Jaffa before it became part of Israel, Abu-Lughod came to the United States in 1950 and helped found the Association of Arab American University Graduates in 1968, then an instrumental organization for providing an Arab voice in America.

After a distinguished academic and publishing career, he was one of two Palestinian academics—along with Columbia University's Edward Said—to meet with Secretary of State George P. Shultz in 1988 in the early steps of an attempted peace settlement between Israeli and Arab leaders.

Abu-Lughod earned a bachelor's degree in 1953 and a master's degree in 1954 from the University of Illinois in Urbana-Champaign. He received his Ph.D. in political science from Princeton University in 1957. He achieved early academic acclaim for his 1963 book *Arab Rediscovery of Europe: A Study in Cultural Encounters.* His reputation was cemented in 1970 when he published *The Arab-Israeli Confrontation of June, 1967,* a book reprinted in three languages.

From 1957 to 1961, he headed the social science division of the UNESCO education center in Egypt, and after several visiting lecturer posts, he arrived at Northwestern in 1967. He became a U.S. citizen in 1975.

Abu-Lughod was chairman of Northwestern's political science department from 1985 to 1988, but he left in 1992 to return to the West Bank, where he had since been a vice president and professor at Bir Zeit University.

While returning to his native land to help rebuild social institutions there, he insisted on independence from the governing Palestinian Authority.

Witty and charismatic, Abu-Lughod lured others to the Middle East, said Fouad Moughrabi, a political science professor on leave from the University of Tennessee in Chattanooga and the director of the Qattan Center for Education Research and Development in Ramallah.

"He was a very dynamic, very charming person," Moughrabi said. "He was a very good leader, and this is important in this part of the world, to have that kind of leadership quality."

Lughod is survived by his former wife, Janet Lippman; a son, Jawad; and three daughters, Lila, Mariam, and Deena.

FRIDAY, JULY 27, 2001

Dr. Alf H. Altern, Ninety-One; Chicago Dentist, Norwegian Civic Leader
By James Janega, *Tribune* Staff Reporter

Dr. Alf H. Altern, ninety-one, a Chicago dentist knighted by King Olav V of Norway in 1981 for the central role he played in the city's once-burgeoning Norwegian American community on the Northwest Side, died of congestive heart failure Friday, July 13, in the Norwood Park Home.

Altern, a respectful man given to formal dress, practiced dentistry on West Fullerton Avenue for sixty-two years; served on the board of directors at the Vesterheim Norwegian American Museum in Decorah, Iowa, since 1962; and was well known for his involvement in an array of Norwegian cultural groups in the Chicago area.

He began his dentistry practice in 1932, at a time when sixty thousand or so Norwegian immigrants lived in Humboldt Park and Logan Square, a concentration that gave the neighborhoods the largest Norwegian population in the world outside of Oslo and Bergen in Norway.

"Norwegians did very well in this country," Altern told the *Tribune* while being visited by King Harald of Norway, the son of King Olav V, in Chicago in 1995. "They were in demand here as laborers, electricians, and carpenters. But most of the ones who came here went to night school to learn English, and they all pushed their kids to do well in school."

Against that backdrop, Altern was a familiar figure. His business thrived within the heavily Norwegian neighborhood, and he served on the board of the local Fidelity Federal Savings Bank from the mid-1940s until 1995. He was active in the Normennenes Singing Society, the Sons of Norway, the Norwegian Pioneer Social Club, and, later, the Scandinavian Club in Arlington Heights.

Altern was born in Chicago, the son of recent Norwegian immigrants who settled on the Northwest Side. He graduated from Schurz High School and Crane Junior College before attending Northwestern University Dental School. He graduated in 1932 and set up shop on the Northwest Side. Except for interruptions to serve as a navy dentist during World War II and the Korean War, he had remained there since.

As a child, he met the former Ruth Amelia Chrystie through their mothers' shared interest in traditional Scandinavian embroidery. They married in 1942, and his wife died in 1989.

Janet Pultz, executive director of the Vesterheim Museum, called Altern significant among Chicago's Norwegian community because of the longevity of his practice within it and for the link he continued to provide to an era when Chicago was a focal point for Norwegian culture.

"He was very active in promoting the preserving of Norwegian heritage," Pultz said. "He was one of the originals here, a great supporter of all things Norwegian."

Because of his active involvement in Norwegian culture in Chicago—from hosting visiting diplomats (and doing their dental work) to serving as a conduit of artifacts and information to the Vesterheim Museum in Iowa— Altern was appointed to the Royal Order of St. Olav by the late King Olav V of Norway.

Since retiring in 1995, Altern resided in the Norwood Park Home, where he served on the board of directors for twenty years.

Altern is survived by two daughters, Norma Altern Smith and Beverly Trusdell, and three grandsons.

TUESDAY, AUGUST 14, 2001

Julius B. Szygowski, 105;
Anticommunist Diplomat Represented Poles in Exile
By James Janega, *Tribune* Staff Reporter

Julius B. Szygowski, 105, who represented the government of Poland in Chicago before World War II and its democratic government-in-exile once the communists rose to power after the war, died Sunday, August 12, in St. Francis Hospital, Evanston, where he had been hospitalized for pneumonia.

Szygowski was a cultured and romantic figure who never recognized

Poland's communist government and worked to collect and preserve the papers of the country's former leadership after the 1945 communist takeover.

During the 1950s and 1960s, he corresponded with fellow former Polish officials headquartered in London, while for nearly forty years he and his wife regularly opened the doors of their North Side home to recent Polish immigrants in Chicago and local Polish dignitaries who likewise refused to acknowledge Poland's communist leaders. Pictures prominently displayed in his home showed Szygowski with various members of European royalty.

"He was almost like a Don Quixote. He and the patriots were trying to do something that would never happen," said Szygowski's son, Mathew. "They kept the fire burning, even though it had no power."

Of Chicago's Polish population— among the largest in the world— Szygowski always remained an important figure. He headed local Polish banking and veterans groups and was a prolific writer who drafted articles for Polish historical journals as well as a witty memoir of his World War I experiences and a history of his family dating to 1439.

"I would say from the political point of view, he was a number one man," said Grazyna Kahl, a member of the board of directors of the Polish Youth Association in Chicago and a distant family member. "He was a diplomat of the old era: impeccable. He was a linguist, a connoisseur, had beautiful old manners."

Szygowski was born in Poland in 1896 and had a whirlwind military career during World War I that included service in the Polish and Austrian armies, including a term in an Italian prisoner-of-war camp. He left the Polish army to study law at the University of L'vov and received a law degree in 1925.

He joined Poland's foreign consulate after that, serving over the years in Slovakia, Mexico, the United States, and Canada. He was transferred to Chicago as consul general in 1944. He made headlines the next year by refusing to personally turn over the consulate's keys to communist officials in the new Polish government.

In 1979 Szygowski was named minister plenipotentiary to the United States for the Polish government-in-exile, and in 1989 he voted from Chicago in the election that returned a noncommunist government to Poland. In the early 1990s, he was awarded the Restitution of Poland Medal by then-President Lech Walesa for his work over the years.

Besides his son, Szygowski is survived by nine grandchildren and eighteen great-grandchildren.

THURSDAY, AUGUST 23, 2001

Dr. Jorge Prieto, Eighty-Two; Physician to City Immigrants

By James Janega, *Tribune* Staff Reporter

Dr. Jorge Prieto helped to bring clinics to Chicago's immigrant communities.

Dr. Jorge Prieto, eighty-two, an immigrant physician who became a household name by treating Chicago's Mexican immigrants in the 1950s and pioneering Cook County's practice of locating clinics in immigrants' neighborhoods, died Tuesday, August 21, of heart failure. He had been recovering from an amputation surgery in St. Francis Hospital in Evanston.

He was a quiet, unassuming man who nonetheless found himself at the forefront of medical, immigrant, and workers' rights causes.

He became an icon for a generation of Mexican Americans living in Chicago, a city that at the time barely recognized their existence, let alone provided for it.

"He was revered," said Henry Martinez, founder and executive director of the Mexican Community Committee in Chicago. "When you look at what health services were provided by the city many years ago, there weren't these health clinics. But he came on the scene and said somebody's got to serve these individuals. And he started providing."

First as a neighborhood doctor, then as the founding chairman of the Family Practice department at Cook County Hospital, and later as president of the Chicago Board of Health in the mid-1980s, Prieto made medical services available to immigrants, both legal and undocumented.

The precedent set the pace for city and county services for years to come, said Dr. Bernard Turnock, former director of the Illinois Department of Public Health.

"He championed the role the Chicago Department of Health needed to play in terms of providing access to primary care service and coordinating that role with the County Hospital," Turnock said. "He clearly was one of the most important and compassionate public health leaders in the city in a long time."

Prieto was the son of an exiled mayor of Mexico City and spent much of his childhood in Texas and California. When his family returned to Mexico in 1933, he continued his education there until 1943, when he went to the University of Notre Dame to study bacteriology.

Driven by his family's immigrant experience in the 1920s, he decided to become a physician to Mexican immigrants in the United States. He returned again to Mexico, studied medicine in Mexico City, and, after fulfilling an internship and social service requirements in Mexico, came to Columbus Hospital in Chicago for his second internship.

He was licensed to practice medicine in Illinois in 1953 and spent the next twenty-five years making house calls in Little Village, charging little and sometimes accepting food in return for services. He joined Cesar Chavez and the United Farm Workers on their California march for a contract in 1966, and Prieto was active in the Catholic Archdiocese of Chicago Cardinal's Committee for the Spanish Speaking.

In the early 1970s, he served as director of community medicine at Cabrini Hospital and was named chairman of the new Family Practice department at Cook County Hospital in 1974, where he stressed that physicians training there serve disadvantaged communities.

While at County Hospital, he established the South Lawndale Health Center, since renamed in his honor. In 1984, Mayor Harold Washington named him president of the Chicago Board of Health, a policy advisory board from which Prieto urged greater contact between doctors and the communities they served. He left the board in 1987.

Prieto was the first recipient of the Latino Institute's Dr. Jorge Prieto Humanitarian Award in 1984, delivered weekly commentary on Latin American culture for Hispanic Television of

Chicago until 1997, and was inducted into the Chicago Senior Citizen Hall of Fame the same year.

"He was a doctor who carried a sense of history with him," said Chicago author Studs Terkel. "In all the discussion we have about immigration, he represented the riches that are brought by immigrants, and he enriched our community very much."

Prieto is survived by his wife, Luz Maria; two brothers, Guillermo and Pedro; four sisters, Felisa Carrillo, Emma Negrete, Socorro Martinez, and Teresita Sheridan; four daughters, Luz Maria, Carmen, Margarita, and Lupe; five sons, Dr. Jorge Jr., Dr. Francisco Javier, Antonio, Carlos, and Miguel; thirteen grandchildren; and a great-grandson.

FRIDAY, APRIL 19, 2002

Niza Miranda De Colom, Seventy-Six; Welcomed Many to Humboldt Park

By James Janega, *Tribune* Staff Reporter

To many of the city's Puerto Rican immigrants, Niza Miranda De Colom will be remembered for her graystone on North Francisco Avenue in the Humboldt Park neighborhood.

There, the short, busy woman with the keen sense of humor and stern sense of self-reliance was one of the first Chicagoans the immigrants met, a hostess who in the 1950s and 1960s took in Puerto Rican families new to the country as temporary boarders.

She helped many of them find jobs and more permanent housing, much of it in Humboldt Park, where she and her husband were among the first Latino residents.

Colom, seventy-six, died Monday, April 15, of cardiac arrest in her home.

At her wake Wednesday and Thursday nights in the West Kelvyn Park neighborhood, Colom was remembered for working a factory job at Zenith when she wasn't running cash registers at three

family businesses, for bringing in extra money by sewing clothes in her dining room, and for instilling a sense of independence in her children, one of whom became a Chicago alderman.

"If anyone was hungry, the door was always open. She would have bingo games on Saturday. There was always something going on, some type of game, some type of dancing," said her daughter Janice Colom Kahn. "She would always have guests in the house."

The former Niza Miranda Acevedo was born in Manati, Puerto Rico. Things were particularly strict in her family, she would tell her children, and after their parents' deaths she and her nine brothers and sisters were raised by older siblings, several of whom were schoolteachers.

It was the late 1970s before she agreed to wear pants, her daughter said. In a later rebellious streak, she thought up ribald jokes with her friends (which never seemed that bad to her children) and occasionally sneaked a cigarette "when she was really naughty," her daughter said.

Colom was married in 1950 to Andres Colom, a Puerto Rican serving in the U.S. Army. Shortly after their wedding, he came to Chicago while Mrs. Colom remained in Puerto Rico to raise the first two of their three children, their daughter said.

She came to Chicago in 1954, a difficult move that later motivated her to help others undergoing the same transition. Hard work was a kind of liberation for her, her daughter said.

On weekends, she towed her children to neighborhood homes, where she did a word-of-mouth hairdressing business. During the week, she did seamstress work at home. In the 1960s, she helped her husband run a record shop, beauty salon, and barbershop he opened near North and Washtenaw Avenues. She worked through the 1960s and 1970s as an assembly line supervisor at a Zenith factory on the Northwest Side—all the while stashing away money so her children could go to college.

Though she left Zenith in the late 1970s, she never really retired. Colom continued working in her husband's stores, made clothes for her children and grandchildren, and planned the weekend events she held in her home.

In addition to her daughter and husband, Colom is survived by two other daughters, Adelmees Quintana and Ald. Vilma Colom (35th); two stepsons, Ramsey and Sebastian Colom; a sister, Pachina Miranda; six grandchildren; and four great-grandchildren.

WEDNESDAY, SEPTEMBER 25, 2002

Andre Gabor, Ninety-Two; Head of Import Firm, Advocate for the Arts
By Barbara Brotman, *Tribune* Staff Reporter

Andre Gabor, ninety-two, who left Hungary as World War II loomed and became an international businessman and arts supporter in Chicago, died Monday in Northwestern Memorial Hospital of cardiac fibrillation. Still working at the time of his death, Gabor was chairman of Kemeny Overseas Products Corp., a Chicago-based distributor of tin mill products.

A debonair figure who spoke seven languages, Gabor exuded a sophisticated European sensibility that led his daughters' awestruck friends to refer to him privately as "the Count."

"He was a gentleman to the nth degree," said David Filkins, who was hired by Gabor as an intern at Kemeny and is now president of the company. "He was witty; very self-assured. . . . He had very interesting friends from all different political and artistic backgrounds. It would be a marvelous evening to be invited to the Gabor house."

Gabor, who lived on the Near North Side, was born in Budapest, Hungary. He earned a doctorate in economics and political economy at the University of Budapest, and he served in the Austro-Hungarian army, where he was one of the last Jewish recruits to enter the officer corps.

His commanding officer caught him reading a Zionist tract, an offense for which he could have been jailed. But Gabor defended Zionism so eloquently that the officer became his mentor. With the growing power of Adolf Hitler in Germany, the officer got him an honorable discharge and urged him to leave the country. He left in 1937 and got his parents and several other relatives out of Europe.

In Chicago he worked as import manager at Mandel Brothers department store and then at Sears, Roebuck and Co. In 1946 he and a childhood friend, Emery Kemeny, started a business exporting tin plate, a thin steel coated with tin. "He told me that being a businessman surprised him," Filkins said. "He was a scholar; he loved the theater." Indeed, in 1956, he was a cofounder of the Studebaker Theater,

along with Theodore Rossman, Lewis Manilow, and Second City cofounder Bernard Sahlins.

He met the former Clara Bolcskey in Baden-Baden when he showed up at her formal birthday party in his tennis whites. They married in Vienna and had two daughters, whom they raised on Chicago's North Side.

"We traveled in Europe every summer for three months," said his daughter Andrea Gabor, an author and professor of journalism at Baruch College in New York. "For him, life was about living to the fullest."

He played tennis until he was eighty-eight, and learned to use a computer at ninety-one.

Clara Gabor died in 1994.

In 1996 Gabor married Barbara Vaughan. "He had such a vitality about life," his second wife said. "He once told me he had been to every country of the world."

Gabor is survived by his second wife, Barbara Vaughan Gabor; two daughters from his first marriage, Andrea and Antonia; two daughters from his second marriage, Sierra and Shana Vaughan-Gabor; and two granddaughters.

TUESDAY, OCTOBER 1, 2002

Branko Vukotich, Seventy-Nine; Architect Was Born into Montenegrin Royalty
By Sufiya Abdur-Rahman, *Tribune* Staff Reporter

Branko Vukotich, a member of a Montenegrin royal family, was a man whose honor and pride never

dissipated. The seventy-nine-year-old died Wednesday, August 28, of esophageal cancer in Northwestern Memorial

Hospital, but because he forbade his friends from seeing him in less than perfect condition, they learned of his death only last week.

Vukotich was an architect who after retiring spent countless hours in libraries and bookstores reading and chatting with people of like mind.

"He was an independent thinker, an analytical mind. He used to say, 'I don't live with chairs, furniture. I live with books and ideas,'" said his friend Branko Mikasinovich.

Vukotich was born in Yugoslavia, the nephew of Queen Milena Vukotic of Montenegro. The Vukotic family played a leading role in Montenegro before the Petrovic family came to power. His family's status was something Vukotich never took advantage of but was instilled in him, Mikasinovich said.

He was held in an Italian concentration camp during World War II and could have been released if he had mentioned his aunt, the queen, but he refused. "He didn't want any special treatment," Mikasinovich said.

Vukotich studied philosophy at a university in Rome on a scholarship. "'Who but fools are studying philosophy?'" Mikasinovich said Vukotich would say. "'I should have been a dentist or something like that.'"

But he was a thinker, and for a long time he had been thinking about coming to America, where there were endless possibilities for an intellectual, Mikasinovich said. Vukotich, who was fluent in Italian and Russian, became a designer for the Chicago architecture firm Holabird & Root in the 1950s and retired about twenty years ago.

Since retirement, he spent most of his time reading international newspapers and books and philosophizing about politics and social problems.

He was married to a Yugoslavian newspaper editor named Mira for about ten years, but they divorced without having children. He has no known survivors.

SEPTEMBER 9, 2004

Paul J. King Sr., Eighty-Nine; Founder of Chicago's First Black-Owned Produce Firm
By Barbara Sherlock, *Tribune* Staff Reporter

Paul J. King Sr. was convinced there was a larger market for the greens, okra, and crowder peas he was selling in the late 1940s to small black-owned grocery stores. With a clever ploy, he enticed the national chains on the city's South Side to stock the same produce.

"He saw a niche," said his son, Paul Jr. "He said to them: black people eat this produce and you don't sell it. So what I am going to do is give you three boxes of each of these on Thursday, and if you don't sell them by Monday, I will take them back."

They sold, and King's already-successful produce business soon included ten National Tea stores that ordered sixty cases of those items every day, his son said.

"They took the gamble. I think that was brilliant. Imagine a black guy with only a high school education having that kind of tenacity," his son said. "If you ever go to a grocery store and see collard greens, like at Dominick's and Jewel, my dad is responsible for that."

Formerly of Chicago's Chatham neighborhood, King, eighty-nine, was the founder of P.K. Produce, Chicago's first black-owned produce company. He died of fluid buildup in his lungs on Friday, September 3, in Sherwin Manor Nursing Center in Chicago.

Born in New Orleans, King moved with his mother, Olivia, and twin sister, Marie, to the South Side at age three after the death of his father, Joseph. The family expanded when his mother married Charles Brown, who had three children.

A graduate of Englewood High School, King started his produce company in 1935. Rising at 3:00 AM, he would travel to the South Water Market on the city's Near South Side to buy wholesale fresh fruits and vegetables that he sold to people and independent stores in his neighborhood.

Two years later, he married Frances Lindsey and they moved into her mother's two-flat for a year before renting their own apartment a block away. In 1953 they bought a bungalow in Chatham, making them among the first blacks to live in that neighborhood.

In 1944 King joined the army and served in the European theater during World War II. His wife and a family friend continued the business until his discharge two years later, when he decided to approach the national chains to buy his greens.

About the same time, he began to suspect that the South Water merchants were hiking the prices they quoted him for their wholesale produce because he was black. King went to produce farmers in Highland, Indiana, and they began to bring their produce directly to King's business at Seventy-first and State Streets.

The move was effective, said his son, because the South Water merchants soon lowered the prices they quoted King and even extended him credit.

His client roster eventually expanded to include the Chicago Board of Education, the Cook County Jail, the Lincoln Park Zoo, and major grocery store chains.

About nine years ago, he gave his business to Richard Thomas, who had been working for him since 1983.

"Everything I know about the business I learned from him," said Thomas, owner of T&T Food Service. "He was a very tough man during a very tough period. There were very few black produce companies around, and he survived in a pretty racist atmosphere. Things are very different now, but at that time we as blacks were not doing that kind of thing."

King was a constant source of inspiration to his children.

"I got every bit of my example from my father," said his son, who owns UMB, one of the state's largest minority-owned construction firms. "He never missed a day of work . . . and his persistence was an example to me. Everything good about me, I learned from my father."

In addition to his son and wife, survivors include his daughter, Claudia Yunker; a stepsister, Janet Tucker; and five grandchildren.

SECTION

III

Faces Behind Cultural Landmarks

It is a city where a self-made man might create museums devoted to American art, where its wealthiest citizens and institutions might vie for a single woman's needlework, where the tallest edifice in the world was set, window by window, by a man who hung on the outside of the building as it climbed into the sky.

SATURDAY, JUNE 29, 1996

Daniel Terra, Eighty-Five; Founded City Art Museum

By Alan G. Artner, *Tribune* Art Critic

With $2,500 borrowed from a friend, Daniel J. Terra went on to become one of the wealthiest men in Illinois, founding two museums devoted to American art and serving as the country's first ambassador-at-large for cultural affairs.

Terra, who in recent years had shuttled between homes in Chicago; Washington; D.C.; and Vernon, France; died Friday at the age of eighty-five from a heart attack suffered Wednesday in Washington.

"Few people in the history of the arts in Chicago have had the commitment to create an entire museum in the heart of the city," said James N. Wood, director of the Art Institute of Chicago.

"Dan Terra helped immensely in making Chicago an artistic center and one of the few cities in the nation that can boast a museum devoted to American art of all periods. His presence and patronage will be sorely missed."

The son of an Italian lithographer, Terra studied chemical engineering and, in 1940, borrowed money to start Lawter Chemicals, now Northbrook-based Lawter International Inc., a company making additives for printing ink.

Terra was also chairman and a major shareholder of Lake Forest–based Mercury Finance Co., a successful nationwide specialist in financing used cars.

Terra credited his first wife, Adeline, with getting him to look seriously at American art. He subsequently became a member of the Art Institute's committee on American art.

In 1980 Terra opened the Terra Museum of American Art in a converted 1,100-square-foot florist's shop in Evanston. The same year he also became national finance chairman for Ronald Reagan, raising $21 million for his presidential campaign.

After Reagan's victory in November, Terra was offered his choice of several ambassadorships, and he invented a purely ceremonial one that took him across the country to speak on behalf of American art.

"Ronald Reagan has said that I've done more for American art than any other man in the history of the country," Terra liked to contend, adding: "It's absolutely true."

When in 1987 he moved the museum to its present location at 666 North Michigan Avenue, Terra further displayed his enthusiasm by dressing up as Uncle Sam and singing "I'm a Yankee Doodle Dandy" at each of the four inaugural parties.

But the crowds he expected to overrun the museum did not come. Amid a constant reshuffling of staff members, Terra imperceptibly began withdrawing himself to a new interest in France, near Claude Monet's famous home and gardens in Giverny.

In 1992 he opened the Musee Americain, a twenty-six-thousand square-foot space devoted to American Impressionist artists who had been influenced by Monet. Shortly thereafter, he also began restoration of the house of Monet's friend, American artist Lila Cabot Perry. Terra was decorated by the minister of culture of the French government for his efforts.

Both museums are supported by the Terra Foundation for the Arts, and their operations will be relatively unaffected by Terra's death, said Stuart Popowcer, director of the Chicago institution.

Terra is survived by his second wife, Judith, and a son, James.

WEDNESDAY, AUGUST 9, 2000

Donald Mussay, Seventy; Shaped City Skyline
By James Janega, *Tribune* Staff Reporter

For a while in the early 1970s, Donald R. Mussay Sr. had the best view of Chicago the city had to offer. He worked on the outside of the Sears Tower as it was being constructed.

As foreman of a team of glaziers, it was his job to ensure the giant building's windows were set correctly, just as he had for the John Hancock Center and a number of other architectural titans in Chicago. In fact, in a city famous for its glass-and-steel skyline, Mussay set in place an awful lot of the glass.

Mussay, seventy, died of non-Hodgkin's lymphoma Tuesday, July 18, in Howard Young Medical Center in Minocqua, Wisconsin.

A puckish man (to needle an office worker inside, he once pretended to hang on for dear life to the outside of a skyscraper), Mussay spent much of his life specializing in the exacting work of building skyscrapers.

He said it was because such work paid an extra few cents an hour, said his daughter Kathleen Johnson, but the job was also a challenge. In the two years Mussay spent working on the Sears Tower, wind would rock the building back and forth as much as eighteen inches, while glare from the sun would cause window openings to expand from the heat.

But the work had its rewarding moments, his daughter said.

"You can actually see so much more than on the inside of the building," she said. "He could see in every direction, and sometimes, there'd be a cloud coming in, and it was like, oh gosh, you're going up to heaven."

Mussay was raised in Chicago near Fullerton and Central Avenues, then the edge of a city that bordered on farmland.

He never graduated from high school, instead hitchhiking as a teen down Route 66 to California, then making his way up to Seattle, where he worked a series of odd jobs. He was a busboy, a gas station attendant, and a shipyard repairman before becoming a glazier in the mid-1950s.

Back then, setting glass wasn't as glamorous for Mussay as it would one day become: his first jobs were boarding up windows after late-night fires in rough neighborhoods. One night, the floor of a building literally moved with rats trying to escape from charred walls soaked from the fire hoses.

And though he worked so much in the city, Mussay was at heart an outdoorsman, the teen who traded his home on the edge of the prairie for a hand-to-mouth existence among the towering firs and redwoods near Seattle.

He went mushroom picking in area forest preserves and smelt fishing in Lake Michigan harbors. After retiring in 1992 he went to northern Wisconsin, where he and his wife of forty-seven years, Doris, had spent so many of their summer vacations.

All that time in the outdoors gave him a sense of perspective that standing on top of skyscrapers never did, his daughter said. For all the tall buildings he helped create, she said, "I think he was more impressed with the redwoods."

Besides his wife and daughter, Mussay is survived by two sons, Donald Jr. and David; another daughter, Susan Simpson; a brother, Marshall; a sister, Virginia Grizzaffi; eleven grandchildren; and a great-grandson.

TUESDAY, FEBRUARY 20, 2001

Martin de Maat, Fifty-Two; Second City Teacher
By James Janega, *Tribune* Staff Reporter

Martin de Maat, fifty-two, the artistic director for Second City's training centers whose nurturing advice and laid-back support boosted the early careers of Chris Farley, Tim Meadows, Tina Fey, and many other successful comedians, died Thursday, February 15, in Cabrini Medical Center in New York.

The cause was pneumonia, said Sheldon Patinkin, chairman of the theater department at Columbia College in Chicago, where de Maat had been an artist in residence.

De Maat was also an artistic consultant at Second City, a faculty member of New York's Video Associates, and a consultant to the Annoyance Theater in Chicago.

De Maat was four years old when his aunt Josephine Forsberg, an improvisation teacher in Second City's early days, took him to work with her.

Despite a lifetime in comic theater, de Maat remained more reserved than the famously manic students he later taught.

"He wasn't a performer; he was a teacher and a director," Patinkin said. De Maat's strength was in mentoring others, Patinkin said. "Martin was wonderful at handling them. He was an extraordinarily caring human being. He was good at recognizing talent and helping train it."

His first performances were in children's shows under his aunt's direction, and he began studying improvisation at age nine with Viola Spolin, the mother of Second City's first director, Paul Sills.

De Maat was a teen when he began teaching at Second City, though his earliest steady jobs with the comedy theater—while he was still in comedy classes—were as a dishwasher and box office attendant.

"I don't know a Second City without Martin because he literally grew up there," Second City producer Kelly Leonard said. "Martin was many people's first introduction into the world of entertainment at Second City. It's an awesome responsibility that he was handed somewhat casually and that he took very, very seriously."

Recently, de Maat's directing credits included *Tell Me That You Love Me, Junie Moon* at the Bailiwick Arts Center, *Sleeping Beauty* at the Theatre Building, and *Two All Beef Parodies* for Second City, among others.

His master classes have been featured at the Chicago Improv Festival, Northwestern University, the University of Chicago Graduate School of Business, and the Zen Center of San Francisco.

"Martin really believed in helping people achieve the most and be the best they could be," said Rob Chambers, director of the Second City Training Center.

There was a New Age tenor to his comedy classes. De Maat saw improvisation as a kind of comic self-help method.

"Most of us are often looking for approval," he told the *Monthly Aspectarian* magazine in August 1998. "It's that approval that has us in our minds worrying about what we're doing as we're doing it."

"In this work," he said, "there's only approval."

De Maat is survived by his sister, Patty.

MONDAY, APRIL 2, 2001

Stephen S. Prokopoff, Seventy-One; Led Museum of Contemporary Art in 1970s
By Ruth E. Igoe, *Tribune* Staff Reporter

Stephen S. Prokopoff, seventy-one, the director of Chicago's Museum of Contemporary Art from 1971 to 1977, died of non-Hodgkin's lymphoma Wednesday, March 28, in the University of Iowa Hospitals in Iowa City.

Born and raised on Chicago's Northwest Side, he attended Saturday classes at the Art Institute of Chicago as a child. By 1952 Prokopoff had earned bachelor's and master's degrees in art at the University of California at Berkeley.

In the late 1950s Prokopoff went to Paris on a Fulbright fellowship for painters, a trip that would foster a lifelong love for the city. He returned to earn a doctorate in art from New York University in 1962.

Prokopoff taught at a number of small colleges, including Skidmore College in Saratoga Springs, New York, where he taught both painting and art history. In 1966 Prokopoff began directing the college-affiliated Hathorn Gallery. That part-time position quickly turned into a full-time job.

After a year with the gallery Prokopoff was recruited to lead the University of Pennsylvania's Institute of Contemporary Art. He remained there for five years, initiating several prominent exhibits, including the Spirit of the Comics, which examined their impact on fine art; the Graphic Art of Robert Rauschenberg; and Christo: Monuments and Projects.

Such work caught the attention of Chicago's Museum of Contemporary Art, which hired him in 1971 after the museum's first director, Jan van der Marck, left.

"It was a very rich time in American art, and it was a good place for him to be," said his wife, Lois Craig.

During Prokopoff's tenure, museum staff increased membership and began forming the keystones of a permanent collection. At the time of the museum's tenth anniversary in 1977, that permanent collection included more than 100 works. Prokopoff's work also included writing many of the catalog essays that accompanied the exhibitions.

In 1974 Prokopoff served as commissioner and co-organizer of the American section of the Sao Paulo Bienal, an international art exhibit where he featured the Chicago imagists.

"He was a champion of certain schools of work that are characteristic of the San Francisco Bay Area and the Chicago area—in other words, places other than New York," recalled artist friend Ellen Lanyon. "He was always very genuinely interested in their world and developing their work."

Prokopoff also earned a reputation as an artist's museum director, bringing his painter's eye to exhibition installation.

"Prokopoff functioned best as a curator," wrote *Tribune* art critic Alan G. Artner in July 1977. "He never appeared stronger than when surrounded by artworks. Seeing him during installation was to see a professional selflessly working toward the solution that would put art before all else."

As with most of his museum positions, Prokopoff continued to teach while in Chicago. Soon after his arrival, he was named the first Robert B. Mayer Visiting Professor in the art department at the University of Chicago.

Prokopoff went on to the Institute of Contemporary Art in Boston, where he stayed for five years. He then spent another decade in Illinois with the Krannert Art Museum at the University of Illinois at Urbana-Champaign. It was there, in 1984, that Prokopoff organized the first exhibition in the United States of the Swiss psychiatrist Hans Prinzhorn's collection of art of the insane.

In 1992 he took a directorship at the University of Iowa Museum of Art, where he remained until his retirement in 1999. There, his 1996 exhibition, Henry Darger: The Unreality of Being, attracted widespread critical attention to outsider art, which does not fit well in any category.

After retirement, he and his wife began spending more time in their Paris home. Prokopoff also enjoyed many interests, including playing his violin. About his many pursuits, his wife recalled her husband once said: "There are many roads to roam, and they are all wonderful."

Other survivors include his father, Stephen; two sons, Alexander and Ilya; three stepchildren, Stephen, Carolyn, and Jennifer Craig; and one grandchild.

SATURDAY, NOVEMBER 24, 2001

Julia "June" Price Reedy, Ninety-Five; Helped Secure Botanic Garden Property
By James Janega, *Tribune* Staff Reporter

Julia "June" Price Reedy, ninety-five, a lifelong gardener and self-taught horticulturist who served on the committee that obtained the land for Chicago Botanic Garden in Glencoe, died in her Glenview home Wednesday, November 21. Her family said she had been recovering from a stroke.

Reedy, for whom the garden's fourteen thousand–volume June Price Reedy Horticultural Library is named, was an avid backyard gardener in River Forest and later in Glenview. She had served as a flower show judge in Chicago and was a director of the Chicago Horticultural Society.

On the women's board of that group, Reedy and several others lobbied to secure land and proper zoning from the state of Illinois for what became the 300-acre Chicago Botanic Garden in 1965.

Because of her continued contributions to the garden, it dedicated its rare-books library to her in 1986.

The former Julia Price worked in the late 1920s as a teacher for Highland Park elementary schools.

She married Thomas J. Reedy in 1930 after meeting him on a double date at an ice rink. Reedy helped her husband nurse his new refrigeration company through the Depression and build it into a larger firm afterward.

"She was very loving and very passionate about what she loved. She was like a laser beam if she was interested in something," said her grandson, also Thomas J. Reedy. "She was a doer. If there was something that had to be done, she'd get it done."

At various times, Reedy served as president of the Oak Park Hospital Women's Board and chairwoman of the board of trustees of River Forest Library.

Known in later years for her white hair, sharp memory, and sunny personality, Reedy was a genealogist who researched her family's ancestry back to William the Conqueror. Reedy was also active in her local Skokie Valley chapter of the Daughters of the American Revolution as well as the Mayflower Society.

In addition to her grandson, Reedy is survived by a son, Thomas W. Reedy; a daughter, Mary Lou Ahlering; eight other grandchildren; and twenty-seven great-grandchildren.

TUESDAY, OCTOBER 12, 2004

Dorothy Friend, Ninety-Three; Took Needlepoint in New Directions
By Barbara Sherlock, *Tribune* Staff Reporter

Dorothy Friend's medium was traditional, but her final product rarely was. As a needlepoint enthusiast, designer, and teacher, Friend sought to move the craft beyond its predictable appearance on a pillow—although she also enjoyed those creations—to more unusual objects, such as stair risers and old commodes.

Her designs ranged from original to custom adaptations of eighteenth-century and contemporary artists. A multireligious tapestry in the chapel of the Rehabilitation Institute of Chicago and a vestment of the late cardinal Joseph Bernardin are examples of her work.

Her students most often were among the wealthier of society who, under her suggestion and instruction, created items representing their interests or to coordinate with the color schemes of their homes, said her son Arthur. Others created needlepoint canvases of favorite pets, one of Friend's more popular marketing ideas, her son said.

"Her thing was to create unusual pieces that were personalized, not what you would think of as your usual needlepoint," he said.

Friend, ninety-three, former proprietor of The Needlery, a studio located for decades in a 100-year-old house near Superior and Rush Streets, died of cancer Friday, October 8, in her Lake Shore Drive home.

"The kind of work we do will always be in vogue," she said in a 1978 *Tribune* interview. "Heirloomed quality is important. Needlepoint should be as individualized as possible."

Born Dorothy Hess in Baltimore, she fell in love with medical student Arthur Koff when he came into the rare bookstore where she worked.

The couple married in 1934 and moved to Chicago so he could accept a teaching position at the University of Chicago and set up practice as an obstetrician.

Together, they rewrote a popular baby keepsake book into one that also chronicled a child's medical history. To market the books, she created examples and displayed them in doctors' offices.

Her husband died in 1954. Four years later, she married Henry Friend, who died in 1972.

Friend became enraptured by needlepoint in the 1960s through a correspondence course of the Embroiders' Guild in London. Her desire for in-depth instruction led her to travel three times to England to the Royal School of Needlework to study under the famous needlepoint teacher Nancy Kemmons.

In 1967 Friend opened The Needlery, where she and her small staff crafted custom designs and where she also provided lessons by appointment.

"She was very clever, very shrewd, and an excellent businesswoman," said her niece, Diane Pelham Burn, who lives in England and accompanied Friend during her travels there.

"She spotted something that was particularly American, in which things in a room all matched a color scheme," said Pelham Burn. "She would tell clients it would be terribly nice to have a cushion—or covers for their bridge table or wastepaper basket—that picked up the colors and tones of the room's decor. They would end up looking custom-made, because they were. It was a real gap in the market that she filled."

Friend also came up with the idea to purchase antique miniature chairs and sell them to clients who had grandchildren. She would sell the chairs with supplies and a design for a seat cover.

She had a long list of ideas for objects that could be used in needlepoint, from stepladders and jewelry boxes to old commodes. All her canvases and yarns were purchased in England, as were many of her needles. She had an expansive collection of thimbles.

The studio closed in the late 1980s.

She was passionate about raising funds for medical research and had been president of Mother's Aid of Chicago Lying-In Hospital.

A star high school basketball player, she unwound after work by playing a game with her sons.

Other survivors include another son, Robert; two grandchildren; and four great-grandchildren.

Neighborhood Personalities

If your spouse had mere months to live, how would you spend them? Would you have the courage to spend twenty more years at it, if a reprieve were granted? Such was the choice Charley and Hobart VanDeventer in Streator, Illinois, faced.

In Chicago, Ruth Levin worked for sixty-one years in the same Near West Side clothing store. On the South Side, Ethel Muhammad Sharrieff urged her father, Elijah Muhammad, to allow women more equality within the Nation of Islam.

They are antiques dealers, gym teachers, and neighbors reclined in lawn chairs. In a city of neighborhoods, they are the people who make the city what it is.

THURSDAY, OCTOBER 22, 1998

Carol Stoll, Ninety-Four; Ran Celebrated Bookstore

By Meg McSherry Breslin, *Tribune* Staff Reporter

Sitting behind the cash register just inside the wide window of her famous bookstore, a cigarette dangling from her mouth, Carol Stoll was a master at luring in customers with simple charm and a few forceful words.

"People would march in and out of that store and she would hold court," said a longtime friend, Steve Cogil Casari. "You'd walk in and she'd say, 'Darling, you need this book.' And boy, could she sell books."

Stoll, who sold books and collected scores of friends as a saleswoman and later proprietor of the Oak Street Book Shop in Chicago, died Wednesday in her Near North Side home. She was ninety-four.

For many of her customers and friends, the closing of Stoll's bookstore on 54 East Oak Street in 1989 represented the end of an era in bookstores in Chicago. For twenty-three years, she had helped operate a truly old-fashioned store, consisting of a small, narrow room full of books stacked to the ceilings overseen by a proprietor who knew most of her customers by name and wouldn't hesitate to hop in a car to make a delivery.

In her years as a partner at the store with Arlyne Wimmer, and after she became the sole proprietor in the early 1980s, Stoll would wake up before dawn to pore through stacks of books herself. A voracious reader, she wanted to feel confident in her personal recommendations to clients.

For years, she kept coffee mugs with the names of her favorite customers engraved on them. When they stopped by, she'd offer free coffee, pastries, and a lively conversation.

Stoll was a feisty woman who dressed impeccably, often with ornate hats and a flower on her lapel. And she never hesitated to offer her opinions, which for many customers was her charm.

"She once told Lawrence Sanders in front of me that his last book was so bad he must be in the cocktail hour of his life," Casari said. "She just smiled and said, 'You can do better than this, Larry.'"

Big-name customers like Sanders, playwright David Mamet, film critic Gene Siskel, and dozens of artists and actors frequented the book shop for years, partly because of Stoll's unusual collection of movie scripts and plays and the store's location, next to the Esquire Theater.

A native of Chicago, Stoll began working at the bookstore just days after Wimmer opened it in the early 1960s. She had always been attracted to books and the ideas they represented, and the bookstore quickly became a perfect fit, said her granddaughter, Kathy Halbreich.

From the beginning, Stoll worked seven days a week with rarely a day off and little help, other than an occasional worker to assist in lugging around stacks of books after a fresh delivery.

"Books just always seemed absolutely a part of her life," her granddaughter said. "It was a kind of commitment to ideas and to people who wrote books and people who read books."

When her Oak Street location became more trendy in the 1980s, Stoll's rent climbed, and she was eventually forced to give up her lease in 1989.

"Closed for Keeps," was the hand-written sign announcing the end of a literary institution. "I will tell you, I am very sad," she told the *Tribune* near the closing day. "Every morning I've gotten up—I couldn't wait to get here. Opening a crate of books is just like Christmas. It's thrilling!"

Stoll's husband, Harry Stoll, preceded her in death. She is survived by a daughter, Betty Halbreich; two grandchildren; three great-grandchildren; and a sister, Helen Oppenheim.

MONDAY, MARCH 22, 1999

Martin Oster, Ninety; Owned Dry Cleaners
By James Janega, *Tribune* Staff Reporter

Martin Oster, ninety, of Evergreen Park, who worked in the dry-cleaning business for fifty-three years and literally built his first dry-cleaning store by hand, died Friday in Little Company of Mary Hospital and Health Care Centers, Evergreen Park.

Oster was born in Chicago but moved with his parents to the family farm in what was then the Austro-Hungarian Empire as a boy, according to his daughter, Carolyn Jucewicz.

When he was eighteen, Oster returned to Chicago and landed his first job in a dry-cleaning shop. Eight years later, he married his boss' daughter, Anna Miller, and the couple moved to Evergreen Park in 1941. Oster, with the help of his two sons, Martin J. and Ronald, built and opened his own dry-cleaning shop in Evergreen Park in 1948.

"He always wanted to have his own, and he achieved that," Jucewicz said. Over the years, Oster opened two other shops, in Oak Lawn and Worth, where he tried to oversee everything, sometimes arriving for work at 5:00 AM.

Oster tried to return home by midafternoon every day to work in his garden.

"He loved to garden. That was what he did when he wasn't working," Jucewicz said.

Survivors also include a son, Martin J.; a sister, Anna Kluver; eight grandchildren; and six great-grandchildren.

SATURDAY, JUNE 12, 1999

Ruth Levin, Eighty-Eight; Veteran of Maxwell Street; Clothing Store Worker for More Than Seventy Years

By James Janega, *Tribune* Staff Reporter

Ruth Levin, who started working as a temporary switchboard operator at a Near West Side clothing company in 1927 and stayed on as the company's bookkeeper until last week, died Wednesday in Northwestern Memorial Hospital.

Levin, eighty-eight, had a life steeped in the history of the Jewish tailors and immigrant installment buyers in the Maxwell Street area. She was born in the Humboldt Park neighborhood and graduated from Tuley High School before starting work at the switchboard of what was then Associated Clothing Co.

She stayed at the company—now known as the Meyerson Associated Clothing Co.—through the years and was eventually entrusted with its bookkeeping duties.

"She's been down in that area and knows all the old-timers and their kids since she was sixteen," said her granddaughter Carla Gliebe.

"She lied about her age," said Max Israel, co-owner of Meyerson Associated Clothing Co. "She said she was eighteen so she could get the job."

"She was a very nice lady, very efficient. She's going to be very hard to replace," Israel said.

From her seat at the back of the men's clothing store, near Roosevelt Road and Clinton Street, Levin saw the area change from Chicago's crossroads for Russian and Polish Jews, where merchants hawked goods on the sidewalk, to an open-air flea market and year-round blues fest, to one of the city's hottest and most contested pieces of real estate once the University of Illinois at Chicago moved next door.

Levin's daughter Harriet Kornit said the store's location and family atmosphere fulfilled her mother's love for being around people.

Kornit said that between answering phones and writing checks and squaring up accounts, her mother kibitzed with customers and coworkers.

At her desk near the original Maxwell Street, where installment dealers once went door-to-door to collect weekly payments to purchase discounted garments—an early line of credit for immigrants who couldn't get the same treatment at department stores—there was much to kibitz about.

"She would talk to people about their families and what they did and the kind of work they did. She was just very interested in people," Kornit said.

In addition to her daughter and granddaughter, Levin is survived by another daughter, Evelyn Howard; a brother, David Kapper; two other granddaughters; a grandson; a great-granddaughter; and a great-grandson.

TUESDAY, JANUARY 18, 2000

Susanne Willson, Thirty-Seven; Antiques Dealer
By James Janega, *Tribune* Staff Reporter

Even amid the moddish, modernist furniture that Susanne Willson collected and dealt in, the painting on her living room wall turned heads.

As eclectic and manifold as its owner, it depicted three women standing in front of a Persian rug; one was naked, another laughing, the third concerned.

None of her friends or family understood her fascination with it.

"She liked things that were playful, fun, exciting, innovative," said her husband, Linas Smulkstys. "She liked to do things differently."

A student of Chinese political science who once starred in a Taiwanese soap opera, Willson, thirty-seven, was a newcomer who carved a niche in Chicago's cluttered antiques market. She died Thursday, January 13, in her Gold Coast home of cancer.

The daughter of a military physicist, she spent much of her childhood in Germany, England, Greece, and Italy. After her high school graduation in the United States, she went to Europe on a two-month backpacking trip.

After earning a degree in Chinese political science at the College of Wooster in Ohio, she went to Taiwan to improve her Mandarin. A year later, she was acting in a soap opera there. She later returned to the United States to attend graduate school in Indiana and took a job in a coin laundry.

After earning a master's degree in Chinese studies, Willson moved to Chicago, got married, and worked briefly in the corporate world.

But it was after her decision in 1995 to go into the antiques business—specifically, into the brightly colored, form-bending furniture of the 1950s, 1960s, and 1970s—that Willson settled down and made a name for herself here.

Her Andersonville store, Really Heavy Antiques, was always hip and fun, said Gene Douglas, a partner at Gene Douglas Decorative Arts and Antiques. Another friend, Dominick Manella, said a good eye for rare items allowed her to make "a fortune" with 100 pieces of machine-age jewelry from England.

In addition to her husband, Willson is survived by her parents, Peter and Ingrid Willson.

WEDNESDAY, JANUARY 26, 2000

Joseph Colucci, Ninety-Two; Bathhouse Owner
By James Janega, *Tribune* Staff Reporter

Joseph Colucci ran a bathhouse, sold cars, was a member of the Near West Side Democratic organization and fought off charges that he had ties to organized crime.

Colucci, ninety-two, died Sunday, January 23, in his River Forest home.

For the past twenty-five years he owned the Division Street Russian Baths, the only bathhouse left in a city that once had fifty.

But while many of Chicago's original bathhouses were decidedly utilitarian—located in areas that had higher concentrations of rooming houses—Colucci's was solely devoted to relaxation.

"We got the best heat in the country," Colucci once told the *Tribune*. "We got people from all over the world. They tell us the heat is tremendous."

Dr. Joseph Brawka, a regular at the bathhouse for the past eight years, said that he has seen judges, lawyers, doctors, and city workers lounging between wisps of steam. Colucci was friend to them all.

"He was just a regular nice guy who was fun to be around," Brawka said.

Depending on who you were, such was not always the case. The same year Colucci bought the bathhouse, a deputy chief of police was demoted to captain for admitting to regularly playing cards with him.

Colucci owned Parkside Motors on the West Side at the time.

In 1972 Colucci was subpoenaed by a federal grand jury in connection with the investigation of an organized crime drug ring. Colucci was never charged, but the pall of suspicion was enough for a police inquiry board to consider consorting with him a violation of departmental ethics policy.

"He was a character. The last of a breed. The last of the true Chicagoans," said Brawka.

Colucci is survived by his wife, Mabel; two sons, Joseph Jr. and James; and two grandchildren.

SATURDAY, MARCH 25, 2000

Barry Rogers, Eighty-One; Was Coach, Friend to New Trier Students
By James Janega, *Tribune* Staff Reporter

Barry Rogers, eighty-one, who as a New Trier High School assistant coach always seemed ready with a fresh towel and a kind word, died Saturday, March 18, in Rush North Shore Medical Center hospice center in

Skokie of complications related to prostate cancer.

Rogers captained a navy supply ship in the Pacific during World War II and had a lengthy freight distribution career, but he was best known during the past twenty years as a sort of morale officer in the New Trier athletic department.

Rogers was on a first-name basis with coaches and students and wore his white hair in a crew-cut stubble.

Though most coaches at the school dreaded towel duty in the locker room, Rogers went at it with gusto, joyfully hurling towels from within a cage in the middle of the room.

He could supply towels to passing students without breaking eye contact with a person who came to him for friendly advice.

"If I would chew a kid out, Barry would be there to console him," remembered Gene Cichowski, New Trier's longtime football coach.

"He would get that kid back up on his feet. He was great for the football team, just for that reason alone," Cichowski said.

Rogers was born in Los Angeles and raised in Seattle. His father died while Rogers was still a boy. His son, Andrew, said the experience left Rogers with a desire to mentor other young people.

He served as chairman of the board for Will Power, an advocacy group for the mentally ill, and came to New Trier after retiring from the transportation industry in the early 1980s.

Neighbors on his block in Wilmette rarely had to worry about finding their morning newspapers; Rogers saw to it they were placed at the foot of their front doors when he walked his dog in the mornings.

For the children who lived on his block, Rogers conducted an informal golf class from his front porch, his son said. And he doled out advice to neighborhood youths as casually and comfortably as he played catch with them on the street.

"He always had the right words at the right time," his son said, adding that his father was pretty good at cheering up adults too.

"After a loss or something, or if some kid would get hurt, you'd turn around and there'd be Barry," Cichowski said with a laugh.

Rogers retired from New Trier in 1997.

Other survivors include a daughter, Elizabeth.

TUESDAY, APRIL 25, 2000

Cirildo Delgado, Eighty; Friendly Face in Pilsen

By James Janega, *Tribune* Staff Reporter

From a lawn chair in front of his Pilsen three-flat, Cirildo Delgado kept tabs on his community, talking to a stream of neighbors that idled past him in the warm months like a receiving line.

He sat there as soon as the spring air would allow, his family said, and he stayed there in wilting summer heat reminiscent of the humid East Texas sun of his youth.

He had the kind of placid, friendly face that welcomed talk—light conversational fare about family members, health, baseball, and boxing.

But the smiling man also held a wealth of stories, tales about picking cotton in Texas, of his proud World War II army service in South Asia, of how his grandparents had raised him when his mother died giving birth to him.

Delgado, eighty, whom everybody called "Lilo," died Saturday, April 22, after suffering a heart attack on a flight from Dallas to Chicago, having just visited family in Texas.

He had grown up there but came to Chicago after World War II to find better work than cotton picking. He spent twenty-nine years working in the U.S. Steel South Works plant, a job he appreciated so much he showed up for work two hours early every day, wanting "to make sure he was there on time and ready to work," said his daughter Leticia.

"He was a man of honor," said his son Arturo. "If you gave your word of honor, he expected people to abide by that. That's the way he lived his life."

He drew his values from the hard-working men he grew up around in Texas, his family said.

He was proud of his service in the army, frequently describing the poverty he saw in the Bengali jungles or on the streets of Calcutta, and took to his job at U.S. Steel with a passion he never explained.

"He took pride in whatever he did. That was one thing that he knew how to do, so he did it well," his daughter said.

"You persevered and you worked hard and you sacrificed to obtain the American dream," said his son.

When he retired in 1985 Delgado seemed to apply himself as much to maintaining relationships with his neighbors and passing on family lore to his children. He performed small kindnesses whenever he could, they said.

In addition to his son and daughter, Delgado is survived by his wife, Maria; five other sons, Mario, Hector, George, John, and Oscar; another daughter, Rosemary; twelve grandchildren; and five great-grandchildren.

SUNDAY, FEBRUARY 18, 2001

Khalid Abdul Muhammad, Fifty-Three; Fiery Ex-Aide for Farrakhan

By James Janega and Noah Isackson, *Tribune* Staff Reporters

Khalid Abdul Muhammad, fifty-three, the controversial and uncompromising Nation of Islam official who served as Minister Louis Farrakhan's assistant until his dismissal over virulent oral attacks on Jews and whites in 1993, died Saturday, February 17.

A spokesman for the family said Reverend Muhammad died of natural causes in Wellstar Kennestone Hospital in Marietta, Georgia. He had been taken to the hospital on Tuesday after suffering a brain aneurysm and was removed from life support Thursday.

Muhammad, a former national spokesman for the Nation of Islam, was more recently the national chairman of the New Black Panther Party. In that role, he led more than a dozen followers to the streets of Jasper, Texas, in 1998 in a display of solidarity with black residents after James Byrd Jr. was dragged to his death by whites.

"Black men and black women must protect themselves," he told reporters at the time. "We must put God first, but we need our guns. And we pray that God will give us the strength to shoot straight."

That same year, he led the Million Youth March in New York City, which drew an estimated six thousand people and ended in a clash between police and participants.

"He will be remembered as a modern-day Malcolm X," said Malik Zulu Shabazz, a spokesman for the New Black Panther Party and an attorney for Muhammad.

In Chicago, Nation of Islam officials praised him for helping to strengthen the organization.

"May Allah be pleased with him," said James Muhammad, editor of *The Final Call*, the Nation of Islam newspaper. "And we call on those who followed him and benefited from him to double the pace in the struggle for complete liberation of black people in America and throughout the world."

Muhammad was born Harold Moore Jr. and began preaching as a child. The quarterback for an all-black high school in Houston, he attended Dillard University in New Orleans. While at the school in the late 1960s, he heard Farrakhan speak and became interested in the black liberation movement.

By the early 1980s, he had become one of Farrakhan's top aides in the Nation of Islam. He served at Nation of Islam mosques in New York and Atlanta until becoming Farrakhan's personal assistant in 1991.

The relationship was short-lived. During a 1993 speech at Kean College in New Jersey, Muhammad referred to Jewish people as "bloodsuckers," called Pope John Paul II a "cracker," and urged violent uprising against whites in South Africa.

Congress quickly denounced the speech, and Farrakhan suspended Muhammad from the Nation of Islam hierarchy. In 1994 a former Nation of Islam minister attacked Muhammad after a speech in Riverside, California. Muhammad was shot in the leg in the attack, which also injured three other people.

"The stormiest time for Mr. Muhammad was when he had to split from his teacher," Shabazz said. "But he was able to survive, and he was still Khalid Abdul Muhammad to the very end. He was uncompromising."

Shabazz said that Muhammad and Farrakhan had since resolved their differences and that Farrakhan had called several times in the past week.

In recent years, Shabazz said, Muhammad had taken to a combination of social service and activism, building the New Black Panther Party and leading programs for drug addicts, the poor, and the uneducated. He lived in New York and Atlanta and spoke at lectures and rallies nationwide.

Survivors include a wife, three sons, and three sisters. Shabazz declined to identify them, citing unspecified security reasons.

WEDNESDAY, SEPTEMBER 4, 2002

Charley VanDeventer, Seventy-Five; Woman Made Her Living by Reveling in Unusual
By James Janega, *Tribune* Staff Reporter

Told her husband would die within months from an inoperable brain tumor, Charley VanDeventer and her spouse—with whom she already had dug graves and opened a drugstore in downstate Streator—decided they had time for one more adventure.

"We sold the drugstore and bought a custom-made International truck and travel trailer and set out to see the United States," said her husband, Hobart. They soon found out his illness had been misdiagnosed, but they stayed on the road anyway, traveling the country until they were broke.

VanDeventer, seventy-five, died of lung cancer Sunday, September 1, in St. Mary's Hospital, Streator.

During the twenty years or so after hitting the road, VanDeventer and her husband panned for gold (with modest success) and tried their hands at treasure hunting (a surprisingly unlucrative profession, her husband said).

After that, they spent years on the Midwest carnival circuit, where they hawked chances to win giant stuffed animals on carnival midways or entertained people with a computerized personality test built around customers' favorite colors.

"They were just the life of the party—they were always into something fun and different," said Marj Jaggers, a longtime friend from Streator, where the VanDeventers returned in the 1980s to retire. "I think it was just an adventuresome nature. She could fit in anyplace that she needed to be. She didn't know a stranger."

VanDeventer was born in Chicago and raised in Berwyn. She graduated from Morton High School in 1944 and met Hoby VanDeventer while they were students at Knox College in Galesburg. They got married in 1948, the day before Mrs. VanDeventer graduated with a bachelor's degree in chemistry. She graduated summa cum laude, with additional majors in physics and math, her husband said.

After living for a year in Ely, Nevada, they moved to Streator, where VanDeventer's in-laws operated a cemetery. Jaggers remembers visiting the VanDeventers' home on the grounds of Hillcrest Memorial Cemetery. The basement was full of pinball games and slot machines, and the parties they threw were memorable, she said.

In 1956 VanDeventer and her husband left the cemetery business and opened Streator-Wayside Drug Store.

For twelve years the VanDeventers ran the drug store with another couple before selling it in 1968. Among their adventures, VanDeventer also took up competitive swimming when she was in her fifties.

Other survivors include two daughters, Valerie Reger and Pamela; a sister, Marjorie Blair; and a grandson.

FRIDAY, DECEMBER 13, 2002

Ethel Muhammad Sharrieff, Eighty; Nation of Islam Leader's Daughter
By Rudolph Bush, *Tribune* Staff Reporter

Ethel Muhammad Sharrieff, eighty, eldest daughter of longtime Nation of Islam leader Elijah Muhammad who gently advised her father to allow women in the organization more freedom of expression and equality, died of heart failure Wednesday, December 11, in her Chicago home.

Born in Macon, Georgia, Sharrieff was always obedient and respectful to her father, a man who united tens of thousands of African Americans under a polarizing message that separated them from mainstream America.

When her father died in 1975 and a great rift between Louis Farrakhan and her brother, Wallace D. Muhammad, split the organization, Sharrieff supported her brother and remained close to Farrakhan. In her life, she was a close friend and contemporary of her father's prodigy, Malcolm X, who left the Nation of Islam before his assassination in February 1965.

Sharrieff's daughter Ea Sharon Sharrieff said of Malcolm X, "My mother loved him, and he treated us like we were royalty."

During the early years of her father's ministry, Sharrieff lived in Detroit and then moved to the South Side of Chicago, where Elijah Muhammad would base the Nation, when she was seven or eight, her daughter said.

As a young woman, she ran a Nation-owned bakery, called Eat Ethel's Pastries, at Thirty-first Street and Wentworth Avenue. She also worked with young women and girls within the Nation of Islam.

In 1948 she married Raymond Sharrieff, who became the head of the Fruit of Islam, the Nation's bodyguard unit.

While her husband rose in the Nation, Sharrieff worked quietly to influence her father's strict restrictions on women.

"She told women to walk beside the men, not behind them," her daughter said. She also suggested her father relax dress codes that required headdress and jackets at all times.

Through the 1960s and 1970s Sharrieff managed the Nation's clothing factory and store on Seventy-ninth Street.

Through tumultuous times, Sharrieff never spoke out about her father's theology.

For much of her life, Sharrieff took great delight in traveling the world and had toured the Middle East, Egypt, and Europe. For many years, she spent a good deal of time with her husband in the Bahamas. There she tutored and cared for children of all races.

In addition to her husband and daughter, Sharrieff is survived by her other daughters, Aleatha, Claramarie, and Zainab C.; her son, Hasan Sharif; fourteen grandchildren; and eight great-grandchildren.

SECTION

V

Politicians

It is hard to imagine Chicago without Harold Washington, its first black mayor, or the political characters who challenged his short and historic tenure. It is harder still to imagine the challenge facing Michael Bilandic, a son of immigrants who succeeded the first of two Daleys in Chicago's twentieth-century mayoral dynasty.

The city was home to Illinois governors who saved the state from bankruptcy or built its highways, and a focal point for the township that may boast America's oldest elected politician, 105-year-old Emma Schweer. Chicago's politics influenced the national stage as the twentieh century grew older.

The Windy City was named not for its weather, after all, but for its politicians.

TUESDAY, DECEMBER 21, 1976

Richard J. Daley, Seventy-Four; City's Boss for Twenty-One Years
By *Tribune* Staff Reporters

Mayor Daley asks for a veto override in the state capitol in 1975 .

Richard Joseph Daley was squat, tough, Irish, and smart, and he governed Chicago with a firm hand during an era when cities were supposed to be ungovernable.

He laid out expressways, built airports, sent up skyscrapers, and tore down slums.

He was the boss—"the man on five" they said on the fifth floor of City Hall where he had his office—and nobody ever had the clout to make it otherwise.

He possessed vast and unquestioned power, and he could wield it unmercifully to make or break those with ambitions for public office in the city, the state, or the nation. Yet he also could exercise it with the gentleness a doting father might show a favored daughter.

And he loved his city; he never aspired to be more than its mayor.

He served longer than any other mayor in Chicago's history, holding office at a time when such cities as New York City, Los Angeles, and Philadelphia had become political graveyards for their mayors. He did it by building a Democratic political organization of the old-fashioned kind—a machine, though he hated that word.

Through the organization he turned a theoretically weak mayor's office into a distillation of power. And he turned the theoretically powerful city council into a rubber stamp.

Scandal frequently raged around him. His machine was accused of vote-stealing, his closest aides were accused of bribe-taking, and even his sons were accused of influence-peddling.

But no scandal ever touched Daley himself. He acquired great power but never great wealth. All his life he lived simply and modestly in the Irish neighborhood of Bridgeport, an all-white working-class area of bungalows and corner bars.

His home life with his wife, Eleanor, and their seven children was intensely private. But away from home he loved the public push-and-shove of politics. He delighted in parades, banquets, speeches, and ribbon-cutting. He was a hand-shaker, a baby-kisser, a campaigner who could run the legs off aides half his age.

In 1974 he suffered a stroke and underwent surgery. After four months of recuperation at his Grand Beach, Michigan, compound, he was back at work, leading the pack.

Most of the time he was a careful diplomat, so soft-spoken that it was frequently difficult to hear what he was saying. Yet he could explode in purple-faced rage when provoked. Perhaps his most famous scene occurred on live, nationwide television when he stood on the floor of the 1968 Democratic National Convention and howled in protest at Sen. Abraham Ribicoff (D-Conn.), who was denouncing the city for its handling of thousands of demonstrators who had come to Chicago to protest the war in Vietnam.

His speech frequently was ungrammatical, and his famous malapropisms were treasured by friends and enemies alike.

"We must rise to ever higher and higher platitudes," he once said, and to a critic he once declared: "I resent the insinuendoism."

Probably his most-quoted remark was one made after the 1968 riots during the Democratic National Convention when the Chicago Police Department was accused of contributing to the unrest rather than suppressing it.

"The police are not here to create disorder," he said. "They are here to preserve disorder."

Some of his most memorable remarks were directed at the press, with which he carried on a running battle.

"They have vilified me," he said of the press. "They have crucified me; yes, they have even criticized me."

And his tongue could cut like a knife. "We have had a lot of dishonest newspapermen in this town," he once said during a news conference. "We still have. I could spit on some from here."

If he made enemies, he also made friends. He was ready with a kind word for any member of the vast army of precinct workers, police, firemen, park workers, and regular voters who caught his eye.

Striding through the lobby of City Hall, he frequently would break away from his aides and grasp the hand of someone he recognized, such as the son of a retired patrolman.

"I knew your dad," he would say. "He was a fine man."

He would leave behind him a man flushed with pride and happiness, a man who would never fail to vote the Daley ticket.

He was born May 15, 1902, the son of a metalworker whose bungalow was at 3602 South Lowe Avenue, less than one block from the house at 3536 South Lowe Avenue, where Daley lived out his life. Daley herded cattle in the stockyards to earn money for school, graduating from the Catholic school system and going on to become the first of his family to receive a college degree, and then a law degree.

In 1927 he entered the Democratic Party ranks as secretary to the late Ald. Joseph P. McDonough, (13th).

He became secretary to the county treasurer, then deputy county controller.

In 1936 he became a state representative—as a Republican. But he immediately made it known where he stood when he sat down in the Capitol with his Democratic colleagues. He subsequently was elected to the state Senate as a Democrat. He also was state revenue director and county clerk, and the only election he ever lost was an attempt to become county sheriff.

He emerged as a major political figure in 1953 when, in a struggle with the forces of Col. Jacob M. Arvey, he took effective control of the Cook County Democratic Committee. From there he built a formidable political base so that when Mayor Martin Kennelly was dumped from the ticket in 1955, Daley garnered the nomination.

In the election, he won with 708,222 votes, and for the rest of his mayoral career he kept that number on the license plates of his official car.

He was reelected again and again, achieving an unprecedented sixth term in 1975, despite sensational scandals that occurred throughout his tenure. These included the Summerdale police scandal of 1959; the racetrack stock scandal of 1971; the furor over the Paul Powell shoebox cash hoard; a succession of convictions against policemen accused of taking part in shakedowns; and the indictment and conviction of some of his closest friends and political associates, among them former governor Otto Kerner, former alderman Thomas Keane, and former county clerk Edward Barrett. Even his sons were accused of using their influential name to reap windfall fees in their law practices.

Daley's own ethics were questioned in 1974 when it was disclosed that he and his wife were the secret owners of Elard Realty Co., a firm heavily involved in buying and selling real estate and which controlled approximately $280,000 of his assets.

Mayor Daley presides over a 1972 city council meeting.

Daley said Elard was created 17 years earlier to protect the titles of his properties from potential lawsuits by disgruntled taxpayers against the city and himself as its mayor.

He dissolved the firm in the spring of 1976.

Yet Daley weathered all those storms. He kept the trust of his mighty political machine, and at the banquets it was the custom for the party faithful to introduce him as "the greatest mayor in the history of the world," or as "the greatest civic administrator who ever lived."

"Good politics," Daley liked to say, "is good government."

He never doubted that the way he ran his machine was good politics or that it produced good government. Only a short time before his death he fell to reminiscing with newsmen about his two decades in office.

He said it was the strength of his Democratic organization that made Chicago work.

"The idea is to have good candidates, good issues, and dedicated people who go from door to door and talk to other people," he said. "That's the secret of politics, and we have found the most successful politics is on a door-to-door basis."

It was a kind of success that carried Daley's influence all the way to the Oval Office of the White House, and to the Capitol in Springfield.

Democratic presidential candidates— and Democratic presidents—sought Daley's backing and advice. Adlai E. Stevenson—both the father and son— looked to him for support, as did John and Robert F. Kennedy and Hubert H. Humphrey. Through his control over the vast Chicago metropolitan area, he wielded immense power over the state legislature and the governor's mansion.

Never, however, did he seek an office higher than that of mayor of Chicago.

He said he was offered the gubernatorial nomination in 1960, but "I didn't think you could have an Irish Catholic for president and one for governor, too." Similarly, he turned down proposals that he seek the vice presidency.

Much of his national power, however, was expended to improve his city.

He obtained billions of dollars to spend on public works, from new sewers to new street lights to O'Hare International Airport—which he persisted in calling "O'Hara Field."

He brought major improvements to the city's rapid transit system, and one of his major political efforts was winning a close referendum victory for a Regional Transportation Authority.

The reason, he said, was love.

"I've been mayor for nineteen years," he once said. "I would have to have a type of love to keep moving on. I do love Chicago and its people. Years ago, when I was around the stockyards area, I never thought I'd be mayor. I never thought I'd have the opportunity."

THURSDAY, NOVEMBER 26, 1987

Harold Washington, Sixty-Five;
Mayor's Legacy a New Direction for Chicago Politics
By Kenan Heise and Dan McCaughna, *Tribune* Staff Reporters

Harold Washington, the first black mayor of Chicago, who surprised the city with his election, his survival skills, his reform measures, and his political acumen, died Wednesday of a heart attack.

He had been mayor since April 29, 1983, serving for four years and seven months. He was sixty-five years old.

Mayor Washington was taken to Northwestern Memorial Hospital shortly after 11:00 AM Wednesday after collapsing at his desk in City Hall.

In his first four years in office, Mayor Washington won first the "Council Wars" struggle for control of city government and then a second term and a decisive majority in the Chicago City Council.

Illinois Appellate Court justice R. Eugene Pincham expressed the view of many allies when he said: "We didn't know how good a product we were getting. There's nothing in his past to indicate how good he would be."

But not everyone in the city agreed, and Mayor Washington in April was denied the landslide victory over his chief opponent, former alderman Edward Vrdolyak (10th), that had been predicted and that would have capped his council control victories.

His principal opposition came from the white ethnic wards on the Northwest and Southwest Sides, but he also lost or did poorly in lakefront wards. Still, he won solidly in the black wards, did quite well in the Hispanic ones, and captured enough white votes to win a clear victory (53 percent) and to carry a majority of his supporters into office.

His legacy to the city is a new direction in its political life: Washington gave minority voters far more political control than they ever could have envisioned. He uprooted entrenched politically protected people and policies, bringing into city government many reformers and new perspectives.

And, finally, he began a process of paying attention to inner-city wards that had been ignored or slighted in city services while presiding over the fastest growth of the Loop in this century.

For all his promises of reform, however, the mayor did not completely dispel the cynical belief that politics and city government in Chicago are backroom affairs governed by the mayor's cronies.

Never was that more apparent than when Michael Raymond, a convicted con man, became a government informant and posed as a corrupt executive of a bill-collecting firm. Raymond wined and dined allies of the mayor in an attempt to gain lucrative city business for his firm, Systematic Recovery Service. The FBI videotaped the passing of alleged bribes, leading to the convictions of two former aldermen who had been loyal to the mayor.

Washington, an independent Democrat, started in political life working as a South Side precinct captain for the Cook County Democratic Party. The family lived near Forty-fourth Street and Michigan Avenue on the South Side, where Washington's father was a lawyer and a Methodist minister. The elder Washington also was a Democratic precinct captain, even before Franklin D. Roosevelt converted most blacks from Republican to Democrat.

Mayor Washington recalled that, as a boy, he helped his father ring doorbells for the Democratic Party. "He was my only hero," the mayor said. "He was a good man. He stood for something. He was firm, but fair."

Washington's first term as mayor was a turbulent one, marked by confrontation and racial polarization. His administration was dominated by a running battle with white regular Democrats who controlled the city council. The feud was dubbed "Council Wars"—from the movie *Star Wars*—and it attracted national attention.

As the city's first black mayor, he became a hero in the black community, and his fights merely enhanced his image among his political base.

As a reformer, he was credited with encouraging honest government.

Though he began his career as a loyal member of the Democratic organization, Washington spent much of his time as mayor warring with the Democratic machine that has run Chicago for more than fifty years. His prime target was the patronage system, which had allowed the machine to enhance its power by providing jobs and contracts to supporters.

Aided by federal court rulings that barred hiring and firing for political purposes, Washington ended the long-standing mayoral practice of hiring city workers who brought a letter of recommendation from a party leader.

He promised that only a limited number of his top policy-making officials would be hired on the basis of political loyalty. All others were to be hired on merit. Opponents scoffed at such promises, calling them a smokescreen behind which the mayor provided city jobs and contracts to his loyalists.

The mayor's opposition to patronage also angered some of his black council allies, many of them longtime regular Democrats who had hoped that a black mayor would provide jobs for their constituents.

It had been a coalition of black leaders, led by radio performer and community activist Lu Palmer and Rev. Jesse Jackson of Operation PUSH, who had gone to Washington in 1982 and asked him to run for mayor.

Washington, then in Congress, was reluctant but said he would consider it if the coalition could register fifty thousand black voters, which appeared to be an impossible demand.

But a registration drive, piloted by Palmer and others, resulted in more than one hundred thousand newly registered black voters, which virtually pushed Mayor Washington into the mayoral campaign, where his theme became "It's Our Turn."

The mayor was born in Cook County Hospital on April 15, 1922. He was the fourth of eleven children of Roy and Bertha Washington.

When his parents were divorced, he remained with his father. He attended Forrestville Elementary School and DuSable High School in Chicago. At Du Sable, he was a track star, winning the 1939 city championship in the 120-yard high hurdles and placing second in the 200-yard low hurdles.

He also was a middleweight boxer in high school and in Depression-era Civilian Conservation Corps camps, which he attended during summers.

He spent World War II in the Army Air Corps, where he was a first sergeant in a unit helping build landing strips in the South Pacific.

As the result of a wartime romance, he married in 1942. He was divorced in 1951. There were no children, and he never remarried.

After the war, he attended the new Roosevelt University in Chicago. He graduated in 1949 after being elected senior class president. He then went to Northwestern University Law School.

Washington graduated in 1952 and was admitted to the Illinois bar in 1953. The next year he took the first in a series of political jobs that would keep him on public payrolls for most of the next thirty years.

When his father died in 1954, Washington succeeded him as a precinct captain in the Third Ward and in his city job as an assistant Chicago corporation counsel under Mayor Martin Kennelly.

He remained a lawyer for the city until 1958. In 1960 he was hired as an arbitrator for the Illinois Industrial Commission, a state agency that determines the amount of workers' compensation payments awarded to people injured on the job.

By the early 1960s, he had become deeply involved in Third Ward politics, emerging as a protégé of Committeeman Ralph Metcalfe, then the alderman, later to become a congressman from the South Side.

Mayor Washington ran Metcalfe's campaigns for alderman and, later, for Congress, and in 1964 he was rewarded with a seat in the Illinois House from the South Side Twenty-Sixth District.

He spent the next twelve years in the Illinois House, becoming chairman of the Judiciary Committee. He sponsored bills on civil rights, open housing, minority hiring, small-business problems, currency-exchange reform, and medical malpractice.

He led a drive to save financially impoverished Provident Hospital and steered to passage a bill creating the Illinois Department of Human Rights. He also sponsored the state law making Dr. Martin Luther King Jr.'s birthday, January 15, a state holiday.

Mayor Washington's colleagues found the future mayor to be a voracious reader and an articulate speaker. He could quote from the classics and was fond of using flowery language in speeches and barbed criticism aimed at political foes.

Washington's strong baritone voice often boomed out from the back rows of the House chamber, and fellow legislators said he was one of the few lawmakers who could change votes by eloquence.

He turned out to be different from most of the organization politicians sent to the capitol by Mayor Richard J.

Daley's machine. He asked questions, did not always follow orders, and on occasion tried to put together his own coalitions behind particular legislation.

After two terms, Daley decided to dump him for his independence. But Washington had become a highly visible and popular legislator among his constituents, and he easily won reelection.

Just as his political career was beginning to blossom, he was staggered by problems in his personal and professional life.

In 1970 his law license was suspended after the Illinois Supreme Court's Attorney Registration and Disciplinary Board found that he had accepted retainers from five clients and then failed to perform promised legal services.

The suspension was for a year, but by the time it was to have expired, he was in tax trouble with the federal government. As a result of his tax difficulties, the law license suspension remained in effect until 1975, when it was lifted by the state supreme court.

In 1972, while a state representative, Mayor Washington served thirty-six days as a federal prisoner in Cook County Jail after being convicted in U.S. District Court in Chicago for failing to file income tax returns for the years 1964, 1965, 1967, and 1969.

He was sentenced to two years in prison, but federal judge Joseph Sam Perry suspended all but thirty-six days. Prosecutors said Washington hadn't filed returns for nineteen years, but was prosecuted for only the most recent four years because the statute of limitations prevented the government from bringing him to trial for the earlier years.

His legal problems did not hinder his political career, however, and in November 1976, he was elected to the state senate. Washington had, by then, severed his organization links. Metcalfe, his mentor, had broken with Daley in 1972 over the issue of police brutality, and Washington joined him in the antimachine camp.

In 1975 Washington was one of many independents who tried to persuade Metcalfe to run against Daley for mayor. When Metcalfe backed out, Washington became disillusioned and for a time considered quitting politics.

In the spring of 1977, after Daley's death, Washington decided to run against his successor, Mayor Michael Bilandic, the former Eleventh Ward alderman picked by the city council to succeed Daley.

Many blacks had been angered at the way party bosses had chosen Bilandic as acting mayor over Ald. Wilson Frost (34th), a black who held the title of mayor pro tem under Daley.

But Bilandic had no trouble winning the special mayoral primary against Washington and other Democrats, plus the special mayoral election against a Republican. In that primary, Washington got only 11 percent of the vote—73,705 of more than 700,000 cast.

He was defiant. "You have not heard the last of Harold Washington," he told a group of admirers. And he indicated that his break with the machine was total.

The next year, he repulsed another attempt by the organization to defeat him for reelection, winning his senate seat by just 239 votes.

He took on the organization again,

defeating the machine's man, U.S. Rep. Bennett Stewart, who had gone to Congress in 1978 after Metcalfe's death, in a four-way Democratic primary in 1980 for Metcalfe's old congressional seat.

The district was one of the more Democratic in the country, and in November, Washington was easily elected to Congress from Chicago's First District. Getting reelected in 1982 was a snap. Other things also were going his way.

In the November 1982 election, an upsurge of new black voters from Chicago almost defeated Gov. James Thompson, a Republican who had been expected to win easily.

To an experienced politician like Washington, the new black voters carried an important message: a black person could be elected mayor in 1983. Indeed, Washington had decided to run several months before black leaders assured him that he would be the only serious black contender. He announced his candidacy on November 10, 1982.

The campaign was aided by the fact that he had two white opponents: Jane Byrne, the machine candidate who had replaced Bilandic as mayor in 1979, and State's Attorney Richard M. Daley, heir to the most potent political name in Chicago.

Washington was by far the least known of the three. But he changed that with an aggressive approach during a series of televised debates, which raised his visibility and gave him credibility with his political base, black voters.

"I'm running for mayor because Jane Byrne is destroying the City of Chicago," he said in the first debate. He accused Byrne of "fighting for control of city patronage and fat cat city contracts for her cronies."

His 1970s jail sentence and law license suspension increasingly became issues in the campaign. But Washington kept up the attack on Byrne and came in first in the Democratic primary with 36 percent of the vote, mostly from black neighborhoods. Byrne and Daley got 34 and 30 percent, respectively, mostly from white areas.

The primary victory meant that Washington was the Democratic Party's nominee for mayor. His 419,266-vote total was nearly six times what he had received in 1977.

In Chicago, winning the Democratic primary is usually the same as winning the election. But not in 1983. The primary victory stunned the Democratic machine, and his race, independence, and legal problems turned his Republican mayoral foe, former state representative Bernard Epton, into a viable candidate. Many Democratic regulars, unable to accept Washington, backed Epton—some openly, some covertly.

The campaign was often ugly. The bitter racial tone of the contest attracted national attention as television viewers and newspaper readers across the nation were reminded that Chicago was considered to be the most segregated big city in the country.

In the April 12, 1983, general election, the city split largely along racial lines. Epton carried some white wards by ratios of 36–1. But Washington carried black wards by as much as 99–1. In addition, Washington got 79 percent of the growing Hispanic vote, which represented 14 percent of Chicago's population.

Washington won the election by a 39,568 majority, receiving 656,727 votes to Epton's 617,159. The key to his victory was support among Hispanics and liberal whites along the city's lakefront.

WEDNESDAY, MAY 11, 1988

Richard Ogilvie, Sixty-Five; Former Governor
By John Camper and Jon Van, *Tribune* Staff Reporters

Former Illinois governor Richard B. Ogilvie, sixty-five, a no-nonsense politician who helped rescue the state from near-bankruptcy and governmental obsolescence, died Tuesday, a day after suffering a heart attack in his Loop law office.

Governor Ogilvie, who continued to play an important role in local government and Republican politics after leaving office in 1973, died at 5:23 PM in Northwestern Memorial Hospital.

A hospital spokeswoman said that "damage to his heart as a result of a massive heart attack suffered yesterday in his office was too severe for his heart to recover despite maximum medical and mechanical support."

Ogilvie was taken to the hospital after being stricken about 11:30 AM Monday in the thirteenth-floor offices of his former law firm at 19 South LaSalle Street.

Short, stocky, serious, and non-telegenic, Ogilvie was out of place in an era of charismatic, blow-dried politicians who put personal popularity first and governmental programs a distant second.

Nevertheless, Ogilvie had enough political skills to win three successive elections—first for Cook County sheriff in 1962, followed by Cook County Board president in 1966, and finally governor in 1968—before losing a close reelection race in 1972, largely because of voter resentment against the state income tax he unpopularly pushed through while in office.

Although Ogilvie retired from public office, he never retired from public life. He was mentioned as a potential candidate for Chicago mayor before every election, and mayors and governors frequently looked to him to help solve tough government problems.

"Dick Ogilvie's contribution to the state of Illinois will be long remembered," said Governor James R. Thompson. "He was a true public servant and one that I and millions of other Illinoisans had the privilege of calling governor.

"He always spoke his mind and had the strength of character to stand behind issues he believed in, such as the state's first income tax," Thompson said.

Ogilvie had been slated to become chairman of the Chicago Housing

Gov. Richard B. Ogilvie (right) chats with Sen. Charles Percy.

Authority (CHA) board under a reform plan put together in recent weeks by Mayor Eugene Sawyer.

Sawyer called Ogilvie's death "a great loss to the city and state. Governor Ogilvie was a fine public servant. I looked forward to working with him as we tried to resolve some of the problems in CHA, and he indicated he was trying to give back to the city that has been so kind to him."

It would have been similar to the role Ogilvie had filled successfully in 1985, when Thompson and former mayor Harold Washington put him in charge of supervising the completion of the $312 million McCormick Place annex project, which had been plagued with cost overruns and construction problems.

After losing to Democrat Dan Walker in the 1972 gubernatorial contest, Ogilvie had pursued a financially rewarding career as a lawyer with the venerable Chicago firm of Isham, Lincoln & Beale. He made millions as trustee for the bankrupt Chicago, Milwaukee, St. Paul & Pacific Railroad Co. from 1977 through 1985, and Ogilvie was chosen last month to become trustee for the bankrupt Chicago Missouri & Western Railway Co.

"He was probably the most straightforward man I've ever met, and certainly the most straightforward politician," said Chicago attorney A. Daniel Feldman.

Ogilvie and Feldman were longtime colleagues at Isham, Lincoln & Beale, which recently dissolved amid much-publicized squabbling. But Feldman noted that Ogilvie "was rock solid through a very difficult time, and when we needed him, he was there."

The firm's demise came two years after a much-heralded merger between Isham, Lincoln & Beale and Reuben & Proctor. Ogilvie was a key player in fashioning the marriage of the two firms, as was lawyer Don Reuben.

"My wife [Jeanette] and I are very sad at the loss of a longtime and good friend, and a distinguished man," Reuben said. "His loss is Illinois' loss."

Ogilvie had joined Wildman, Harrold, Allen & Dixon on May 1.

Ogilvie is best remembered for his courageous sponsorship of the state income tax in 1969. Almost every responsible public figure admitted privately that the income tax was necessary to save the state from financial ruin, but few were willing to support it publicly.

Ogilvie took the lead. And although Chicago mayor Richard J. Daley and many Democratic legislators ended up supporting the tax, it was Ogilvie who took the heat.

"I told him," said Chicago Republican chairman Lou Kasper, "'You have to be careful with this income tax, Governor.

It could hurt you politically.' His reply was, 'I have to do what I have to do. I am the governor, and this has to happen.'"

Fred Bird, his press secretary at the time, recalled, "Ogilvie's mistake was that, being a rather direct sort, he didn't soften people up. Other governors waited until their states had payless paydays to build up pressure for an income tax, but Ogilvie wasn't willing to let things reach that stage."

Bird said Ogilvie's other major accomplishment was "bringing a number of bright, young people into government, where they were given responsibility, turned loose, and not subject to embarrassment by tawdry doings."

One of them was Chicago lawyer Michael Schneiderman, his policy adviser on environmental issues.

"There was no one in state government fighting hard for pollution control, so Ogilvie did," Schneiderman said. "His solution was to completely rewrite the laws to create agencies that were aggressive in dealing with the problems. This was not a universally popular thing to do politically."

Ogilvie vastly increased state spending on education; pushed through a $900 million bond issue for highways, airports, and mass transit; and created a new Bureau of the Budget to manage the state's finances professionally.

Though Ogilvie was skillful at dealing with other politicians, even his strongest supporters admitted he was not terribly popular with the public. This was partly because of his dour expression, the result of serious facial wounds suffered as a tank commander in France during World War II. But beyond that, his aides said, he just didn't like the glad-handing and small talk that come naturally to most politicians.

"He was never comfortable with the fluff of politics," recalled John Kolbe, his assistant press secretary and now a political columnist for the *Phoenix Gazette.* "For a lot of politicians, the fluff is the essence of the job, but Ogilvie would rather be in an office with department heads, knocking heads and making things work."

Dr. Renee Hartz, chief cardiac surgeon on the team that treated Ogilvie at Northwestern Memorial, said the former governor's heart was enlarged to at least twice normal size. This was likely caused by the strain of pumping because of Ogilvie's severe high blood pressure, she said.

Dr. Barry Kramer, another doctor at Northwestern, said a blood clot in Ogilvie's left main artery evidently totally closed the left anterior descending artery, which already was 90 percent closed by plaque buildup in artery walls. The left circumflex artery was 100 percent closed by plaque buildup.

It is likely that the clot closed the artery and triggered the massive attack, Kramer said.

The medical team also discovered dead heart tissue near the right artery, indicating that at some time in the past, Ogilvie had suffered a milder heart attack, Hartz said.

A native of Kansas City, Missouri, Ogilvie completed high school in Port Chester, New York, and graduated from Yale University and the Chicago-Kent College of Law.

He first gained public notice as a crime-busting assistant attorney general in Chicago in the late 1950s and early 1960s. His biggest catch was mob boss Anthony J. Accardo, whom he convicted of income-tax evasion—a conviction Accardo managed to overturn on appeal.

He parlayed his fame into an upset victory for sheriff in 1962 and won election as county board president four years later. He was the last Republican to hold that office in the county.

Ogilvie was never particularly close to Thompson, and in 1978, with characteristic directness, he said Thompson's proposal for a nonbinding statewide referendum on limiting taxes was "a meaningless gimmick." Ogilvie also incurred the wrath of Chicago Republicans by endorsing Democratic mayor Jane M. Byrne for reelection in 1983.

He is survived by his wife, Dorothy, and a daughter, Elizabeth Simer.

FRIDAY, JULY 27, 2001

Emma Schweer, 105; Crete Township Institution

By James Janega, *Tribune* Staff Reporter

Emma Schweer, the longtime Crete Township tax collector who, at 105, was widely believed to be the oldest elected politician in America, died Wednesday, July 25, in St. James Hospital and Health Centers in Chicago Heights.

She succeeded her husband in the post in 1965 and was reelected seventeen times, most recently in April. She continued to be an institution even after her position became less significant when Will County took over tax-collection duties in the 1970s.

Though the position was unpaid and largely ceremonial, the people of Crete Township considered it a tradition to continue electing her to the office, said Crete Village Administrator David Wallace.

"There are just some things you don't change," he said. "I think the type of person that Emma Schweer was warranted that. I think it commanded respect, and I think that's why it lasted as long as it did."

With her husband, she was the co-owner of Schweer Gas & Appliance on Main Street, learned how to fly in the 1930s, and volunteered to train pilots during World War II. Though her family said she was driven by a gritty, do-it-yourself mentality, almost everyone in town remarked that Schweer was an elegant woman in every respect.

"I was probably five or six years old and I met her when we were paying our

Emma Schweer, a longtime tax collector, was a Crete Township institution.

light bill at the store she operated. She was a very proper figure, always very businesslike, always dressed impeccably," said Crete mayor Mike Einhorn, recalling an encounter some forty-five years before. "She's been pretty much constant," he added.

Schweer was born in Iowa in 1896. Her family moved to a farm near Crete when she was four. She graduated from Trinity Lutheran School in town at a time when classes were still conducted in German, and she attended business college in Chicago Heights.

She met her future husband, Art Schweer, at a local roller rink. After working briefly as a secretary for an insurance company in Chicago, she married him in 1923.

Partners in Business, Politics
They went into business together, first in a small wooden building on Main Street and later by branching into operation of an airport in Homewood. She served as his deputy when he held the township collector's post from 1933 until his death in 1965 and said she took it over afterward out of respect for him.

For a few years, Schweer was responsible for typing tax bills, collecting real estate and personal property taxes, and shuttling tax revenue back and forth between township taxing bodies and the county seat in Joliet.

State law required that the post remain even when it became unnecessary in Crete Township in the 1970s.

After that, "her position and running kind of took on a life of its own. It just evolved," said Einhorn. "She kept doing it. She could have just walked away but didn't. Not only did she run, but she won. It was probably at that point that she became somewhat of an institution."

Out of respect for Schweer—a staunch Republican who filled her white frame house with elephant figurines—the local Democratic Party has not slated anyone to run for collector since the late 1980s, township Democratic chairwoman Norenna Schumacker told the *Tribune* in April.

"She was a symbol of consistency and loyalty," said township Republican chairman Joseph Battaglia. "She gave a lot of pride to the members of the Republican Central Committee. She gave a lot of substance to the Republican Party."

Still, she had to be talked into running again at age 101. Crete Township Assessor Ronald Koelling said that to avoid a similar argument this year, he nominated her at the township Republican caucus last January without first telling her.

"A big cheer went up from the audience—there were probably 300 people. She got a big round of applause," he said. "And she was nominated without question."

Pride in the Post
If she was reluctant to run a few years ago, it was not because she disliked the job, said her great-niece Jeannine Aull, adding that Schweer was always proud of the post.

"She was really just a little farm girl when she grew up, but when she got involved in picking up her husband's term when he died, that's when she really began to shine," Aull said. "She had to make her own decisions. The numbers, the spreadsheets, that was all a part of her household."

Interviewed in April, Schweer even hinted at considering another run in four more years: "I don't think I'll be around by then," she said. "But if I am and they put my name on the ballot again, I just might give it a shot."

THURSDAY, JANUARY 17, 2002

Michael Bilandic, Seventy-Eight;
A Mayor Who Had Hard Act to Follow

By Gary Washburn, *Tribune* Staff Reporter. *Tribune* reporters Joseph Sjostrom, Christi Parsons, Ronald Kotulak, and David Mendell contributed to this report.

Michael Bilandic accepts the gavel as Chicago's new acting mayor in 1976.

Purple and black bunting was draped over the entrance to City Hall on Wednesday as Chicago mourned Michael A. Bilandic, the quiet and unassuming son of immigrants who rose to become a leader of the city council, mayor of Chicago, and, later, chief justice of the Illinois Supreme Court.

Bilandic, seventy-eight, died unexpectedly late Tuesday at Northwestern Memorial Hospital on the eve of scheduled coronary bypass surgery. He had been admitted to the hospital two days earlier after suffering what doctors described as a mild heart attack.

A former alderman who was the eyes and ears in the city council for his mentor, the late Mayor Richard J. Daley, Bilandic was picked by council colleagues to replace Daley when he died in late 1976. But he will be best remembered for the way his political career unraveled under the weight of record snowfalls in the winter of 1978–1979, which immobilized the city and led to the historic election of Chicago's first female mayor, Jane Byrne.

But his admirers, of whom there were many in the halls of government, say the snow debacle unfairly clouded the reputation of a man who was a dedicated and hardworking official.

Bilandic was a "very good public servant and very committed," said Mayor Richard M. Daley, whose father, the late Mayor Richard J. Daley, had been Bilandic's political sponsor. "He made a strong contribution to the city."

"He had a full and rich and diverse career," said Ald. Edward Burke (14th), a longtime friend. "He served in all branches of government—legislative, executive, and judicial—and will be remembered as a very capable, hardworking, and loyal public official."

In a written statement, Bilandic's wife, Heather, described her husband as "a devoted family man who also loved Chicago and its people, was proud of his Croatian heritage, and grateful for the opportunities which this country provided to his family. He felt deeply honored to have been able to serve as a member of the legal profession and to have participated in three branches of government during a lifetime of service."

After his defeat by Byrne, Bilandic returned to private law practice and then answered what some believe was his true calling when Bilandic was elected a judge, first to the Illinois Appellate Court in 1984 and later to the state supreme court after winning election in 1990.

Every mayor since Bilandic has taken a political lesson from his downfall, launching Herculean salting and plowing operations after even the gentlest of snowfalls. Bilandic had to learn the hard way.

A total of thirty-five inches hit the city over a two-week period, and Bilandic shrugged off the snow, insisting that conditions were improving even as buried cars blocked streets, service on the Chicago Transit Authority faltered, and O'Hare International Airport was tied up in knots.

At one point during the crisis, he urged people to move their cars from streets to school parking lots, which he announced had been cleared. But the mayor apparently had been given faulty information by underlings; unhappy motorists discovered that the lots remained waist deep in snow.

Democratic Primary Loss

Indeed, the city's response to the snow was perhaps the biggest factor in Bilandic's stunning defeat in the Democratic primary a few weeks later.

"He was a gentle and sometimes too nice a guy who got caught in a snowstorm," said Ald. Richard Mell (33rd), who was in the city council when

Bilandic was mayor. "And, unfortunately, that will be part of his legacy. But the real Michael Bilandic was a decent Chicagoan who had the best interest of the city at heart. In all the times I was with him, I never saw him mean-spirited, vindictive, or ever do anything but try to be a good guy. And that's what he was."

Born in Bridgeport in 1923, Bilandic learned Chicago politics in the Eleventh Ward neighborhood that had produced a host of Democratic politicians, including Richard J. Daley.

He graduated in 1940 from De La Salle High School and received a bachelor's degree from St. Mary's College in Winona, Minnesota, and a law degree from DePaul University.

Bilandic served as a first lieutenant in the Marine Corps in the Pacific during World War II.

He became active in the Eleventh Ward Democratic organization in 1948 when then ward committeeman Daley asked him to become involved in party work.

But Bilandic's real political career began in 1969.

That is when the late Matthew Danaher was in line for appointment as the clerk of Cook County Circuit Court and Daley needed a replacement for him as Eleventh Ward alderman. The mayor's choice of Bilandic, whose ethnic roots were Croatian, was a break from precedent in a ward that, for years, had been represented in the council by Irish Americans.

Bilandic was reluctant to give up a law practice that was bringing him a salary estimated at $75,000 a year, but Daley prevailed. The newcomer ran, swamping the GOP candidate.

As an alderman, Bilandic's long, detailed speech making and monotone delivery gave him a reputation as a colorless man. But he was considered effective and well prepared.

"Here is a guy who led the fight on the environment right from the start," said Ald. Bernard Stone (50th), who served on the council with Bilandic. In 1971 Bilandic pushed legislation that banned phosphates from detergents.

A few years later, Bilandic helped shepherd the Lakefront Protection Ordinance through the council as well as a measure revamping zoning requirements that cleared the way for big multiuse developments, Stone said.

With Ald. Thomas Keane (31st) on trial in federal court on charges of conspiracy and mail fraud, Bilandic in 1974 was chosen to replace him both as chairman of the council's powerful Finance Committee and as Daley's council floor leader.

When Daley died on December 20, 1976, council leaders fought each other to fill the vacuum, but it was Bilandic who received the support of the Daley family and ultimately gained the mayoral seat.

Daley, in his later years respected and beloved by a city that had known no other mayor for a generation, had failed to groom anyone as a successor. The new mayor was faced with the unenviable task of filling shoes that no one in Chicago could have filled.

Started ChicagoFest

Nevertheless, Bilandic sponsored new initiatives. During his two and a half

Mayor Michael Bilandic supervises snow removal on LaSalle Street in 1978.

years in office, he organized the first ChicagoFest and arranged city-insured, low-interest mortgage loans for middle-income families. A runner and jogger, he also lent his support to the Chicago Marathon.

Yet Bilandic's personality didn't capture the imagination or adoration of the voters. In an era when politicians were increasingly becoming celebrities in their own right, Bilandic could stroll through the Loop in the city he ran and not be stopped or even acknowledged by a single passerby.

On another front, the mayor's personal life blossomed.

When he took office, Bilandic was a bachelor who lived with his elderly mother. It was during his time in office, when he was in his fifties, that he married Heather Morgan, the daughter of a prominent Chicago businessman. The couple's only child, Michael Morgan Bilandic, was born during his mayoralty.

After taking over at city hall, Bilandic made numerous changes in the city command structure.

In what turned out to be a major tactical error, he ousted Byrne as the city's consumer sales commissioner and forced her to give up her spot as cochair of the Cook County Regular Democratic Organization's Central Committee.

The Response Was Furious

Byrne's attacks on Bilandic and his administration were so strong during the 1979 primary that the mayor at times appeared on the brink of tears as he compared her offensives, combined with media criticism, to the crucifixion of Christ, the Holocaust in Nazi Germany, and the plight of blacks during slavery in America.

After losing the primary, Bilandic returned to private law practice. Although he maintained his Bridgeport home, he and his family spent most of their time in the Gold Coast apartment he also owned.

Five years after his departure from city hall, and without party backing, Bilandic won election to the Illinois Appellate Court's First District, which covers Cook County. At the age of sixty-seven, he ran for a ten-year term on the state supreme court, this time slated by the Democratic Party, and won again. He subsequently was elected by colleagues on the court to a term as chief justice.

Declined Campaign Donations

Bilandic spent $32,000 of his own money on the supreme court election campaign and refused to accept campaign contributions. "This is my last hurrah," he explained. "I don't want to go there encumbered in any manner."

As a jurist who had served in the other branches of government, Bilandic was especially attentive to the separation of powers and respectful of executive and legislative prerogative.

"He always commented, 'Let them do the work they do, and we'll do the work we do,'" said Judge Allen Hartman, a longtime friend who shared the appellate bench with Bilandic. "He was very proper in that regard."

Nevertheless, one of his most important supreme court opinions was highly critical of a common practice in the Illinois General Assembly, where lawmakers rolled unrelated measures into a single bill to drum up enough support for passage.

Writing for the court in *Johnson v. Edgar*, Bilandic struck down a sweeping new law because it violated the Illinois Constitution's prohibition of such bundling. The opinion formed the heart of the court's doctrine on the so-called single-subject rule, and it eventually led to the overturning of several other measures passed by the Republican-led legislature in the mid-1990s.

Bilandic also wrote a revolutionary 1999 opinion in a ruling that health maintenance organizations can be held liable for negligence involving a patient's medical care. The decision opened the door for a flood of HMO lawsuits.

"When it came to things like budgetary matters or municipal law, we always looked to him," said Chief Justice Moses Harrison, who served on the

high court with Bilandic for eight years. "But you also had to admire his general knowledge. He just knew so much."

The court lowered its flags to half-staff, and Bilandic's portrait was draped in black bunting. The city council, meanwhile, began a meeting Wednesday with a moment of silence in the former mayor's honor.

In what turned out to be his last public role, Bilandic in September cast a vote that is expected to influence Illinois politics for years to come. After Democrats won a drawing to gain control of the Legislative Redistricting Commission, Bilandic was inserted on the panel by the party to break a partisan deadlock and cast the tie-breaking vote on a redistricting map that could set the stage for Democratic control of the legislature for the next decade.

Burke said he talked to Bilandic on Tuesday afternoon to wish him well in surgery.

"He sounded strong," the alderman said. "He was in good spirits. He said he was sad he would miss the board of managers meeting of the Chicago Bar Association on Wednesday, but he hoped to be back on his feet in a couple of days."

Bilandic died of a rare and "uniformly fatal" condition in which the wall of the heart ruptures, and not of a second heart attack, according to an autopsy report released Wednesday by Bilandic's physicians at Northwestern Memorial.

Dr. Dan Fintel, his cardiologist, said that he has seen only two other ruptures following heart attacks in seventeen years of practice.

The rupture occurred on the left side and front of Bilandic's heart, the area that was damaged by a heart attack he suffered sometime in the early morning Saturday. That area of the heart was deprived of blood, thereby leading to the death of a small portion of heart muscle.

Instead of scar tissue forming around the damaged area, which is typical, the weakened area burst from the pressure of blood inside the heart, causing the heart to go into acute failure, Fintel said. Such conditions are impossible to detect in advance, even using modern diagnostic equipment, he said.

Heather Bilandic had been visiting her husband for most of Tuesday and left one hour before the rupture occurred at 10:00 PM. A heart team rushed in to try to save the former mayor. He was pronounced dead at 10:30 PM.

Bilandic's doctors said that tests performed Monday showed he had significant blockages in his coronary arteries but added that he appeared to be an ideal candidate for bypass surgery.

THURSDAY, SEPTEMBER 26, 2002

Roman Pucinski, Eighty-Three; Political, Polish, and Proud

By James Janega and Gary Washburn, *Tribune* Staff Reporters. *Tribune* Staff Reporter Matthew Walberg contributed to this report.

Roman C. Pucinski, the silver-haired fixture of Chicago politics who represented the Far Northwest Side for thirty-three years as a congressman and an alderman, died of pneumonia Wednesday in Resurrection Pavilion in Park Ridge.

He was eighty-three and had been under treatment for Parkinson's disease for some time.

Pucinski—"Pooch" to colleagues and friends—served in the U.S. House from 1959 to 1973 and was a Chicago alderman from 1973 until 1991.

"Roman wasn't ashamed to serve in the Chicago City Council," said Ald. Bernard Stone (50th), a longtime colleague. "He wanted to contribute to his community. The one place you can contribute more to your local community than anyplace else is in the city council."

Throughout his career, he was a key representative for Chicago in Congress and for Poles in Chicago, said former U.S. Representative Dan Rostenkowski, who served alongside Pucinski in Washington.

"He was a very prominent individual. He was aggressive, and he brought that aggressiveness to the political, public life. He was a tremendously effective legislator," Rostenkowski said.

"It was at a time when we [new congressmen] were seen and not heard," Rostenkowski said. "Roman wasn't like that. Roman was always heard."

Pucinski stood at the political center of Chicago's Polish community.

Roman C. Pucinski, a longtime U.S. representative and Chicago alderman, stood at the political center of the local Polish community.

"Other than perhaps the president of the Polish National Alliance, if you mentioned a Polish leader, it was Roman Pucinski," said T. Ronald Jasinski-Herbert, public relations director for the Chicago Society Lodge of the Polish National Alliance. "He was recognized within the Polish community as the preeminent Polish politician."

Ald. Edward M. Burke said Pucinski "leaves a legacy of remarkable urban success and hard-nosed gentility," and Mayor Richard M. Daley called him "a dedicated public servant who really cared about Chicago and its people."

But over a long and colorful career, Pucinski knew defeat as well as victory. He lost in his first bid for Congress in 1956, in the 1972 general election for the U.S. Senate, and in the 1977 Democratic primary for mayor.

He grew up in a heavily Polish neighborhood that is now Wicker Park. His youth was shaped by his father's abandonment of his mother and siblings when he was a child and by the Depression in his preteen years when he wore government-issued shoes, said his daughter Aurelia, who followed her father into politics and served as Cook County Circuit Court clerk from 1988 to 2000.

He helped his mother, Lidia, later a personality on a radio station he owned, support their family by selling Magic Washer soap to local grocery stores and chocolate to office workers after school.

Pucinski, articulate and never at a loss for words, had an early interest in public affairs. In January 1939, while still a student at Northwestern University, he became a reporter for the *Chicago Times*, a predecessor of the *Chicago Sun-Times*. He later attended John Marshall Law School but never took the bar exam, his daughter said, because he was too busy covering the 1948 presidential election.

Pucinski joined the Army Air Force during World War II, became a captain, and served as a bombardier in the first B-29 bomb raid on Tokyo in 1944. Back with the newspaper after the war, Pucinski became City Hall reporter, a job that exposed him to opportunities in politics.

He was brought to Washington in 1952, where he served one year as a bilingual chief investigator for a special House subcommittee investigating the Katyn Forest massacre of thousands of Polish military officers by the Soviets during the war.

Urged by Mayor Richard J. Daley to run for Congress, Pucinski entered the Eleventh District race on the Northwest Side in 1956 and lost to the incumbent, Timothy Sheehan, a Republican.

"He understood that in order to get things done for ordinary people, you had to be in a position where people would listen to you," his daughter said. "He loved the problem-solving part of it. That energized him. He loved meeting people, loved wading into a room of strangers to find out what they were thinking, identify with them, and have the chance to represent them."

He ran again in 1958 and won.

After seven terms in Congress, where he was known as Daley's man, Pucinski gave up his seat to run unsuccessfully for the U.S. Senate against incumbent senator Charles Percy (R-Ill.) in November 1972.

The underdog in that race, Pucinski noted a few days before the election that Percy was outspending him 10-1. "We're struggling along on nickels and dimes," said Pucinski.

Pucinski said his proudest achievement in Congress was sponsoring legislation fostering public education, a field in which he was considered an expert. The legislation gave Chicago schools $30 million in 1970 and guaranteed them $38 million the next year.

Pucinski also championed airline safety while in Congress, something for which he was honored many years later. On December 18, 1999, Pucinski was cited by the Federal Aviation Administration (FAA) for his role as a freshman congressman in 1959 when he pressured the government to require cockpit voice recorders in all airplanes that carry at least six passengers. The FAA awarded him the Silver Medal of Distinguished Service during a ceremony in the Polish Museum of America.

Pucinski ran a strong race in the 1977 Democratic mayoral primary, but his main opponent, incumbent Michael Bilandic, who became mayor after Richard J. Daley died in December 1976, won the nomination in a six-way Democratic primary and was elected mayor.

During the mayoral campaign, Pucinski said Daley had "too much power for the good of Chicago." He also blamed Daley and "machine politics" for "allowing the city to deteriorate into a slum and driving jobs out of the city."

Pucinski vowed to decentralize the public school system and give each school its own budget. He wanted to combat school segregation by establishing reading centers on racially neutral ground.

In late 1982 Pucinski considered entering the mayoral race after Harold Washington, then a South Side congressman, indicated he was going to run. Cook County state's attorney Richard M. Daley had already announced, and Mayor Jane Byrne was unofficially campaigning for reelection.

Pucinski decided against another try for mayor, however. In April 1983 he snubbed the Democratic Party and became the eighth Democratic committeeman to announce his support for Republican Bernard Epton against Washington, the Democratic primary winner. Afterward, he remained a leader in Ald. Edward Vrdolyak's majority city council bloc that opposed the Washington administration.

Ever flexible, after Washington's election, Pucinski indicated that white ethnics in Chicago were ready to be reconciled with the new mayor, while noting that the mayor's greatest potential achievement would be to bring black and white people together.

At the same time, Pucinski had been the longtime president of the Illinois division of the Polish American Congress, and he led a number of rallies in Chicago protesting communism in Poland. He supported Poland's Solidarity labor movement, and over the years he helped to raise $1.5 million as the movement gained international prominence.

On New Year's Eve of 1982, he talked to Solidarity leader Lech Walesa in a telephone call made to test the easing of Polish government restrictions on phone communications.

"I almost fell off the phone when Lech answered the phone personally," Pucinski said. Walesa wished Chicago a happy New Year and thanked Chicagoans for food and medicine sent to the Polish people, he said.

In his last campaign for alderman, Pucinski faced six challengers and was forced into a runoff in March 1991, against Brian Doherty, a Republican and a first-time candidate. Doherty waged a vigorous and expensive campaign, arguing that the sprawling middle-class Northwest Side ward paid high taxes and didn't receive enough city services.

Pucinski's first wife, Aurelia, sixty-four, died in April 1983. She had been vice president and general manager of the Pucinskis' family-owned radio station WEDC-AM 1240.

Pucinski later married Elizabeth Simpson, a dean at the University of Wisconsin and an award-winning poet. She died in 1990 at the age of seventy.

Survivors include a son, Christopher; his daughter Aurelia, director of the state's Department of Professional Regulation; a brother, Wesley; a sister, Halina Pawl; and three grandchildren, Rebecca, Elizabeth Anne, and James C. Keithley.

SECTION

VI

Activists

Chicago is known as much for its protestors as it is for its public leaders. Its champions had both local interests and national influence. Among its tireless and most colorful was a lawyer who opposed school segregation and kept a drawing of Don Quixote on his desk. They included, too, a public-relations maven whose fight with multiple sclerosis led him to help draft the Americans with Disabilities Act, and a neighborhood firebrand who once nailed a rat to her alder-man's door in protest of rodent problems on the West Side.

TUESDAY, FEBRUARY 22, 2000

Joseph Dragonette, Sixty-Three; Activist for the Disabled

By James Janega, *Tribune* Staff Reporter

Joseph J. Dragonette, a Chicago publicist who guided developers as they sought public support for downtown building plans, was an activist whose fight with multiple sclerosis led to a seat on the panel drafting the Americans with Disabilities Act (ADA).

A no-nonsense man who understood the Chicago-style nexus of money, politics, and real estate, Dragonette, sixty-three, died Friday, February 18, in the University of Chicago Hospitals of complications related to his disease.

Friends recalled Dragonette as irreverent, whether he was arguing for a downtown that was lively round-the-clock or for greater public access for people with disabilities. "He was really able to shake the starch out of a lot of guys in town," said friend Susan Aaron.

Among other projects, he helped draft development goals for Chicago's Loop, helped secure U.S. landing rights for the supersonic Concorde at Washington Dulles International Airport, and participated in real estate deals from Boston to Los Angeles.

He founded Dragonette Inc., a public relations firm specializing in health-care issues, in 1983.

In 1992, a year after applauding from his wheelchair on the White House lawn the passage of the Americans with Disabilities Act, he was the guiding force behind Project Access, a Chicago-based computer database providing resources to employers trying to comply with ADA guidelines.

Dragonette, whose illness was diagnosed in 1976, had as little patience for people with disabilities who failed to make strides toward employment as he had for his own leg braces, wheelchair, and physical limitations. Yet he worked tirelessly to open doors for people with disabilities.

"No matter how complicated the project," said John McCarron, a *Tribune* writer who covered urban affairs, "Joe either had the answer off the top of his head or could put you in touch with a top professional . . . in minutes."

Dragonette is survived by his wife, Rita Hoey; his mother, June Cerceo; and two brothers, Patrick and Michael Cerceo.

FRIDAY, DECEMBER 1, 2000

Rev. Anthony Janiak, Eighty-Three; Activist Priest

By James Janega, *Tribune* Staff Reporter

Rev. Anthony Janiak, eighty-three, a Catholic priest on the Near Northwest Side who played a central role in urban renewal efforts as they swept through Chicago in the 1960s and 1970s, died of congestive heart failure Tuesday, November 21, in the St. Benedict Home for retired priests in Niles.

"He was always organizing people to fight injustice," said Auxiliary Bishop Timothy J. Lyne, the Catholic Archdiocese of Chicago's vicar for senior priests. "He wasn't a yeller or shouter; he was just a quiet, simple guy who felt he had a responsibility to help people."

In his later years, Father Janiak was a welcoming presence for Hispanics moving into Chicago. Earlier, he had been an organizing force in efforts to revitalize Bucktown, Wicker Park, and surrounding neighborhoods.

A native of Cicero, Janiak graduated from Quigley Preparatory Seminary and St. Mary of the Lake Seminary in Mundelein. He was ordained a priest in 1942.

After a stint at St. Andrew Parish in Calumet City, Janiak served at St. Thaddeus in Chicago and St. Isidore in Blue Island, coming to Holy Innocents Church on North Armour Street as an assistant pastor in 1949.

As the Vatican II pronouncements of the early 1960s shaped the modern church, Catholic priests took on more progressive roles in their communities.

Against that backdrop, Janiak was among the secular and religious members to found the Northwest Community Organization in 1962, targeting dilapidated neighborhood conditions in the then largely Polish neighborhoods of the Near Northwest Side.

"Tony was known for the social action work that he did," said Rev. Andrew McDonagh, a friend and seminary classmate. "A lot of priests were a little timid about taking a stance. However, he was not."

Many Holy Innocents parishioners had become so fed up with living conditions in their old neighborhood that they simply moved out, returning only for church on Sundays. A survey at the time showed that nearly half of the buildings in Bucktown were so worn they merited razing.

With the community organization, Janiak persuaded remaining building owners to rehabilitate their properties, lobbied local banks for low-interest loans, and sought support from businesspeople. At the time, Janiak told the *Tribune* he believed the private effort was the first large renewal project undertaken by a community organization in Chicago. "The need for community planning is recognized," he said in a 1966 interview.

For the next two years, Janiak remained active in redevelopment issues while serving at another North Side church and spoke out in the 1970s against rising heating-oil costs and their effects on cash-strapped parish schools. He was named pastor of St. Helen Church in 1968.

Lyne called Janiak "a quiet man with a quiet man's interests," a voracious reader who often played billiards in his spare time. But he said Janiak was also adept at ministering in Polish neighborhoods into which more and more Hispanic parishioners were moving.

"He was a very happy person, very expressive. He enjoyed working with the people," said Lupita Esparza, a former parishioner at St. Helen. "What really touched everybody was how open he was."

He became a pastor emeritus at St. Helen in 1984.

Father Janiak is survived by a brother, Hipolite.

THURSDAY, DECEMBER 28, 2000

Marshall Patner, Sixty-Nine; Public-Interest Lawyer
By James Janega, *Tribune* Staff Reporter

As the prototype for the logo at public-interest law firm Business and Professional People for the Public Interest (BPI), Marshall Patner sketched a tiny Don Quixote–like figure on a charging steed.

The 1969 drawing not only characterized the populist sentiment of BPI's young lawyers, it spoke volumes about the legal philosophy to which Patner gave his allegiance throughout his career.

Patner, sixty-nine, onetime proprietor of a Hyde Park cafe, a former BPI executive director, and an altruistic attorney who represented clients from the Blackstone Rangers street gang to shareholders at Beatrice Foods, died Sunday, December 24, in Northwestern Memorial Hospital, after suffering a heart attack on the way to his office Friday.

In 1969 he won arguments before the U.S. Supreme Court that upheld

Marshall Patner, a public-interest lawyer, represented clients ranging from the Blackstone Rangers street gang to Beatrice Foods shareholders.

a client's right to publicly protest persistent segregation in Chicago schools, and the American Civil Liberties Union in Illinois considered the case, *Dick Gregory v. City of Chicago*, one of its highlights before the high court.

Earlier, Patner's written arguments persuaded the court to refuse the deportation of Fred Thompson, an outspoken member of the Industrial Workers of the World.

"He had an excellent sense of how to persuade a judge and handle rivals," said fellow Hyde Park attorney and former alderman Leon Despres. "It was his ability to understand people and to establish a contact with them that gave him a special ability in trial work."

A 1949 graduate of Senn High School, Patner earned a bachelor's degree in political science from the University of Wisconsin at Madison in 1953. He married Irene Herman the next year and went to law school at the University of Chicago.

He graduated in 1956 and two years later opened the Medici Café in Hyde Park, a hangout for law students, journalists, and civil rights workers. Unsure if he wanted to practice law after graduation, he instead served for a few years as an aldermanic aide and campaign manager for Despres, a progressive. When Patner entered the legal profession, he gravitated to complex litigation and populist causes.

Through his private practice and cooperative work with the Illinois ACLU in the late 1960s, he represented evicted Chicago Housing Authority tenants, challengers to school board contracts, and Blackstone Rangers leader Jeff Fort. He helped found BPI in 1969 and built the Chicago-area firm into a legal watchdog and research group.

"We had no format, no program at the beginning," he told the *Tribune* in 1994, "just a kind of tone, a sense of wanting to correct abuses as they arose. Whatever strategy worked, we'd do."

The group challenged the proposal to build a third airport on landfill in Lake Michigan, accused the county assessor of giving assessment breaks to the city's largest banks, and joined the call for a special prosecutor to investigate the killing of two Black Panther leaders in a 1969 raid.

As BPI moved into policy work on housing, environmental, and nuclear power issues, Patner's interests remained in litigation. He left the organization on sabbatical in 1974 and founded a prelaw program for African American students at Wilberforce College in Cincinnati. Within a year, he was teaching the still-popular program at Stanford and the University of California at Berkeley. He jokingly attributed the moves to a short attention span.

"My father was very much a romantic," said Andrew Patner. "The one thing he knew he didn't want to do was go to work for a big law firm."

Patner frequently bicycled to work downtown. He filled his Hyde Park home with rare books, furniture he bargained for on Maxwell Street, and antique appliances.

When he returned to private practice in Chicago in 1975, he built a reputation in plaintiffs' law and complex litigation in the corporate era of golden parachutes and shareholders' rights. He was an advocate for Chicago Transit Authority riders groups, taxpayers opposed to leasing agreements at O'Hare International Airport, suburban citizens groups seeking open school board meetings, and disgruntled shareholders at Beatrice Foods.

Patner viewed the corporate issues of his later career in the same light as the populist causes of his youth, his son said.

Patner's wife; two other sons, Joshua and Seth; and a brother, Bruce, also survive him.

FRIDAY, DECEMBER 29, 2000

Felicia Goeken, Seventy-Three; Antiabortion Activist
By James Janega, *Tribune* Staff Reporter

Felicia Goeken, seventy-three, an outspoken, politically active mainstay of Illinois' antiabortion rights forces and a prime mover in establishing grassroots antiabortion rights efforts nationwide, died Sunday, December 24, in her Alton, Illinois, home. She had suffered heart problems for several years.

Goeken, mother of seven children, helped organize the National Right to Life Committee (NRLC) and the Illinois Federation for Right to Life (IFRL) in 1973 and led volunteer networking efforts and lobbying groups to the state capital.

"She was one of our pioneers," said Darla St. Martin, associate executive director of the NRLC. "She had a great deal to do with the expansion of the movement throughout the country."

From her hometown in downstate Illinois, Goeken founded Alton Right to Life and served as coordinator of the NRLC's Volunteer Identification Project.

Goeken was enthusiastic in her leadership of the volunteer project and was convinced a formidable antiabortion rights army could be found among the politically inactive.

"Pro-lifers are there throughout this great nation," she wrote in 1998 to NRLC volunteers. "If you call them, they will come."

The former Felicia Hale graduated from Alton High School in 1944. She married George W. Goeken in 1946 and first testified against abortion before the Illinois legislature in 1969.

"The movement was not well organized," recalled Bonnie Quirke, president of the Illinois Federation for Right to Life.

"She was really one of the reasons it became more organized. She pulled the movement together, recognized that you have to work at all different levels to change public policy."

When the U.S. Supreme Court issued its landmark *Roe v. Wade* decision in 1973, limiting restrictions on abortions, Goeken, a grandmotherly figure described as devout and humorous, rose to the forefront of national efforts to reverse the decision.

She was one of the founders of the NRLC, serving as the organization's secretary and on its board of directors from 1973 until recently. She also cofounded the IFRL and served as its president for six years.

Early in her efforts, Goeken established Birthright of Alton, a volunteer group created to arrange medical treatment and other necessities for pregnant women in need. In the 1980s Goeken led the IFRL's political action committee.

From the time she picked up the cause—her family said it was after a miscarriage—Goeken never set it down.

"She was one of the most tenacious women I've ever known," said Derek Jones, former board member of the IFRL and an administrative assistant in the NRLC. "When she had a point she wanted to make, she made sure it was made, and all the time with a smile on her face," Jones said.

She retired from the IFRL board of directors in 1998.

In addition to her husband, Goeken is survived by five daughters, Valerie H. Lewis, Christy J. Holt, Mary C. Donahue, Julie A. Henkhaus, and Anne A. Hermann; two sons, George W. III and John E.; a sister, Marlene C. Shake; thirty-one grandchildren; and twenty-one great-grandchildren.

THURSDAY, AUGUST 16, 2001

Gale Cincotta, Seventy-One;
Activist Fought Discrimination on Housing Front
By James Janega, *Tribune* Staff Reporter

When the alderman of Chicago's Austin neighborhood frustrated Gale Cincotta in 1970 by not getting rid of rats fast enough, Cincotta demonstrated the mettle that would soon make her one of the most effective community activists in America.

She stormed to the alderman's ward office with 100 neighbors and nailed a rat to his door. The next day, as she later told the story, the city's rat patrol was on the job.

By the time Cincotta, seventy-one, died Wednesday of an infection related to cancer in Loyola University Medical Center in Maywood, her legacy extended far beyond her West Side neighborhood.

She spearheaded efforts that brought a federal prohibition of mortgage redlining in 1979, created an organization that specialized in training other grassroots leaders, led groups that brought about a revamped federal first-time homebuyers program in 1999, and helped secure antipredatory lending measures in Chicago and Illinois this year.

"I think at the grassroots level, she inspired everyday people to have courage to defend their neighborhoods," said Joseph Mariano, who succeeds Cincotta as executive director of the National

Housing activist Gale Cincotta once nailed a rat to an alderman's door.

Training and Information Center (NTIC) in Chicago.

Mayor Richard Daley called her "a visionary and active force for housing issues in the city and, in particular, for development of the West Side. She was instrumental in helping the city formulate its campaign against predatory lending." Amid the waxing influence of community groups after the turbulent 1960s, Cincotta was a guiding force and one of the first to recognize the importance of neighborhood groups looking outside their geographical boundaries.

Seen at first as a frizzy-haired kook, Cincotta was able by the late 1970s to transform herself in the eyes of politicians, big banks, and regulators into an indispensable ally in their growing relationships with the community.

"Gale was a powerful champion for consumers. Her good works will be the legacy for which she'll be remembered," said Gov. George Ryan.

She was also one to hold those in power accountable, said Eugene Ludwig, former comptroller of the currency and head of the office that regulates the nation's top banks.

"Gale Cincotta gave a passionate voice to many underprivileged people in this country," he said. "She was a leader of an important movement, a public servant who knew how to fight for her cause."

She grew up in a three-flat on the West Side. Her father ran a Greek restaurant, and she married a gas-station owner. They had six sons, and Cincotta became politically active in the 1960s because of overcrowding in their schools.

The interest grew into a multi-issue group that also fought blockbusting and school busing and expanded to encompass the entire West Side, then the city, and eventually became the NTIC. The group was so successful that community groups nationwide called for advice. In 1972 the Chicago group held the National People's Action on Housing Conference and followed it with a protest the same year in Baltimore.

By 1977 Cincotta and her cohorts got Congress to pass the Community Reinvestment Act, which required banks to invest in their neighborhoods. She led efforts to fight insurance redlining and organized neighborhood anticrime groups in the 1980s.

"When you're talking about women and leadership and women making a difference, Gale definitely made a difference, and not only that, but changed the banking laws in this country," said Jacky Grimshaw, a vice president at the Center for Neighborhood Technology in Chicago. "And not only that, but also made it possible for people to learn how to organize for change."

"She had this saying," said NTIC housing staff member Jason Kiely. " 'We want it. They've got it. Let's go get it.' "

At the hospital Tuesday, she had some advice for her successor. "She said 'Go get the crooks,' " Mariano said.

Cincotta is survived by five sons, George, James, Ted, Chuck, and Richard; eight grandchildren; and two great-grandchildren.

SECTION

VII

Builders

They built one of the most famous skylines in the world and a blueprint for architecture that the rest of the world continues to follow. Following pragmatism and poetry, Myron Goldsmith's John Hancock Center expanded Chicago's urban ambitions. Shattering preconceptions about building materials and forms, Bertrand Goldberg's corncob-shaped Marina Towers celebrated the cylindrical. They were instant landmarks, both.

Chicago's builders included teachers and critics, architects and drywallers, and their personalities frame the way we see the city still.

WEDNESDAY, JULY 17, 1996

Myron Goldsmith, Seventy-Seven; Renowned Architect

By Blair Kamin, *Tribune* Architecture Critic

Internationally renowned architect, engineer, and educator Myron Goldsmith, who imbued pragmatic modern buildings with poetry and whose research led to such supertall skyscrapers as the John Hancock Center, died Monday at his home in Wilmette. He was seventy-seven.

Goldsmith was a gentle man who had a significant impact on his profession, in whose circles he was widely respected. Yet he was little known to the public, a self-effacing figure in a field that has never lacked for self-promoters.

His built work ranges from the sleekly clean-lined rapid-transit stations of the Dan Ryan and Kennedy Expressways to the boldly geometric Oakland Alameda County Coliseum to the dramatically sculptural enclosure for the Kitt Peak solar telescope in the mountains near Tucson.

Along with the late Fazlur Khan and other engineering colleagues at the Illinois Institute of Technology (ITT), Goldsmith helped devise most of the major steel-and-concrete framing systems used to support skyscrapers in the 1960s and 1970s.

This work, which enabled the building of the X-braced, 100-story John Hancock Center and other very tall towers, guarantees him a permanent place in the pantheon of Chicago architects whose muscular buildings have made their city's architecture unique for the past century.

"He was a man of gentle, sweet disposition," said architectural historian Franz Schulze. "Yet, gentle man that he was, he had very powerful ambition."

Born in the Jewish enclave of Humboldt Park, Goldsmith graduated from Crane Technical High School and the Armour Institute of Technology, now IIT. There, he studied under the master of steel-and-glass modernism, Ludwig Mies van der Rohe, who called him "Goldy."

During World War II, Goldsmith served in the Army Corps of Engineers, designing bridges, ammunition depots, and other large-scale projects. After the war, he joined Mies' Chicago office, where he was paid the humble salary of $1 per hour.

Nonetheless, Goldsmith said he felt "privileged" to work for Mies, for whom he helped produce such seminal modern buildings as the apartment high-rises at 860 and 880 North Lake Shore Drive, as well as the Farnsworth House in far-west suburban Plano.

"What you were learning . . . was sort of money in the bank," Goldsmith once said.

In 1953 Goldsmith received a Fulbright grant that enabled him to study with the other great influence on his career, Italian architect Pier Luigi Nervi, whose forte was the domed or vaulted reinforced-concrete structure.

After a stint in the San Francisco office of architects and engineers Skidmore, Owings & Merrill, where he worked on clear-span hangars big enough to accommodate a DC-8 jet plane while it was being washed, Goldsmith joined the firm's Chicago office in 1958. He became a partner in 1967, and the firm built on his expertise in tall buildings to design towers like the Hancock.

While at Skidmore, he collaborated on projects including the large mammal complex at the Lincoln Park Zoo, the Brunswick Building at 69 West Washington Street, the United Airlines executive office building in suburban Elk Grove Township, and the Republic Newspaper Plant in Columbus, Indiana, which is an elegantly detailed steel-and-glass pavilion that transforms a yellow printing press into a piece of kinetic sculpture.

Goldsmith is survived by his wife, Robin; a son, Marc; a daughter, Chandra; and a sister.

THURSDAY, OCTOBER 9, 1997

Bertrand Goldberg, Eighty-Four; Architect
By Blair Kamin, *Tribune* Architecture Critic

Bertrand Goldberg, whose corncob-shaped twin towers at Marina City are almost as much a symbol of Chicago as the historic old Water Tower and whose vision of thriving, densely populated cities helped trigger the revival now sweeping many of the nation's downtowns, died Wednesday at Northwestern Memorial Hospital in Chicago. He was eighty-four years old.

Once a student of Ludwig Mies van der Rohe, whose right-angled, steel-and-glass buildings set the standard for architects worldwide in the post–World War II era, Goldberg broke with the master to celebrate cylinders, boldly sculpted in reinforced concrete. He considered boxy buildings dehumanizing, calling them "the idea of a man made in the image of a machine." His naturalistic designs found expression in internationally recognized landmarks, such as the shell-like roofs of the Sydney Opera House by Jorn Utzon and Eero Saarinen's swooping, birdlike TWA terminal in New York City.

But Goldberg's significance transcended architecture. In the 1950s, when there was widespread pessimism about the future of cities as places to live, Goldberg posed a vital alternative with the five-building Marina City complex, which shared the twin distinctions of having the world's tallest reinforced concrete buildings and the world's tallest apartment buildings when it was completed in the mid-1960s.

A 1985 book published by the Paris Art Center, *Goldberg: On the City*, describes Marina City as the first mixed-use downtown complex in the United

States to include housing. Though some might dispute that claim, there can be no doubt that Marina City helped pioneer the notion of a "city within a city" and inspired the revitalization now occurring in downtown Chicago and in other American cities.

Variously described over the years as corncobs, flower petals on a stem, refrigerator coils, and radiators, Marina City still defines Chicago's image on travel posters and postcards.

"Marina City will survive close scholarly appraisal well into the next century as a superb example of architectural plasticity as well as a multiple-use facility reflecting Goldberg's concerns about urban amenities," the late *Tribune* architecture critic Paul Gapp commented in 1991 when he ranked Marina City among Chicago's ten most significant postwar buildings.

Goldberg also was a revolutionary transformer of hospital layouts and a promoter of humane public housing. He was, in many respects, as distinctive as his architecture.

With his rumpled hair and simmering eyes, his tweed jackets and stylish shirts, and his courtly, genteel air—now impish, now prickly—Goldberg often seemed more of a poet than an architect. He was once described as a humanist whose medium happened to be architecture.

"We are still trying to find out what we can design that will invite people to form community," he said in a 1994 *Tribune* interview. "We can't force them to form communities, but we can invite them."

He articulated the view that the denser a city is, the better, because only with a critical mass of people in proximity can society provide itself efficiently with such services as transportation and public safety.

Not everyone shared his vision, which accounted for some of Goldberg's most bitter disappointments.

His River City complex, which was to have housed forty thousand people in a network of high-rise towers on the Near South Side between State Street and the Chicago River, was greatly reduced in the late 1970s after city officials deemed it too dense. The result was a single wriggly concrete midrise structure at Polk Street and the Chicago River with 446 apartments, a seventy-slip marina, and an expanse of commercial space, completed in 1986.

A native Chicagoan who was known to many as "Bud," Goldberg grew up in Hyde Park, went to local private schools, proceeded to Harvard University, then went to Germany's famous Bauhaus School of Design, studying there with such giants as Mies.

In 1933 he had to leave Berlin in a hurry after lecturing his landlady on the evils of Nazism, a rash act for a Jew at that time and place.

Influenced by the 1933 Century of Progress Exposition in Chicago, which featured Moderne architecture that was more streamlined than the austere International Style buildings championed by the Bauhaus, Goldberg gradually made his break from Mies and shaped his own approach.

Marina City, which began to be designed in the late 1950s, marked his defining moment. With middle-class families fleeing the city for the suburbs, Goldberg teamed with a special client, William McFetridge, who headed a union of elevator operators and building janitors. The union's membership was bound to suffer if downtown Chicago emptied out.

The result was a complex dominated by cylindrical, twin-tower sixty-story apartment buildings, which had forty stories of pie-shaped apartments above twenty stories of helical ramp parking facilities. Also part of the complex were a slim sixteen-story commercial and office building; a lead-sheathed, saddle-backed theater building; and a two-story commercial building. A horizontal building at the base of Marina City housed a wide range of recreational uses, including a bowling alley, an ice-skating rink, and a marina with berths for 700 boats.

By and large, Marina City succeeded, continuing to retain residents in its closely packed condos despite the crumbling of its commercial portion in recent years. However, new attractions such as a Chicago outpost of the House of Blues nightclub chain are reviving that part of Marina City.

Goldberg also used cylindrical forms in the Raymond Hilliard Homes public housing development in Chicago, which he said with pride had suffered less damage than other public housing projects in Chicago, and in many hospitals he designed throughout the United States. Among the latter are the Prentice Women's Hospital in Chicago, the Elgin State Hospital in Elgin, as well as hospitals in Tacoma, Washington; Milwaukee; Boston; and Phoenix.

To sit with Goldberg at the Tavern Club, high in the Art Deco high-rise at 333 North Michigan Avenue, where he was a member and where the waiters typically would seat him at a table with a view of Marina City, was to feel a part of architectural history.

He once told how he served as a translator when Mies, after immigrating to Chicago, visited Frank Lloyd Wright at his Taliesin compound in Spring Green, Wisconsin. During the visit Wright showed Mies his collection of Japanese prints and, Goldberg recalled, "Wright offered Mies his choice of any one of the prints. Unfortunately for Mies he selected too good a one and he never got it."

Goldberg is survived by his son, Geoff; two daughters, Nan and Lisa; and two grandchildren.

WEDNESDAY, JULY 8, 1998

Alfred Caldwell, Ninety-Five; Architect, IIT Teacher
By Blair Kamin, *Tribune* Architecture Critic

Alfred Caldwell, the firebrand landscape architect and educator who used a distinctive Midwestern style to design such beloved features of the Chicago lakefront as the Lincoln Park Zoo Rookery and Promontory Point, died Friday at his farm in Bristol, Wisconsin. He was ninety-five.

Caldwell was for years a living link to three of the giants of Chicago architecture. He taught under Ludwig Mies van der Rohe at the Illinois Institute of Technology from 1944 to 1958. His own mentors included Frank Lloyd Wright and the eminent landscape architect Jens Jensen, both of whom drew inspiration from the Midwest prairie.

Although Caldwell shaped the northern half of Lincoln Park during the late 1930s while he was a landscape designer with the Chicago Park District, his masterpieces are widely regarded to have been done on a smaller scale.

One, the Zoo Rookery at Fullerton Parkway, is an intimate bird sanctuary with massive limestone walks and walls. The other, Promontory Point, juts into Lake Michigan at Fifty-fifth Street and has thick groves of trees and shrubs that create a ring around a central meadow. Both were completed in 1937 while Caldwell was with the park district.

"He was for our generation the person who carried Jensen's commitment to the native landscape to the present day," said the landscape historian Victoria Ranney. "His landscapes, particularly Promontory Point and the Zoo Rookery, are fairly small, but [they are] gems of the lakefront."

In a 1986 interview, Caldwell explained that he wanted Promontory Point to be "a place you go to and you are thrilled—a beautiful experience, a joy, a delight." But anyone who expected him to always be a nice man talking sweetly about flowers was in for a rude awakening.

Once, when making a point to a student at IIT, Caldwell, eighty-seven years old at the time, pounded the young man's shoulder with a series of jabs that rocked him back and forth on his heels. That sort of behavior was his trademark.

In 1958 IIT's trustees bypassed Mies, who had done numerous steel-and-glass buildings at the South Side campus, and asked the Chicago firm of Skidmore, Owings & Merrill to design IIT's remaining buildings. Caldwell resigned on the spot. However, he returned to IIT in 1981 and remained on the faculty until his death.

Born in St. Louis in 1903, Caldwell grew up in Chicago. He came to detest the violence and squalor of cities and, like Wright, sought to decentralize metropolitan areas and resettle everyone in gardens.

Caldwell worked in Chicago from 1920 to 1931 as an assistant to Jensen, then was the parks superintendent in Dubuque, Iowa. In 1936 he became landscape designer for the Chicago Park District. After serving as a War Department civil engineer during World War II, he joined IIT, where he landscaped much of the university's Mies-designed campus.

Caldwell received numerous professional honors, including the Teacher of the Year from the American Institute of Architects.

Caldwell's survivors include a daughter, Carol Dooley, and a son, James.

SUNDAY, NOVEMBER 1, 1998

Harry Weese, Eighty-Three;
Visionary Architect Known as "Chicago's Conscience"
By Blair Kamin, *Tribune* Architecture Critic

Harry Weese, the renowned architect who shaped Chicago's skyline and the way the city thought about everything from the lakefront to its treasure trove of historical buildings, died Thursday in a veterans home in Manteno, Illinois. He was eighty-three. The cause of death was a stroke, said his daughter Kate.

Weese's eclectic, much-honored body of work here includes the muscular Time and Life Building and the Metropolitan Correctional Center, a slit-windowed triangle whose façades resemble an old computer punch card.

His masterpiece is the subway system in Washington, D.C., whose graffiti-free underground has spectacular concrete vaults that evoke, but do not imitate, the capital's classical monuments.

"Harry believed in democracy. He believed that the public sector was a barometer of society. He couldn't stand a world where there were great individual buildings but the streets were out of order," said Chicago architect Jack Hartray, who worked with Weese for fifteen years.

A planner, a visionary, a consummate city man with a piercing wit, Weese was known in the shorthand of headline writers as "Chicago's conscience."

In his heyday, from the early 1960s to the early 1980s, he presented a humanistic alternative to the sterile, steel-and-glass buildings then being turned out by followers of Ludwig Mies van der Rohe.

When many architects turned their backs on history, Weese embraced it, leading an acclaimed restoration of Louis Sullivan's Auditorium Theater in 1967. Sensitive renovation was long a Weese specialty, embracing everything from the Field Museum of Natural History in Chicago to Union Station in Washington.

"He kept everybody aware of the larger issues. He may have made more of a contribution nationally than in Chicago," Hartray said.

Indeed, Weese's role as a civic tastemaker extended to the Vietnam Veterans Memorial. While others on the competition jury paid little attention to a rough pastel rendering submitted by an architecture student named Maya Lin, Weese lobbied the design into reality, and today the memorial is widely regarded as D.C.'s most emotionally powerful.

Weese was born in Evanston. He graduated from New Trier High School and the Massachusetts Institute of Technology. He served as an engineer on a U.S. Navy destroyer in World War II and established his own firm in Chicago in 1947.

Between then and the early 1990s, when he gave up control of the firm that still bears his name, Weese led the design of scores of significant structures—hotels, office buildings, embassies, banks, churches, city halls, and houses in locales from the Loop to the small-town architectural mecca of Columbus, Indiana. The firm also designed transit systems in cities including Miami.

The Weese firm won several national design awards from the American Institute of Architects, including the coveted Firm of the Year Award in 1978.

Weese enjoyed other triumphs.

He played an early and major role in conceptualizing the Printer's Row area. He took over Chicago-based *Inland Architect* magazine when it was on the edge of extinction and helped to transform it into one of the nation's best design periodicals.

Weese was equally well known for more than thirty years of promoting more creative uses of Chicago's waterfront, though his proposals for man-made islands, marinas, and less-intrusive lakeshore roads went mostly unimplemented.

Other Chicago projects completed under Weese's direction include the 200 South Wacker Drive office building, the Swissotel Chicago, and the restoration of Michigan Avenue the Hotel Inter-Continental.

The base of his lone clunker, the graceless Marriott Hotel on North Michigan Avenue, is now being given a face-lift.

In addition to Kate Weese, he is survived by his wife, Kitty; two other daughters, Shirley Young and Marcia; and five grandchildren.

TUESDAY, DECEMBER 12, 2000

J. Munroe McNulty, Eighty-Four; Headed Firm Known for Drywall Interiors

By James Janega, *Tribune* Staff Reporter

J. Munroe McNulty, eighty-four, former president of McNulty Bros. Co., which worked on the interiors of such famous Chicago skyscrapers as the Hancock and Standard Oil Buildings, died Sunday, December 3, of complications related to cancer in Kendal at Hanover, a New Hampshire retirement community.

Under his direction, McNulty Bros. designed and installed interior walls in skyscrapers, in shopping malls that never repeated a floor pattern, and in buildings where even designing the scaffolding was a major technical feat.

McNulty, formal in person and a perfectionist in practice, was a demanding contractor and voracious reader of technical literature that was often as dry as the plaster he once hung inside buildings.

"He loved details. He wanted to know the physics and chemistry of every piece of material he put into a building," said McNulty's son, Joe. McNulty grew up on the North Side and graduated in 1934 from Choate School in Connecticut. He received an English degree from Yale University in 1938 and, after a few years as an apprentice plasterer in his grandfather's firm, joined the army in 1941. He worked in supply units until 1946.

He returned to his plastering work after the war ended, and in 1948 he married the former Julie Turner.

The McNulty Bros. Co. was founded in 1888 by McNulty's grandfather, Thomas J. McNulty, and made a name for itself during the Columbian Exposition in 1893, when the company did much of the exposition's interior plasterwork. When McNulty succeeded his father as president of the family business in the early 1960s, the company started the transition to drywall. Having already done work inside the Prudential Building, McNulty led efforts to construct interiors in the nearby Standard Oil and Hancock Buildings, the Oakbrook Shopping Center, and other buildings that were

pushing the envelope of interior design.

"In a lot of ways, Munroe had a brilliant mind," said Joseph A. Feldner, president of McNulty Bros. "He wasn't satisfied with just a simple answer. He got into the nitty-gritty."

By the early 1980s, McNulty's company also had worked on buildings seeking to preserve their historic edifices and even oversaw construction of the Miro sculpture that stands opposite the Picasso at Daley Plaza.

He gradually retired and by 1985 was devoting more of his time to fly-fishing. His attention to detail was evident even in this activity, when he studied the insect life near his favorite Montana trout stream.

When his efforts didn't fill his creel with fish, he took the dilemma to naturalists, who subsequently discovered logging, mining, and farming operations along the river had thinned out the bugs—and McNulty's trout. He then worked with naturalists and special interests to turn the problem around.

In 1996 he and his wife moved to Hanover, New Hampshire.

SECTION

VIII

I Met Them Once . . .

At a name like Toad Smith, you can't help but chuckle, even at his passing. With a man like Donald Luchene and his fanciful flamingo collection, you can't help but marvel that the less sense the world makes, the better it seems.

Meet a tennis magician, a public-housing preacher, a dashing drum major, and a beloved Chicago Tribune writer (and friend of Toad's). In short, meet the people of Chicago who made you smile.

WEDNESDAY, NOVEMBER 27, 1991

Toad Smith, Fifty-One; Always Left Them Laughing

By John Husar, *Tribune* Staff Reporter

They eulogized Toad Smith in Sibley, Iowa, the other day, all 300 pounds of him, and then did what he would have them do. They went deer hunting. Next spring, his buddies will spread his ashes around the deer camp to let him nourish another season of growth.

When Toad died at the untimely age of fifty-one, he was becoming an outdoor legend.

Six years ago, after a valve was removed from his diseased heart, Toad asked the doctors for the tissue. They gave it to him in a jar. When he became strong enough to fish, he used his heart for bait and caught a six-pound catfish.

"What else was I going to do with it?" Toad grumbled.

That was going to be part of a book on Toad's skewed wisdom compiled by Mike Fine of Spirit Lake, Iowa, to be called *Toad Logic*.

"For example, he would get up at 4:00 AM, take a shower, and then clean 200 crappies from the night before," Fine said. "He was different."

Toad had become a mainstay of the *In-Fisherman* magazine staff, contributing insight, background, and Toadish humor to a variety of articles and TV specials. His guileless appearance and shambling bulk made him a hit with the everyday guys who saw him on TV. Toad was, even for outdoors TV, a very rough gem.

"Body by Oreo," was the caption under a recent magazine photo of Toad with his gaping smile and brillo beard. He had a few front teeth missing, although a dental post did protrude from one of those gaps.

"There was one way to describe him—ugly," said Fine, who runs public relations for Berkley Co. "Until you got to know him, and then he was beautiful."

Even though Toad couldn't write a lick, he had one book published and a second at the printer's. His buddies polished the stories for him. One book, *Channel Catfish Fever*, was authored with Doug Stange, the *In-Fisherman* editor. Another, *Toad's Tricks to Taking Whitetails in the Corn (and Everything Else)*, was aided by Iowa writer Bob Jensen. It's due out in another month.

Toad had a special touch that allowed him to get away with acts that would shame the rest of us. He could sneak white, squiggly power grubs into restaurant pizza, and strangers would laugh. Let you and I do the same and they'd glower. He could pretend to be a dirty old man and charm the ladies. Anyone else would be humiliated by hostile glares.

Toad's idea of camp fun was to bury elk urine scent pads in buddies' pillows, hide fish under the hoods of their cars, and tie pop cans to ice lines. And he was welcomed back.

Toad loved to sidle up to kids on fishing trips and complain about having "a frog in his throat." He'd make them look, and out would pop a plastic frog.

That went over so well, he graduated to the real thing, letting live, green frogs pop into startled physicians' hands. "He did that once to a doctor on a Canadian lake, and we all laid down and laughed for fifteen minutes," said Fine.

One time, a wise guy, new in camp, had found a way to get Toad's goat, and Toad seemed helpless. "So what can you do to me, anyway?" the guy sneered.

"That was the stupidest thing I've ever heard anybody say," Stange prodded from his place on the sofa. "Why, Toad gives hickeys that can stay with you for six months."

A smile spread across Toad's face. That night, he pounced on the fellow's bed, gaps puckered. "I have a wife . . . I have a wife . . ." the poor soul screamed into the night.

Toad was a consummate outdoorsman, a small-town sheriff's deputy who lived to hunt and fish. He guided some and traveled the world, from Alaska to Bolivia. He once trained and escorted a paraplegic hunter to fulfill a dream of killing an antelope with a crossbow. "He did that not because the guy was disabled but because he liked the guy," Fine said.

He was an outstanding bow hunter for thirty years, a member of the second wave who pioneered the sport. He claimed at least 300 deer, two *Pope & Young* record book black bears just last

spring, plus elk and hundreds of turkeys.

"A neighbor once bragged about his new bow," Fine said. "He hit a pop can two times out of five from twenty yards. Without a word, Toad went across the street, got his bow, and shot three arrows from his porch. He put all three into that can from sixty-five yards."

Fine said Toad hunted and fished all the time not just because it gave him pleasure and delight but because it was his act of rebellion.

"He would philosophize that fish and deer don't lie or cheat. They can't be bought or bribed. They're not impressed by who you are or your power. They only respond to quietude, endless patience, and humility.

"He didn't think fishing and hunting were all that important. But he believed everything else in life was equally unimportant—and a whole lot less fun."

Toad and Fine were caravanning to deer camp in this month's snowstorm when Toad spotted three pheasants in an Iowa field. He left the car, flushed the birds, and got all three with two shots. Then he retrieved the birds through deep snow. His heart couldn't take the exertion, and he died in Fine's arms back on the road.

The point, I guess, is we all know guys like Toad. Cherish them, get their pictures for the wall. Heck, we're all Toads, waiting for buddies to tell our stories someday.

FRIDAY, FEBRUARY 18, 2000

Donald Luchene, Forty-Eight; Flamingo Aficionado
By Maura Kelly, *Tribune* Staff Reporter

For some, plastic pink flamingos in a front yard are tacky reminders of warmer climates. But for Donald R. Luchene, they represented beautiful and elegant birds that fascinated him so much he collected more than three thousand knickknacks, pictures, and replicas of flamingos in his Blue Island home.

The only thing missing was the real thing, family members said.

"They're uplifting, and they are so unique. They are beautiful animals. It's just something that enlightened his heart," said his twin sister, Doreen Wood. "He had a passion for flamingos."

Luchene, forty-eight, known in his town as "Flamingo Man," died Tuesday, February 15, of a blood clot at his heart at Rush-Presbyterian-St. Luke's Medical Center.

His fancy for flamingos began in college, when his roommate collected flamingos dating from the 1930s and 1940s, his sister said. Luchene bought a few at the time as well, but his collection did not really get off the ground until the early 1980s.

Since then, he had gathered flamingos made of glass, wood, papier-mâché, concrete, and plastic. He bought everything he could find with a flamingo motif: flamingo stuffed animals, flamingo lamps, flamingo jewelry, flamingo blankets, and even a flamingo letter opener. He also took his collection with him on the road, hanging a flamingo from his rearview mirror and wearing a flamingo earring.

"They're everywhere and anywhere," his sister said. "We grew to love them."

A friendly man always ready with a joke and a smile, Luchene also collected giraffes and antiques such as Depression glass and stained glass from churches.

He worked at St. Francis Hospital and Health Center in Blue Island as a process storage technician, loading carts of medical supplies, his sister said. Luchene also worked part time arranging flowers.

Luchene graduated from Eisenhower High School and attended Southern Illinois University for two years.

He also is survived by three brothers, Lawrence, Irvin, and Ralph; and two other sisters, Linda Lukis and LaVerne.

THURSDAY, MARCH 9, 2000

Bob Huang, Sixty; Tennis Magician

By James Janega, *Tribune* Staff Reporter

Bob Huang was named Illinois Pro of the Year in 1978 by the U.S. Professional Tennis Association.

On the tennis court, Bob Huang was magic, a slight chap in perpetual motion who could pluck speeding yellow orbs from the air and send them spinning toward places where his opponent wasn't.

Little known outside of Chicago tennis circles, his impact here was nonetheless felt like a smashing overhead serve.

While Jimmy Connors and a brash upstart named John McEnroe dominated the national and international spotlight, Huang taught thousands of Chicago professionals, budding athletes, and suburban housewives how to play the sport as well.

He owned Eden's Tennis Club in Skokie and the Tam Athletic Club in Niles, was the onetime coach of the DePaul women's tennis team, and served as manager of tennis clubs from Harvey to Northbrook. Huang, sixty, died Monday, March 6, in his Lincolnwood home of cancer.

"He was a real artist. He's not that big of a man in stature, but he had great control," said Rod Schroeder, who directs a tennis academy in Niles and a summer tennis camp in Wisconsin. "The tennis racket was like a brush and the court was like his canvas, and he would run you side to side and leave you gasping for air."

Huang owed his livelihood to the rise in tennis fanaticism that came in the early 1970s and raised the sport's public profile. The demand for tennis pros became almost inexhaustible, and competent players found themselves learning on the job how to teach the sport.

"He particularly liked the strategy part of the game, as opposed to the power part," said Alan Schwartz, chairman of the Tennis Corporation of America and Huang's former employer at the Midtown Tennis Club. "Certainly his innate sense of strategy increased his ability to teach at the higher levels."

Born in Taiwan, Huang was the son of a Chinese national soft-tennis champion, a sport played with a softer ball and having a greater emphasis on delicate, well-placed shots. He came to Chicago in 1973 to take over as head professional at Midtown, having already gained a reputation in New York and even overseas for his finesse and control.

He joined the Fullerton Tennis Club in the late 1970s and managed the Holiday Tennis Club in Harvey from 1979 until 1981. Between 1986 and 1990, Huang coached the DePaul women's team while also serving as head professional for the Green Acres Country Club in Northbrook. He bought his own club, Eden's, in 1990 and acquired the Tam Athletic Club in 1996.

He was named Illinois Pro of the Year in 1978 by the U.S. Professional Tennis Association, where he was on the board for a number of years, and he also served as president of the Chicago Indoor Tennis Association.

Huang is survived by his longtime companion, Dyann Yaras; a son, Paul Yaras; and a daughter, Michelle Yaras.

FRIDAY, JULY 21, 2000

John Husar, Sixty-Three; *Tribune* Writer

By Don Pierson and James Janega, *Tribune* Staff Reporters

John Husar, sixty-three, the *Chicago Tribune* columnist who wrote as informatively and passionately about his need for a liver transplant as he did about the outdoors, died Thursday in Northwestern Memorial Hospital, little more than a week after receiving part of a new liver from a live donor.

He knew in depth the creatures and flora of Illinois' streams, lakes, and forests and was among just a few newspapermen to write with authority on the outdoors and the environment. But for the last year, he also shared with readers the details of his struggle with hepatitis C and his need for an organ transplant, announcing his illness in a column the same day Bears great Walter Payton shared with the world his own need for a new liver.

Standing well over six feet, Husar was a giant of a man and, like Payton, seemed similarly indestructible. Yet in subsequent columns, Husar allowed a glimpse into his five near misses with transplants, times when he waited in hospitals as a "backup" in case another recipient could not accept an organ that had been found.

His writing put a personal face on the disparity between the number of people who need transplants and the much smaller number of organs actually available. And because most liver donations come from cadavers, he wrote with raw honesty about the chill he got

Chicago Tribune columnist John Husar was nominated for a Pulitzer Prize in 1980.

from waiting for someone else to die so that he might live.

Until he couldn't write anymore, said his daughter Laura, a photo editor for the *Tribune*, Husar wrote about the outdoors and his illness as well.

"He felt that his readers deserved to hear the truth, and he also wanted to encourage other people to understand what hepatitis C is," his daughter said. "[He hoped], by sharing his story with his readers, maybe more people would come forth and become organ donors."

Though Husar was known as an

outdoors writer for the last two decades, no *Tribune* sportswriter covered a greater variety of sports. His résumé extended from the traditional (football, baseball, and basketball) to the obscure (luge, curling, and women's rugby) to the bizarre, such as motorball (soccer on motorcycles) and dogsledding.

"He could be absolutely trusted no matter what the assignment, but there was never any doubt he thought the best job on the paper would be the outdoors writer," retired *Tribune* sports editor Cooper Rollow said. "He had the curiosity and tenacity of an investigative reporter, coupled with a gentleness that drew people out."

Husar covered eight Olympics, specializing in the Winter Games, and was honored in 1988 as one of six United States journalists picked to carry the Olympic torch in Seoul. He was nominated for the Pulitzer Prize in 1980 for a series on conserving natural areas along the Des Plaines River.

Mainly, he wrote about people. He covered famous athletes from Ali to Pelé and ordinary characters from fishing guides to dogs, always seeking the human-interest element and usually succeeding with a style that reflected his curiosity for whatever and whomever he encountered. He wrote about Walter Payton and Isiah Thomas and Mike Singletary and about their mothers. "He saw a story in just about everything, and he empathized with the story and the characters involved," said *Tribune* writer Mike Conklin.

Early in his career, Husar worked on the Richard Speck murder investigation and the McCormick Place fire. Since 1984 he covered the outdoors with a special passion, adding issues of environment and ecology to reports on hunting and fishing. It was a beat that fit Husar's personality as well as interest, because no subject on the sports pages generates more passion and controversy than the outdoors.

Husar became such an avid outdoorsman himself that he began to share recipes for squirrel, crow, and cattails (from marshes, not alleys). He lamented that he was unable to find a recipe for prairie dog, and then he invented his own. He wrote of the real "Roadkill Cafe" in Montana.

Born in Chicago on January 29, 1937, Husar graduated from St. Rita and played football at Kansas, where he befriended Wilt Chamberlain.

Though not a golfer when he assumed the *Tribune*'s golf beat, Husar's reportorial instincts led him to question mobster ties to the PGA's Tournament of Champions at La Costa Country Club.

With his imposing height and weighing close to 300 pounds, Husar was kinder and gentler than he needed to be, choosing to persuade with his brain rather than his brawn.

"If you asked him a question, you'd better be prepared because you would get an answer, and it would be frank and honest," said Bill Cullerton, former cohost with Husar on WGN-AM's Saturday morning outdoors show.

He traveled the globe on assignment. In 1986 he took a twenty-day, eight thousand–mile journey into Canada's Northwest Territories with *Tribune* publisher Stanton Cook and wrote about the Inuits.

"He found a job in concert with his faith," said his wife, Louise. "He never once harvested an animal without praying over it. It bothered me that doctors kept saying, 'He's not out of the woods yet.' For John, peace was being in the woods."

Husar often acknowledged his gratitude for working "a tough job that somebody had to do."

"Any day spent fishing or hunting is not deducted from the normal span of life," he wrote. "In that case, our families had better prepare for the worst. We'll probably live forever. Each day in the outdoor business is a gift."

In addition to his wife, he is survived by two daughters, Kathryn Coyle and Laura Husar; a son-in-law, Kevin Coyle; four brothers, Michael, Frederick, Matthew, and Edward; one sister, Jez Husar; and three grandchildren. A son, John T. Husar, preceded Husar in death.

THURSDAY, SEPTEMBER 21, 2000

Rev. Louise Reid, Eighty; Preached Compassion and Discipline
By James Janega, *Tribune* Staff Reporter

In her neighborhood on the West Side, the kids just called her Mama Reid.

She had dressed in white from head to toe for several years, and the effect was that Rev. Louise Reid looked like some sort of gray-haired angel when she walked through the Rockwell Gardens housing development near her West Side apartment.

Sometimes rounding up people to attend the Jackson Boulevard Christian Church, where she preached every other Sunday, sometimes walking amid a flurry of youngsters on her weekly trip to a McDonald's restaurant on North Western Avenue, Reverend Reid was a compassionate soul in a place where compassion is often hard to find.

She preached old-fashioned discipline in a place where schoolchildren talk about trouble with the police. And she worried that, even in a place where storefront churches seem as numerous as corner taverns, people weren't getting enough God in their lives.

Reid, eighty, longtime copastor of the Jackson Boulevard Christian Church with her late husband and the church's children-focused leader after his death in 1990, died of complications from a lung tumor Friday, September 15, in Rush-Presbyterian-St. Luke's Medical Center.

"Everybody knew her, and everybody remembered the things she did for all the children, their parents, and their parents' parents," said Rev. Gregory Brown, who took over for Reid as pastor at the West Side church three years ago. "She represented the causes of humanity, to make life closer to what heaven might look like."

Alongside her husband, Reid had worked steadily in the shadow of public

Rev. Louise Reed tells a story to her weekly McDonald's group.

housing developments for five, perhaps six, generations, said Brown.

Her brother Alvin Anderson said she seemed to have as much faith in the young people she worked with as in the religious convictions that motivated her.

"She always saw good in people," Anderson said. "She said, 'This is where I want to be, this is where our kids are.'"

Reid never had any children of her own. The daughter of a minister in Tyler, Texas, the former Louise Anderson grew up as the youngest girl in a family of ten children. She graduated from Tyler's Scott High School in 1937, but after two years at a college in town, she moved to Chicago at the promise of better jobs and the urgings of older siblings.

She had gone back to Texas for an extended vacation when she met Frank Reid, a divinity student in a school near Tyler. The couple married in 1956 and moved to Massachusetts, where her husband went to Harvard University. They came to Chicago in the early 1960s after he was appointed pastor of the Jackson Boulevard Christian Church.

Rev. Louise Reid, for years an assistant pastor, gradually became a copastor, preaching in her teacherlike way every other Sunday by the late 1980s.

Together, Reid and her husband pushed for better living conditions in their neighborhood and for educational opportunities for its residents. The church became an informal community center, with books collected by Rev. Frank Reid passed out to congregation members seeking to broaden their minds.

Since her husband's death, Reid had remained a consistent force in the neighborhood, filling two rows of the church with children every Sunday and getting up at 6:00 AM most days to pick up trash in Rockwell Gardens. Her brother said children and neighbors soon joined her.

"The Lord reveals things to you," she told the *Tribune* in 1989. "It's not guesswork. When the Lord tells you, you know."

Reid also is survived by another brother, Maurice Anderson, and a sister, Gladys Livingston.

FRIDAY, OCTOBER 27, 2000

James Tuach MacKenzie, Ninety-Two; Drum Major

By James Janega, *Tribune* Staff Reporter

James Tuach MacKenzie, ninety-two, the dashing and charismatic former drum major and band manager of the Stock Yard Kilty Band, among the most prominent of Chicago's many pipe bands, died Wednesday, October 25, in his Munster, Indiana, home. He had lung cancer, his family said.

MacKenzie seemed larger than life in many a Chicago-area parade. As he slowly turned to face the crowd, let his baton drop, and stepped off, his broad smile, confident swagger, and formidable Highland regalia commanded nearly as much attention as the skirling bagpipes and thundering drums that followed.

"He was perfect, a born gentleman, and looked like an army man from the tip of his head to the soles of his shoes," said Tom Carroll, a longtime bass drummer with the Kilty Band.

Although Chicagoans may associate pipe bands with St. Patrick's Day, the Kilty Band performs far more often, headlining its own Tartan Balls, St. Andrew Society feasts, special parties, and local Highland weddings.

The group was founded in 1921 by a former pipe major of the Gordon Highlanders, a Scottish regiment in World War I, and one that at the beginning of the war was still in the practice of sending pipers over the tops of trenches with charging infantrymen.

MacKenzie moved to Chicago from Scotland when his father, a World War I

James Tuach MacKenzie, of the Stock Yard Kilty Band, was frequently seen in the St. Patrick's Day Parade.

Canadian army recruiter, was posted here to recruit British enlistees.

He graduated from Bowen High School on the South Side, worked as a stone cutter, and attended the University of Illinois at Urbana-Champaign in the 1930s. During World War II, he went to flight school and in 1944 graduated first in his class from the Merchant Marine Academy in New London, Connecticut. He spent the next year or so training merchant sailors. Later he embarked on a long career in auto sales and financing.

But it was in front of the Kilty Band that he was most widely known, marching in a kilt and wearing a sly grin, offering nods to gentlemen as he passed and winks to ladies. And oddly enough, MacKenzie played neither pipes nor drum.

When he tried learning the pipes, his wife quickly put an end to it, family members said.

Exactly when he joined the band remains a matter of dispute, with some estimates placing his arrival shortly after his merchant marine days and others saying it couldn't have been earlier than the mid-1960s.

His daughter Judy Holzer said it was while she took Highland dancing lessons at the old Stock Yard Inn in the 1960s, where the band had long made its headquarters.

Being a genial fellow, she said, her father hit it off with the members of the band and apparently inspired confidence enough that they soon asked him to handle their business affairs and parade-leading duties.

The story seemed in keeping enough with MacKenzie's personality, said his sister Katherine Kendall: "When he [got] on a plane, he immediately knew everybody in range, the names of the crew, and very often ended up in the cockpit," she said. "It was in his nature."

His renown at one time extended outside the band as well, and a couple of times—once in honor of Great Britain's visiting Prince Philip—it was MacKenzie who led masses of Chicago-area pipe bands.

He attended all of the band's practices and continued marching with the band, though less often, until he was ninety.

MacKenzie also is survived by a son, David; another daughter, Nora Loughlin; ten grandchildren; and six great-grandchildren.

WEDNESDAY, MAY 8, 2002

Ira Kipnis, Eighty-One; Real Estate Lawyer, Professor, Raconteur
By James Janega, *Tribune* Staff Reporter

Ira Kipnis, eighty-one, a quiet man whose life experiences and intelligence made him an intimate of some of Chicago's most illustrious residents, died of cancer Sunday, May 5, in his East Lake Shore Drive condominium.

Though he was the lawyer who helped Jupiter Realty Corp. conclude real estate transactions on, among others, the Chicago Stock Exchange Building, the Drake Hotel, and the McClurg Court Center, friends said that was more or less just a job for Kipnis and that he was better known for holding court each Friday afternoon in Kiki's Bistro.

In that Near North restaurant—and for decades before that at Riccardo's on Rush Street—Kipnis dined at a boisterous back table with such luminaries as former *Playboy* publishing president Nat Lehrman, former Chicago Symphony Orchestra cellist Eddie Druzinski, law firm founder Richard Mandel, Illinois Institute of Technology communications department chairman John Tarini, ABC-Channel 7 news anchor Joel Daly, and the late Columbia College president Mike Alexandroff.

"It was always kind of illustrious—illustrious at a Chicago level—but Ira was always the kingpin," Tarini said.

An author with thousands of books in his library and several degrees on his résumé, Kipnis had given up a career as a history professor by invoking the Fifth Amendment at a 1953 Senate hearing investigating supposed communist activity at the University of Chicago.

He responded by obtaining a law degree from the same university, said law partner Mandel, which he then used to make a killing in real estate legal transactions downtown.

"He was considered by most in his profession as the authority on ground leases and other complicated real estate matters," Jupiter Realty developer Edward Ross wrote in a letter to Mandel.

Yet what interested many of Kipnis' friends is that his plan had been to become a classical pianist. A native of the Austin neighborhood, he received a master's degree in music from Northwestern University in 1943.

He joined the army the next year and chucked his musical ambitions until retirement, when he devoted himself to practicing on his Steinway.

After World War II, he entered a doctoral program in history at the University of Chicago and received a Ph.D. in 1950. His 1952 book, *The American Socialist Movement 1897–1912*, is still considered an authoritative work.

An offshoot of that period was a fascination with George Bernard Shaw, whose leftist views appealed to Kipnis so much that he became an authority on Shaw's writings.

He was invited back by the University of Chicago to teach Shaw's works in the 1970s, in addition to courses in constitutional law and American history, said his stepson Jeffrey Wolfson.

He retired in the early 1990s but returned to real estate law after the 1995 death of his wife, the former Anita Sherman.

Other survivors include a son, David; another stepson, Ronald Wolfson; a brother, Gilbert; and four grandchildren.

Cop and Robbers

Say "Chicago" anywhere in the world where people don't speak English, and it happens immediately—their hands curl into handguns. "Chicago," they say knowingly. "Bang, bang." Of course.

If ever a town's mystique was founded on cops and robbers, it is Chicago. The city is what it is because of men like Al Capone and Eliot Ness—but also for the mark of reputed Chicago mob boss Joseph Ferriola, or "Pops" Panczko, Chicago's most famous thief, or Captain Frank Pape, the city's toughest cop.

In Chicago, the superlatives mattered.

SUNDAY, MARCH 12, 1989

Joseph Ferriola, Sixty-One; Chicago Mob Figure
By Kerry Luft and Jacquelyn Heard, *Tribune* Staff Reporters

Reputed Chicago mob boss Joseph Ferriola, sixty-one, died Saturday in a Houston hospital, apparently of heart problems.

Ferriola, who once had a heart transplant, died at about 2:50 AM at Methodist Hospital, a spokeswoman said. She said Ferriola had been a patient of Dr. Michael DeBakey, one of the world's foremost heart specialists.

Ferriola's death came less than six months after federal officials said they believed that he had been replaced as operations chief by Sam Carlisi, seventy-four, of Bloomingdale. Carlisi is a convicted tax cheat and protégé of imprisoned mob boss Joseph Aiuppa.

But in the wake of Ferriola's death, authorities anticipate that John DiFronzo of River Grove will take over for Carlisi. DiFronzo, owner of a car dealership on Chicago's West Side, is regarded as a member of the mob's ruling elite and within the past three to five weeks has emerged as the operating boss, easily pushing aside Carlisi and the ailing Ferriola.

DiFronzo is regarded by officials as a no-nonsense hoodlum and is expected to rule as a dictator rather than seeking his lieutenants' advice. "This is a firm, iron-fisted guy," a federal investigator said.

The local mob's leadership has been in disarray since 1985, when Aiuppa and several other top Chicago mob figures were convicted of skimming untaxed profits from a Las Vegas casino. Ferriola, already weakened by poor health, then took over as crime boss.

His three-year tenure as head of the Chicago syndicate was notably shaky. His health and a lack of confidence in his ability to fend off legal attacks by the FBI and the criminal division of the Internal Revenue Service helped lead to his deposition as mob chief, authorities believe.

The FBI and IRS both have increased prosecution of mob leaders in recent years, mostly on racketeering and extortion charges. Because Ferriola failed to thwart the law agencies, authorities said he did not enjoy the confidence of the syndicate's rank and file.

Unlike former mob bosses Anthony Accardo or Aiuppa, Ferriola never did enjoy uncontested allegiance from the local underworld. Some authorities contended that he was not, in later years, as ruthless as his predecessors, and that led to his downfall.

Others believed that he was a caretaker for Aiuppa and that over time the imprisoned boss lost faith in him. Still others say that Ferriola's own underlings, unhappy with his inaction and concerned for his health, persuaded him to step down.

Ferriola was a product of Chicago's Near West Side. He became an enforcer for Sam Giancana, one of the most dangerous gangsters in Chicago history. Giancana was shot to death in his Oak Park home in June 1975.

For several years, Ferriola headed the mob's gambling operations in northern Cook, Lake, and McHenry Counties. He also excelled as a roving crime boss, overseeing several projects for various underworld chieftains. At one time, he was called "Mr. Clean," because he owned three Chicago dry-cleaning businesses.

He also described himself as the owner of a sanitation company based in Cicero.

In 1970 Ferriola and four other mobsters were convicted on charges that they conspired to operate a multimillion-dollar interstate gambling ring. He served about three years of a five-year sentence.

In the 1970s and early 1980s, Ferriola also was the mob's chief enforcer. Federal agents at the time described him as "a cold-blooded terrorist" and one of the most feared men in the mob.

By 1981 he was seen as Accardo's heir apparent, at a time when the older man had virtually retired because of poor health. This gave Ferriola almost total control over the syndicate's day-to-day operations.

However, he never fully superseded Aiuppa until 1985, when Aiuppa and other gangsters were on trial in the casino-skimming case. Ferriola apparently had the blessing of Accardo, who by then had retired. Accardo reputedly was one of Ferriola's advisers after the younger man had taken over.

Almost immediately, Ferriola built a $500,000, fourteen-room home in west suburban Oak Brook, a mile away from Aiuppa's home.

Soon afterward, the battered bodies of Anthony Spilotro, the Chicago mob's Las Vegas chieftain, and his brother Michael were found buried in an Indiana cornfield. Anthony Spilotro had been seen as another contender for the syndicate's top spot.

But by that time, Ferriola already was suffering from cancer and heart problems.

At the time of his death, federal prosecutors reportedly were seeking a series of indictments against Ferriola for operating a continuing criminal enterprise.

Those who faced indictment with Ferriola included several of his top lieutenants as well as mob soldiers.

TUESDAY, MARCH 7, 2000

Police Captain Frank Pape, Ninety-One; Called "Chicago's Toughest Cop"

By James Janega, *Tribune* Staff Reporter

In his thirty-nine years with the Chicago Police Department, Capt. Frank Pape spent two decades as head of the department's robbery detail, was the subject of forty-nine articles in detective magazines, and provided frequent grist for the TV series *M Squad*.

He was involved in sixteen shootouts with criminals; nine times, he shot and killed the offender. When he ran the station house in Englewood, relatives said, he called a meeting of the area's habitual criminals and told them to knock it off. They did.

Captain Pape, ninety-one, known in magazines and newspaper accounts as "Chicago's toughest cop" for much of his career, died Saturday, March 4, in his Park Ridge home.

"I never started a fight in my life, but I'm not going to take any lip from a hoodlum," Pape told *Coronet* magazine in 1949. "I represent the City of Chicago, and Chicago stopped taking orders from gangsters a long time ago."

But Pape could remember life the other way. He became a police officer in 1933, two years after Al Capone went to jail for tax evasion.

There was always enough work to go around during his first few years on the force, and his partner died in his arms after a cops-and-robbers shootout in 1945.

Yet despite his stature in police circles as a guy who got things done—and the kind of notoriety among criminals that bred jail-cell assassination plots—Pape gave evidence to neither reputation at home.

A modest, soft-spoken man, his own children didn't know what their father did for the police department until they were almost in their teens, said Judy Clark, Pape's daughter.

Instead, Pape, who also earned a pilot's license in the 1940s, was famous

Capt. Frank Pape was known as "Chicago's toughest cop" for much of his career.

among neighborhood kids for taking them on weekend airplane rides or dipping his wings as he flew over his children's schoolyard during recess.

He found jobs for unemployed neighbors and helped buy bicycles for their children. And when he hit the street, it was always with a rosary given to him by his daughter in his pocket.

"'This is just what I do for a living,' he'd say," his daughter recalled. "He was one of the most lenient types of fathers."

He later said that was because he

hardly knew his own father; Frank Pape's dad died when he was a boy. Working first as a paper boy and later in a sheet metal factory, he was responsible from an early age for helping support his mother and sister. But working for the police department was like coming home for him.

"He was the Babe Ruth of the police department," said Phil Cline, now deputy chief of the organized-crime division, in a 1994 interview with the *Tribune*. "When I came on the job in the seventies, all we heard about was Frank Pape. He had the reputation that when criminals heard that he was looking for them, they'd turn themselves in. He was the kind of guy we all wanted to work for."

That expertise was wanted elsewhere, also. From 1961 to 1965, he took a leave of absence to head the security detail at Arlington, Washington Park, and Balmoral racetracks, where track owners were concerned about gambling syndicate bookmakers, many of

whom Pape and the men who followed him knew on sight.

At the same time, local businessmen tried to draft him into running for Cook County sheriff.

When he retired in 1972, Pape's tenure with the department included the end of one era in policing and the birth of another. He was hired by a department when cops wore fedoras and natty suits and carried tommy guns on raids.

In 1963, a jury forced him to pay an $8,000 judgment for violating the civil rights of a murder suspect. He told the *Tribune* in 1994 that he wouldn't join the police department nowadays because the methods had changed so much.

"He always said 'You have to stand up for the rights of the decent citizens,'" said his son-in-law, Richard Clark. "He was thorough and he was persistent, and he was never going to stop."

In addition to his daughter, Pape is survived by his wife, Kitty; a son, Jerry; and seven grandchildren.

THURSDAY, OCTOBER 17, 2002

Paul Crump, Seventy-Two; Convict Became Author on Death Row
By Rudolph Bush, *Tribune* Staff Reporter

Paul Crump, seventy-two, a convicted murderer and jailhouse author who, in a case that focused national attention on prisoner rehabilitation, was spared from the electric chair thirty-five hours before he was scheduled to die, died of lung cancer Thursday, October 10, in Chester Memorial

Hospital in Randolph County.

At age twenty-two, Crump was convicted of fatally shooting Theodore P. Zukowski, chief security officer at the Libby, McNeill & Libby food plant in Chicago.

Crump was sentenced to death row in 1953, where he entered as a barely

Paul Crump, convicted of murder, entered prison as an illiterate man but left as an author.

literate man and spent the next nine years reading the great books and writing about his experience as one of the condemned.

In 1962 he published *Burn, Killer, Burn*, a novel about a man who committed suicide rather than face execution.

He became a personal friend of writers Gwendolyn Brooks and James Baldwin and a cause célèbre among activists who argued he was rehabilitated.

"This was the quintessential case for rehabilitation," said Rob Warden, executive director at the Center on Wrongful Convictions at Northwestern University. "Paul Crump, at the time he committed the crime, was, if not illiterate, next to it. Then he became this remarkably eloquent writer."

The same year Crump's book was published, he was scheduled to die. Only a day and a half before his execution did Gov. Otto Kerner commute the sentence to 199 years in prison.

Crump spent the following years in state prison, seeking parole.

"Guilt has its own bars, and remorse is a punishment that a person carries to the grave," Crump told the parole board.

In 1993, after forty years in prison, he won his freedom. But beset by mental illness and trouble with alcohol, his remaining years were marked by struggle.

Crump lived on the South Side with his sister Andra Maxine Spells. He was diagnosed as a paranoid schizophrenic, and his illness caused bizarre behavior, such as piling garbage in front of his sister's front door and locking the elderly woman outside the house.

In 1999 she received an order of protection against him, which he violated. In 2001, despite Spells' defense of him as a nonviolent man, Crump was ordered into the custody of the Chester Mental Health Center, where he remained until his death.

Gwendolyn Jones, his only surviving sibling from a family of thirteen children, does not know much about her brother's life, she said.

"He was my brother and I loved him, and I tried to take care of him and that's all I know," she said.

Among his survivors his sister listed a wife, Maureen; two daughters, Jerry Shaw and Sandra Gunn; and several grandchildren.

TUESDAY, DECEMBER 3, 2002

Joseph "Pops" Panczko, Eighty-Five; Career Thief Whose Crimes, Geniality Became Legendary

By James Janega, *Tribune* Staff Reporter

Joseph "Pops" Panczko, eighty-five, who, with more than 200 arrests between 1940 and 1994, was Chicago's most storied thief, died last week in Our Lady of the Resurrection Medical Center. His family declined to comment about how or when he died.

Bullet-scarred but talkative, Panczko had a genial personality that erased any perception of him as a hardened criminal whose past included sixteen years of prison time and hundreds of thousands of dollars in stolen property.

"I guess you go from being a crook, a thief and, just like anything else if you live long enough, you become a charac-ter. He was a character," said his onetime court-appointed lawyer, Marc Kadish.

For sixty years, no lock in Chicago was safe from Panczko, who had a reputation for committing his criminal acts in a gentlemanly, nonviolent manner: Panczko once returned a cocker spaniel he had accidentally stolen with a car.

But his last years were bitter, beginning when his younger brother—fellow burglar and sometime accomplice Paul "Peanuts" Panczko—ratted him out in the 1980s and became a federally protected, relocated witness.

One of six children born to Polish

immigrants on the West Side, Panczko stole peanut butter as a boy to help feed his family during the Depression. He moved on to stealing coats in grade school, chickens from the Fulton Street market as a preteen, and racks of fur coats, typewriters, and diamonds later on. He often worked with younger brothers Peanuts and Butch.

He was shot the first time in January 1948, when police arrived to find Panczko helping an accomplice carry stolen liquor from a downtown restaurant.

A year later, a private detective shot Panczko while he was exploring a truck filled with furs.

In 1957 a police officer hiding in a Wilmette jewelry store nearly took off Panczko's head with a shotgun blast.

When he was healthy enough to stand trial, jurors found him innocent after ten ballots. They believed his story that the store was unlocked—and that he had to use its bathroom after searching for a house to buy for his mother.

Panczko had been arrested so often by the 1950s that he needed a notebook to remember which judge he was appearing before each day.

Outside of an arrest in 1994 for allegedly passing a counterfeit $20 bill, his final tangle with authorities was in a $500,000 jewel heist. He was convicted in 1985 after his brother Peanuts turned federal witness and persuaded Panczko to plead guilty. He was released in 1990 after four years in federal prison.

"All my life," he told a hushed courtroom in that case, "I stole. That's my racket."

Panczko was considered to be an

Joseph "Pops" Panczko, one of Chicago's most storied thieves, started out by stealing peanut butter during the Depression.

exceptional thief. The nail file he kept in his wallet could defeat the fist-size padlocks favored by jewelry couriers. He once was arrested for "possession of burglary tools" just for being seen with a screwdriver. He bragged that he could find the sweet spot on a car trunk so it would open wide when he smacked his hand against it.

And he relished his renown with Chicago crime reporters, whose hundreds of news articles made him Chicago's best-known felon.

Former *Tribune* reporters Edward Baumann and John O'Brien wrote a book about the Panczko family, *The Polish Robbin' Hoods*. Ovid DeMaris'

1969 book *Captive City* devotes thirteen pages to Panczko. *Life* magazine gave him a full-length piece, complete with a cartoon showing him riding a screwdriver like a witch's broom. Columnist Mike Royko dropped his name often, and filmmaker Michael Mann once tried to make a movie about Panczko's life.

He charmed lawyers as well, even when he would profess from the witness box that he was a thief. (He pronounced it "teef.") He was so recalcitrant that he once even stole files from his own lawyer's office.

"It was the only thing he knew how to do," Kadish said.

"I had no idea what was true or not," Kadish said of Panczko's endless tales about when crime paid—or the sometimes humorous tales about when it didn't. "But I'll say this: he was a welcome relief from deadly gangbangers who were blowing people away."

Panczko's final encounter with police was two years ago when three men and a boy posing as gas company workers were foiled burglarizing his Northwest Side bungalow.

When smirking detectives told Panczko they needed to fill in a blank listing his profession, he replied: "Retired."

"I'm over with crime," he told reporters. "My feet hurt."

SECTION

Celebrities in a Sports Town

We knew them for the "Hey, hey!" or "Holy cow!" they shouted, crackling over our radios, for the sweet number 34 on a jersey that seemed to glide over, twist past, and torment gridiron tacklers. In a sports town like Chicago, celebrity was conferred not by money or Hollywood films, but from the fantasy world of sports, where our ambitions and frustrations were played out every week. Our heroes were our athletes and those who worked closely with them.

THURSDAY, FEBRUARY 19, 1998

Harry Caray, Seventy-Eight; He Took Us Out to the Ballgame; Legendary Cubs Broadcaster Had a Passion for Life and Simple Secret for Success: He Was Fun

By Ed Sherman, *Tribune* Staff Reporter

Harry Caray's signature "Holy cow!" could be heard from the neighborhood bar to the White House.

Harry Caray was fun. It was that simple. Fun was the theme of one of his trademark lines. On a hot summer afternoon, with a ballgame either languishing or careening toward its finish—it didn't matter—Caray would chortle, "Ah, you can't beat fun at the old ballpark."

Caray made baseball's most exciting moments more fun. He made baseball's mundane moments—and Lord knows there are many—fun.

He had fun with names, those he intentionally pronounced backward ("Yastrzemski spelled backward . . .") and those he unintentionally mangled or mispronounced. Even Cubs great Ryne Sandberg was called Ryne Sanderson at times, or merely "Ryne-berg," and he gave up trying on Ken Caminiti.

He wasn't just a man of the fans. On occasion he sat with them, calling games from the bleachers on both sides of town. He knew where to have the most fun.

Only Harry Caray could take a tired old baseball custom like the seventh-inning stretch and transform it into a memorable, magical, albeit off-key Chicago ritual.

For 162 days and nights during the baseball season, the man with the gravel voice, windowpane glasses, and trademark "Holy cow!" salute was a once-in-a-lifetime life of the party.

The party will never be the same.

Caray died Wednesday in Rancho Mirage, California, after collapsing during a Valentine's Day dinner Saturday with his wife, Dutchie. Doctors said his heart suddenly changed rhythm, restricting oxygen to his brain. He never regained consciousness, dying at 6:10 PM Chicago time, according to Harlan Corenman, spokesman for the Eisenhower Medical Center.

The orphan from St. Louis, whose real name was Harry Christopher Carabina, died only a few days short of his birthday, March 1. According to *Who's Who in America*, Caray was born in 1919, making him seventy-eight, but

the Cubs media guide lists his birth date as 1920. Even with those dates, there was always speculation that he was a few years older.

Caray's death brings an end to a remarkable fifty-three-year career as a baseball play-by-play man, raconteur, and bon vivant. He was to have teamed this season with his grandson Chip, the son of Caray's son Skip, a broadcaster for the Atlanta Braves.

"I just wish everyone who ever goes on the microphone could have the good luck Harry had in connecting with the fans," said Jack Brickhouse, another Hall of Fame Cubs broadcaster and a contemporary of Caray's. "The guy was what we all hoped to be as a broadcaster."

"He did well wherever he went," said St. Louis Cardinals great Stan Musial, Caray's all-time favorite player. "The Cubs fans loved him, the White Sox fans loved him, the Cardinals fans loved him. He loved life, and he loved people."

Caray's appeal went from the common man to the White House. First Lady Hillary Rodham Clinton, a native of Park Ridge, said she and President Clinton were saddened to hear of his death. Caray sang "Take Me Out to the Ball Game" at Mrs. Clinton's fiftieth birthday party last year.

"In Chicago, Harry was a larger-than-life symbol, and like all Chicagoans, I valued him not only for his contribution to the game but also his love and zest for life," Mrs. Clinton said in a statement.

For the past twenty-seven years Caray worked in Chicago, arriving in 1971 to spend eleven years with the

White Sox and the past sixteen with the Cubs.

During that time, Caray became nothing less than an institution, his stature perhaps unparalleled for a sports figure who never hit a home run or threw a strike. A roll call of Chicago icons during the last quarter-century would include Michael Jordan, Mike Ditka, Walter Payton, and, yes, Harry Caray, a personality who was bigger than the athletes he covered.

Caray helped define the local sports landscape and more. He was emotional and unfailingly passionate about the teams he covered. Chicago fans are tough on their heroes; so was Caray. At times he got into trouble with players for being brutally honest about their shortcomings. Yet they were plentiful— in only seven of his twenty-seven years in Chicago did his team win as many games as it lost.

Calling a game in which White Sox shortstop Bee Bee Richard already had made a couple errors, Caray once reported: "Richard just picked up a hot-dog wrapper at shortstop. It's the first thing he has picked up all night."

His candor only served to increase his appeal. Fans tuned in to hear what Caray had to say.

"He could be critical, contentious, and bombastic," said Vin Scully, the Dodgers' Hall of Fame announcer. "Or he could be lovable and full of praise. It all depended on the play of his team. He said what he honestly felt should be said, like a fan, and sometimes at the expense of his own team."

But Caray was more than a broadcaster. Howard Cosell, who once dismissed Caray as "a cheerleader," was a tough critic himself, but he was loathed. Caray was beloved.

In a town that likes to have a good time, Caray led the parade. On the air, his laugh, sounding more like a full-throated gargle, often followed a joke or an insight about something mundane. Off the air, with a beer in hand, he was a nightlife legend. He was nicknamed the "Mayor of Rush Street," running unopposed.

Caray was bawdy and raw, a hearty fellow who didn't know the meaning of "last call." Chicagoans accepted him as one of their own because he was.

Caray had a simple explanation for his appeal.

"I think people will remember me as a guy who brought a little enjoyment while he broadcast," Caray said in 1994. "I think even my detractors will have to tell you I am honest. I am honest in my descriptions, and I am honest in my life. I know that you only come around once in this life. You better try to enjoy yourself and try to find as much happiness as you can.

"For a poor orphan boy from St. Louis, I think I have done pretty well."

The legend had a rather modest beginning. Caray grew up in a poor section of St. Louis and was raised by an aunt after being orphaned in childhood.

"I was the only one in my neighborhood who didn't end up in jail," he once said.

Caray had hoped to become a ballplayer himself, attending a Cardinals tryout camp as a teen. Rejected, he turned to radio.

Caray broke into radio when he

brashly wrote a letter to a station manager at KMOX in St. Louis, suggesting that the station's baseball announcers were dull and he could do better.

The station manager called him in and was impressed enough with his bravado to help Caray get a job at WCLS in Joliet.

In 1945 Caray went back to St. Louis and was hired by KMOX to be the third announcer for Cardinals games. When the sponsor couldn't decide on a number one announcer, Caray went to beer baron Ed Griesedick, the main sponsor, and persuaded him to make him number one. For twenty-five years, Caray was the voice of the St. Louis Cardinals, and the combination of his distinctive style and KMOX's booming fifty thousand–watt signal helped make his voice a beacon throughout the Midwest.

"I always thought I'd die at the microphone doing a Cardinals game," Caray said.

It didn't work out that way. After a falling-out with the Busch family, the Cardinals fired him after the 1969 season, and he spent 1970 broadcasting the Oakland A's for then-owner Charlie Finley. Chicago would be his next stop—and his last.

Caray's Chicago beginnings were as humble as his childhood. When he signed with the White Sox in 1971, the team was without a major AM radio outlet, forcing him to broadcast games on a five thousand–watt AM station in LaGrange and on a small FM station in Evanston.

It didn't matter. By Caray's second year he was drawing larger audiences on WTAQ than the fifty thousand–watt

giants he was competing against.

Caray's popularity zoomed when Bill Veeck bought the team in 1976. He teamed Caray with color analyst Jimmy Piersall, and they formed a combination as outrageous as and often more entertaining than the games.

It was Veeck who noticed how the fans sitting under his broadcast perch reacted to Caray singing "Take Me Out to the Ball Game" during the seventh-inning stretch. So one night he stuck a public-address microphone in the booth, and suddenly a tradition was born, off-key warble and all.

Caray's often controversial tenure with the Sox ended in 1981 when the team was purchased by Jerry Reinsdorf and Eddie Einhorn, who wanted to start a pay-TV venture.

The shocker came when Caray jumped to the Cubs for the 1982 season. Sox fans were angry, and so were Cubs fans—77 percent disapproved, according to a *Tribune* poll. But more tellingly, 44 percent of Sox fans said they were going to follow Caray to the North Side.

It showed how strong Caray's pull was on his fans. With superstation WGN-TV as his outlet, Caray helped create a national following for himself and the Cubs, sending the team's popularity to unprecedented heights.

"He is the single greatest salesman of the game who ever lived," said Caray's WGN-TV sidekick, Steve Stone.

In the winter of 1987, Caray suffered a stroke, and for the first time in his career he missed a game. In fact, he missed the first six weeks of the 1987 season, and in his absence, celebrity guests ranging from Brent Musburger to Bill Murray to George Will took his place. But nobody could replace him. When he came back in May of that year, the broadcast was a big enough event to warrant a call from a former Cubs broadcaster, President Ronald Reagan.

Caray reached a milestone in 1989 when he was inducted into the Baseball Hall of Fame. During the ceremonies at Cooperstown, Caray acknowledged the fans.

"You can't possibly stand here and not feel the presence of the legendary figures who have been here before," Caray said. "The more I think of all the history which surrounds me, the more inadequate I feel."

As Caray's career moved into the 1990s, his age at times started to show. He would get names wrong and sometimes be confused by a play. His critics told Caray it was time to retire.

"Never," was his response, and he plugged on.

In an era when the young baseball announcers sound like cookie-cutter A, B, or C, bland and indistinguishable, Caray remained entertaining, even with the mistakes.

"So what if he mangles a few words and gets the names wrong," Stone said. "In the end, what difference does it make? The object of baseball is for everyone to enjoy themselves. In the seventh inning, no matter where we go, everybody stands up and looks to the booth, looks to Harry. He is a people magnet."

Caray eventually did make a concession to age. Overcome by heat in Miami in July 1994, he fell and knocked himself unconscious. At that point he decided to limit his travel, eventually restricting himself to home games only.

Yet Caray never talked of retiring. He was enthusiastic about the upcoming season and the chance to work with his grandson. And above all, it still was baseball, Caray's first and only love.

In 1995 Caray talked about how he would like to go out. A quiet mourning period wasn't part of the plan.

"I've threatened to be cremated and have my ashes strewn over Comiskey Park and over Wrigley Field, and I really should hold some ashes back for St. Louis," Caray said. "I've also mentioned this to my wife. I want her to take some of the money I've accumulated and just throw a party where people eat and lift a drink up to me either upstairs or downstairs—and I'll give you two guesses to where it'll be."

Harry Caray is survived by his wife, Dutchie; five children; five stepchildren; fourteen grandchildren; and one great-grandchild, and by baseball fans throughout the city. His city.

FRIDAY, AUGUST 7, 1998

Jack Brickhouse, Eighty-Two; Chicago Loses Another Giant, Hall of Fame Sportscaster; A Man Who Defined the Word *Versatility* Dies Just Six Months after the Death of Harry Caray

By Michael Hirsley, *Tribune* Staff Reporter

Jack Brickhouse was known as the voice of the Cubs, Bears, and White Sox to a generation of Chicago sports fans. Lesser known were the occasions when that same familiar voice interviewed presidents and a pope.

Because of his versatility, Brickhouse was truly the man for all seasons in broadcasting. From sports to politics and beyond, he was a protean presence at WGN radio and television.

Brickhouse, eighty-two, died at St. Joseph Hospital Thursday morning, after cardiac arrest. He had been hospitalized February 27 with a brain tumor. That prevented him from attending the funeral of friend and colleague Harry Caray.

Now, within a span of six months, Cubs and Sox fans are mourning the passing of the two broadcasters who called the teams' games for most of the past half century. Brickhouse was inducted into the Baseball Hall of Fame in 1983, Caray in 1989.

"Jack was one of the most intelligent men I ever met. He was a perfectionist," Vince Lloyd, a longtime broadcast associate, said from his home in Sioux Falls, South Dakota.

Lloyd said there was nothing contrived about Brickhouse's trademark enthusiasm. He recalled Brickhouse asking him one day in the early 1950s,

"Who do you think has the best job in town?"

When Lloyd offered the name of a veteran sportscaster at another station, Brickhouse rebuffed him.

"No, I do," he said. "I'm doing everything I like to do."

"He's a significant portion of this station's history," WGN-Channel 9 station manager Jim Zerwekh said of the man who was the station's first on-air voice and lived just long enough to witness its fiftieth anniversary.

"He was a giant in our business," Zerwekh said. "He will be missed."

"You could make a case that he's the greatest broadcaster in Chicago history, not just sports," said John McDonough, vice president of marketing and broadcasting for the Cubs.

McDonough consoled Brickhouse's widow, Pat, and family Thursday.

"The Cubs organization is just devastated by what happened," McDonough said. "Losing two Hall of Fame broadcasters in less than six months ... It's hard to fathom. It's a very somber, sad time."

Ed McCaskey, chairman of the board of the Bears, said he had been at a dinner with Brickhouse, his longtime friend, last month.

"He told me he'd been swamped with fan mail since his hospitalization. Jack always made it a point to answer his mail, and he said he'd gotten someone to help him. He was determined to answer them all."

WGN consultant Jack Rosenberg, a former colleague and coauthor of Brickhouse's autobiography, said his friend was "very intelligent, a grammarian and a student of Shakespeare" despite lacking a college education.

And at age eighty-two, despite lingering effects from Brickhouse's hospitalization, "he told me at lunch a little over a week ago that he had a couple of good ideas for projects that we should talk about soon," Rosenberg recalled.

After eight weeks of therapy at the Rehabilitation Institute of Chicago, Brickhouse recently had increased his schedule, including doing a guest-announcer stint with Lloyd and former telecast partner Lou Boudreau last month at Wrigley Field.

Brickhouse was an apt name for the robust 6'3" broadcaster whose assignments took him to a variety of professional sporting events. Whether he was announcing baseball, football, basketball, boxing, wrestling, or golf, he was a solid practitioner.

Brickhouse. "Solid" defined Jack Brickhouse, a pro's pro on radio or television.

And for the acknowledged "Voice for All Seasons," broadcasting went far beyond the fields and arenas of sports.

He covered five national political conventions. He did man-on-the-street interviews, as well as one-on-one sessions with six presidents. He tape-recorded an audience with Pope Paul VI that won a radio award.

His distinctive voice told us what was happening at ballroom and barn dances, at Franklin Roosevelt's 1945 inauguration and upon Roosevelt's death later that year, in Mages Sporting Goods commercials, during World War II blackouts in Chicago, and at the parade welcoming Gen. Douglas MacArthur to the city.

He filed reports from fires and murders as well as dances and parades, from planes, ships, and mine shafts as well as dance halls and street scenes.

On an August Venetian Night in Grant Park, he read "Casey at the Bat" at Petrillo Bandshell, with the Chicago Symphony Orchestra playing in the background.

He reported from Golden Gloves amateur boxing bouts at Chicago Stadium, with heavyweight champion Joe Louis once serving as his broadcast sidekick, and from the streets of Bangkok and Paris as part of a report on global attitudes toward America.

But for all of that, Jack Brickhouse is best remembered for the two words he uttered with unbridled enthusiasm whenever the occasion presented itself: "Hey-hey!"

For nearly four decades, Brickhouse gave that signature call to home runs hit by Cubs and White Sox players. He did White Sox games on WGN radio from 1940 to 1943, on WJJD radio in 1945, then on WGN-TV from 1948 through 1967. He called Cubs games on WGN radio from 1940 to 1943 and WGN-TV from 1948 through 1981, when he retired and passed the microphone over to Caray, his friend and soon-to-be fellow Hall of Famer.

Although they alternately were praised and criticized as "homers" who rooted too ardently for the home team, Caray had a harder edge when a team disappointed him. If Caray was baseball's raucous fan, Brickhouse was its Renaissance man, each game another addition to his broadcasting repertoire.

And as different as their styles were, what Brickhouse and Caray shared was the realization that baseball was entertainment and the ability to convey a sense of fun to their audience.

Born John Beasley Brickhouse on January 24, 1916, at Methodist Hospital in Peoria, he was the son of 6'5", 225-pound John William "Will" Brickhouse and 5'1", 90-pound Daisy, who were thirty-nine and fifteen years old, respectively, when they married.

Brickhouse said that his parents were as different in personality as in size and age. Will was an extrovert theater sales manager, sideshow barker, and would-be entertainer; Daisy was a hardworking hotel cashier and hostess. They were separated before Will died of pneumonia, leaving Daisy a widowed teenager with two-year-old Jack.

Reared by his mother and grandmother, Brickhouse delivered newspapers as a grade-schooler. A second marriage failed for his mother.

In dedicating his autobiography to her, Jack wrote, "God couldn't be everywhere, so he created Mothers."

Brickhouse attended Peoria Manual High School, serving as sports editor of the school paper, then made a short run at college, enrolling at Bradley University. He didn't get a degree until many years later, when he was awarded an honorary doctorate after his career achievements led to his being named to the university's board of trustees.

His short time on campus, however, did open the door to broadcasting. Brickhouse entered Peoria radio station WMBD's "So you want to be an announcer" contest in 1934, envisioning winning the $50 first-prize watch and pawning it to stake a job-seeking trip to the West Coast.

He didn't win any of the four prizes. But someone at the station was impressed sufficiently to give him a one-week tryout. Two weeks later, the eighteen-year-old college dropout was a part-time announcer and part-time switchboard operator at WMBD, earning $17 per week.

Four years later, he was the only sportscaster in town, doing Bradley University basketball play-by-play, making $48 per week, and dating his future bride, Nelda Teach. They had a daughter, Jeanne, before their marriage ended in divorce.

Brickhouse's move from Peoria to Chicago was facilitated by another Hall of Fame baseball broadcaster for WGN, Bob Elson. After arranging an audition for his Peoria protégé, "the Commander" sent a terse wire that Brickhouse subsequently framed for his wall. "Remember, if asked, you have a thorough knowledge of baseball," Elson's message instructed.

After working alongside Elson, Brickhouse took over WGN baseball broadcasts when Elson joined the navy in 1942. A year later, Brickhouse left for a stint with the marines.

Brickhouse became WGN-TV's first

voice in 1948. The station's first telecasts featured Golden Gloves boxing from the Chicago Stadium, wrestling from Marigold Arena, and baseball from Wrigley Field and Comiskey Park. Brickhouse did them all.

The year before, he and renowned bowling announcer "Whispering" Joe Wilson did Cubs games on WBKB, Chicago's first TV station.

Brickhouse's hey-hey days are best remembered as seasons of futility when the best a Cubs fan could hope for was that the North Siders might outdo their crosstown rivals, the White Sox.

It rarely happened—the Sox won a pennant in 1959, with Brickhouse calling the clincher from Cleveland, and remained contenders for much of the 1960s. The Cubs, despite the presence of future Hall of Famers Ernie Banks, Billy Williams, and Fergie Jenkins, were largely a second-division team until 1969, when Brickhouse's call of Willie Smith's game-winning pinch-homer on Opening Day set the stage for one of the most memorable seasons in Cubs history.

Alas, it ended in the disappointment of a September collapse, furthering Brickhouse's image as a long-suffering, seldom-complaining nice-guy narrator of a team's trials and errors. But he could be critical when the occasion warranted it.

Brickhouse had a long if mostly private feud with Leo Durocher, blaming the manager for losing control of the Cubs as they went from nine and a half games ahead to eight behind the New York Mets in the final six weeks of 1969.

He debated Howard Cosell on Irv Kupcinet's TV show and dismissed Cosell's tough-critic persona as "a put-on," albeit "a clever put-on by a clever man." And he turned on his beloved Bears when they switched radio allegiance to WBBM from WGN in 1976.

But at his most critical, Brickhouse tempered his words with objectivity. And he showed he could take criticism, responding to those who disliked his style simply by citing his longevity and laughing at those who joked about his talent.

In his 1986 autobiography *Thanks for Listening*, he recounted joining in the laughter after one such ribbing from comedian Tom Dreesen.

At a WGN-TV-sponsored event attended by numerous athletes and sports dignitaries, Dreesen introduced "Hall of Famer Jack Brickhouse" and added, "Do you realize that tens of thousands of people grew up not knowing anything about football because they listened to Jack Brickhouse and Irv Kupcinet on the Bears' broadcasts?"

He then imitated an oft-heard exchange between the two broadcasters: "Right, Kup?"

"That's right, Jack."

Jack and Kup did Bears broadcasts for twenty-four consecutive seasons.

The Bears assignment ended abruptly when the team switched stations. But Brickhouse had a lot more time for reflection on his Cubs career before retiring.

During one such moment, as he prepared for his five-thousandth baseball telecast in August 1979, he assessed his strength succinctly in an interview.

"If I'm anything, I'm versatile," he said. "There is nothing I have not done in this business."

Feeling he had been blessed with "an announcer's voice," he said, "Some guys who know more about sports than I can ever hope to know just don't sound that way behind a mike.

"My strength is that I can take a piece of copy on a subject I know little about and sound authoritative."

In 1980, a year before he retired, he married Pat Ettelson, who ran her own public-relations firm.

He was preparing to attend Caray's funeral on February 27 when his left leg went numb, sending him to Northwestern Memorial Hospital for tests and subsequent surgery for a brain tumor. Though he couldn't make the Caray service, he recalled a note his friend had written him on the occasion of his five-thousandth telecast.

"I'm proud of his work and of our friendship," Caray wrote. "His success

assured, there is nothing left to wish him but continued good health and a long life. . . . Hang in there. Too few like you are left."

That was a couple of seasons before Brickhouse passed the Cubs' broadcasting reins over to Caray. It was long before they and we would realize that Caray would work sixteen more years after his predecessor retired . . . and that Brickhouse would outlive his successor.

Because they loved the game, because they could enjoy good plays regardless of the final score, because they could focus on the joy of the moment when one of the good guys hit a home run, and because they could ignore the reality that such moments rarely accumulated into success at season's end, we can still find the fun in their words.

Like a scratchy recording from a phonograph on the other side of a half-opened window:

"It might be . . . It could be . . . It is . . ."

"Back, back . . . hey-hey!"

TUESDAY, NOVEMBER 2, 1999

Walter Payton, Forty-Five; Chicago's "Sweetness" Dies of Cancer
By Don Pierson, *Tribune* Pro Football Reporter

Walter Payton, the Bears Hall of Fame running back and the NFL's career rushing leader, died Monday of cancer that was a complication of his rare liver disease.

Payton, forty-five, was diagnosed with primary sclerosing cholangitis (PSC), a disease of the bile ducts. The only treatment is a liver transplant, but

his cancer precluded that option.

"A known complication of this liver disease is this type of cancer," said Dr. Greg Gores of the Mayo Clinic, where Payton received treatment after revealing his disease to the public last February. "Unfortunately, Walter's malignancy was very advanced and progressed extremely rapidly."

One of Walter Payton's coaches, Fred O'Connor, said of the legendary athlete: "God must have taken a chisel and said, 'I'm going to make me a halfback.'"

Teammates who had stayed as close as Payton allowed them to still expressed surprise. Payton died at noon at his suburban home with his wife, Connie, son, Jarrett, and daughter, Brittney, with him.

Mike Singletary, a teammate and fellow Hall of Fame player, said he prayed and read scripture with Payton over the weekend.

"Outside of anything I've ever seen— the greatest runs, the greatest moves— what I experienced this weekend was by far the best by Walter Payton," Singletary said.

Jarrett Payton, a freshman football player at the University of Miami, was called home Thursday. He addressed the media at Bears headquarters in Lake

Forest only hours after his father's death, thanking medical people, the Bears, Payton's teammates, and Chicago fans.

"The last twelve months have been extremely tough on me and my family," Jarrett said. "We learned a lot about love and life. Our greatest thanks goes out to the people of Chicago. You adopted my dad and made him yours. He loved you all."

Former Bears coach and Hall of Fame player Mike Ditka called Payton "the greatest Bear of all," and Bears owner Virginia Halas McCaskey paid special tribute to the only Bears player other than founder George Halas to graduate from the playing field to the team's board of directors.

"After Brian Piccolo died [in 1969], my husband Ed and I promised ourselves we wouldn't be so personally involved with any of the players," Mrs. McCaskey said, fighting back tears. "We were able to follow that resolve until Walter Payton came into our lives."

In thirteen seasons with the Bears from 1975 through 1987, Payton set NFL records for yardage (16,726) and rushing attempts (3,838) that still stand. His ten seasons with 1,000 or more yards, his 275 yards in one game, and his seventy-seven games with more than 100 yards rushing also are records that have not been broken.

From the time he arrived as a twenty-year-old number one draft choice from Jackson State in 1975, Payton's relentless running style and charismatic personality earned him the admiration of Chicagoans starved for sports heroes. For years, Payton patiently carried a team with less talent until his effort was rewarded with a Super Bowl season in 1985.

When Payton retired, the man who drafted him, general manager Jim Finks, said: "He's rare in his whole approach to this business. He has answered the call every Sunday for thirteen years at a very demanding position. He's rare in that he never compromised his privacy or his family for extra dollars. He has handled notoriety as professionally as anybody I've ever known, by being himself. He let his work speak for itself."

Payton was diagnosed with PSC in the fall of 1998 and revealed it at a press conference on February 2 after he felt compelled to explain a dramatic weight loss. PSC is a rare disease in which the bile ducts inside and outside the liver narrow because of inflammation and scarring. This causes bile to accumulate in the liver and results in damage to liver cells. It is a progressive disease that leads to cirrhosis and liver failure. The exact cause of PSC is unknown.

In February, after preliminary tests at the Mayo Clinic, Payton said: "They did a biopsy of the ducts and came up with no cancers or anything else." Payton went on to say he was treating the disease the same way he treated football injuries during a career in which he missed only one game.

"I'm looking at it as a sprained ankle or a twisted knee," he said. "I have to stay positive. Nobody else can make me stay positive. I have to do that. Then whatever happens, happens. If in two years something happens and I get a transplant and my body accepts it and I go on, that's fine. And if in two years I don't, then that's the way life was meant to be for me."

Payton set the standard for durability and productivity by a running back, outlasting and outgaining all who went before. Marcus Allen later played in more games, but nobody ran with a football more times for more yards.

In a sport defined by runners from the time football's unwitting inventor picked up a soccer ball and ran with it, Payton outdid them all, leaving Jim Brown, O. J. Simpson, Tony Dorsett, Franco Harris, Eric Dickerson, John Riggins, Joe Perry, Earl Campbell, Jim Taylor, Larry Csonka, Paul Hornung, Steve Van Buren, Ollie Matson, Hugh McElhenny, Marion Motley, Ernie Nevers, and Jim Thorpe in his wake.

In a city proud of its tradition of runners from Red Grange to Bronko Nagurski to Beattie Feathers to Bill Osmanski to George McAfee to Rick Casares to Gale Sayers, Payton outperformed them all.

Arguments over who was the "greatest" runner revolve around style and opinion. Simpson and Dorsett and others were faster. Brown and many others were bigger; Brown still has the highest yards-per-carry average at 5.22. Sayers and McElhenny were fancier. Campbell and Nagurski and Csonka and Riggins were more powerful, although pound-for-pound, nobody was stronger than Payton.

Ditka, the Bears coach for Payton's final six seasons, described him simply as the best football player he had ever seen because he did so many things so well. Payton found time, for example, to catch more passes than either Lenny Moore or Frank Gifford, two running backs who became the first great flanker-backs as the passing game developed.

Payton was such a superb blocker that coaches liked to save clips to show friends. "He's a thrill to watch for a football man," said Abe Gibron, who missed being Payton's first coach by a year.

"All this folderol about the rushing record never meant anything to me," said Finks, who drafted Payton in 1975 after firing Gibron. "In fact, Walter's rushing yards are probably the most overrated element of his play. For instance, there's no better blocker in the NFL. None. He flattens linebackers, knocks down ends, attacks nose guards. And the irony is that he's competing against one-dimensional players."

Jack Pardee, his first Bears coach, was so defensive-minded that he once included Payton's pursuit and tackling ability after interceptions as two of Payton's assets. His first position coach, Fred O'Connor, set the stage for a legend by declaring after first glance: "God must have taken a chisel and said, 'I'm going to make me a halfback.'"

No man ever played harder; no kid ever loved it more. Payton bounced up from tackles, often helping the tackler to his feet after delivering the first blow with his Popeye-sized forearms. The style was calculated to suggest invincibility, a ruse exposed on the Bears sideline when Payton would surreptitiously seek pain-killing medicine from trainer Fred Caito or rub an ankle when it was really a knee that hurt. He didn't want anyone to know.

Payton missed only one game in his

career and was livid about it, blaming Pardee and O'Connor for punishing him after he missed practice time with a sore ankle in his rookie year. He could have played and forever after demanded an asterisk be added to preserve what he believed was a perfect durability record spoiled by vindictive coaches.

Payton routinely turned the drudgery of practice into a sight to behold. The Bears could have sold tickets to watch him, and probably would if he were playing in this more commercial time. Payton never was formally diagnosed with attention deficit disorder, probably because he couldn't sit still long enough to be tested. In football, he was able to put his relentless movement to good use during practices as well as games.

In nontackling drills, he would sometimes break through the line and run backward or engage in a dance routine with a defensive back before flipping the ball into an unsuspecting belly. When it was time to rest, he would throw passes on the sideline, often catching high-velocity thirty-yarders with one bare hand. When it was a kicker's turn to practice, Payton would shag balls and throw them back at the kicked balls. It was not uncommon for him to hit them in midflight. Once he did it twice in a row, convincing stunned onlookers he could indeed do anything he wanted. Payton also was the team's backup kicker. If he ever ran out of ideas, he would walk fifty yards down the sideline by himself—on his hands.

No shirttail was safely tucked at practice. If a player was in sweat pants, he risked indecent exposure every time he turned his back on Payton. At the end of one practice, as tired players dragged themselves to water coolers, Payton leapfrogged over the head of a 6'4" assistant coach on the way to the locker room.

"My lasting memory will be more of practice, going outside day in and day out and seeing Walter in a state of perpetual motion," said safety Gary Fencik, who played with Payton for twelve of his thirteen seasons. "If he's not running the ball, he's on the sideline throwing it or kicking it. I think that reflects how much Walter really loves playing football."

Teammate Dan Hampton added: "You see a lot of players who are jaded on the job. Yet here's one of the greatest of all time and he's still trying to be the best tailback on the tenth-grade team."

In his best games, Payton merely hoisted the Bears on his shoulder pads and carried them as far as he could. In a 7–0 struggle against the Buffalo Bills, he provided the air attack as well as the ground game by sailing so high over the Bills' defensive line for the game's only touchdown that Buffalo nose tackle Fred Smerlas said, "He was like a fly. I was halfway standing up, and he still leaped over my head."

"Some of the things I do—I amaze myself," Payton once said. "I don't realize I do them until I see the film."

Against the Minnesota Vikings in 1977, he set the NFL single-game record of 275 yards, punishing a team that prided itself on defense and knew it had only one person to stop. The Bears managed to eke out a 10–7 victory, embarrassing offensive coordinator Sid Gillman. Gillman couldn't figure out how a team with a runner who gained 275 yards could generate only ten points.

Against the Packers in Green Bay in 1985, Payton rescued a sorry display of cheap shots and fights by running for 192 yards in twenty-eight carries, including the winning touchdown on a 27-yard run. The close 16–10 call kept the Bears undefeated.

"I thought Payton's exhibition was maybe as good as I've ever seen a guy with a football under his arm play," Ditka said.

Former Bears personnel chief Bill Tobin, who had an easy time scouting Payton at Jackson State, said, "I don't even consider him a rare breed. I just consider him a total, special, special individual. He's a complete phenomenon, in my opinion, and the best player I've ever, ever seen or hope to ever see."

By the 1985 season, some considered Payton an afterthought on a team so devastating on defense and so full of characters that he appeared to be along for the joyride in his eleventh season. Not so. He was still the main man, as his 1,551 yards demonstrated. His failure to score a touchdown in the team's splendid 46–10 rout of the New England Patriots in Super Bowl XX still haunts Ditka, who forgot about him, and quarterback Jim McMahon, who blames himself for not changing Ditka's plays.

Payton was portrayed as a selfish pouter after that game. Although consistently moody and unpredictable, Payton claimed he was not so upset about the failure to score as he was about the anticlimactic Super Bowl experience. It wouldn't have been the winning touchdown anyway.

"I was expecting the Super Bowl to be the greatest game I ever played, but on a scale of one to ten, I'd give it a two. If it had been 14–12, maybe it would have meant more," Payton said later.

"Here's a guy who had the most heart I've ever seen in a football player," McMahon said. "He wanted to do whatever it would take for the team to win. He was the greatest, and he didn't act like it."

Opponents joined teammates in praising Payton.

"To give you an idea of what the rest of the league thinks about Payton, in our film sessions, our defense actually applauded when they saw Payton make some of his runs," said Bud Grant, the former Minnesota Vikings coach.

Said Jim Brown, "I'm a very, very critical individual, and I'm only impressed by what I think is greatness. And I saw Walter run two plays, and he was the most impressive back that I've seen come into the league in a long time."

Gale Sayers loved what he called Payton's "continuation of the first effort. Some people call it second effort, some call it third effort. If Walter gets hit, people might tend to relax on him. He'll keep driving; he's always trying to squirm out of things."

Payton once said he would like to be remembered along the lines of former Cincinnati Reds star Pete Rose.

"Charlie Hustle," Payton said. "Somebody who stands for hard work and total effort. I want to do everything perfectly on the field—pass blocking, running a dummy route, carrying out a fake, all of it."

Off the field, Payton lived a fast,

frenetic, and elusive life similar to the one he lived on the field. It was not exemplary in all ways, as anyone who ever rode with him in a car can attest. He once was arrested for doing ninety-four miles per hour in a thirty-five-mile-per-hour zone in Lake Forest and was later unable to turn his lead foot into a long or successful career as a race driver. Payton listed as hobbies "drums and privacy," an unusual combination of pastimes.

Wife Connie once told writer Jeannie Morris: "He never tells me anything. I almost have to pry everything out of him, and I don't think he really likes that, but that's the only way. . . . I don't think a man should keep so much inside. He keeps everything inside and I don't think even Walter's that strong of a person."

On the field, he was as strong as they came. Former Bears conditioning coach Clyde Emrich said the 5'10", 204-pound Payton would casually pick up 100-pound dumbbells and press them with one hand. His running style helped him avoid crippling injuries. Caito, the Bears' former trainer, said Payton bent his knees at only a thirty-degree angle as opposed to some backs who bend almost ninety degrees. Payton swung his legs from his hips and ran on his toes, not planting his feet long enough for anyone to get a shot.

"Most injuries happen to someone in a relaxed state, and Walter's never relaxed," Emrich said.

The style mirrored his personality.

"I think he had a previous life," brother Eddie Payton said. "He must be the reincarnation of a great white shark.

If he stops moving forward, he will die."

Never a breakaway back, Payton said, "That first fifteen yards I'm wide open, but I don't know what my speed is on long runs. My burst is so strong, I burn up so much energy on my takeoff, maybe I run out of gas."

Payton said his nickname "Sweetness" came from "the girls at Jackson State." Then he raised his voice an octave: "No, I really got it from the men." Then he changed his mind: "No, I really got it from the other college players at the College All-Star Game."

Whatever, "Sweetness" never really fit Payton's rock-hard, slam-bang approach. He said what he loved about the game was the contact, the violence.

"He came back to the huddle once after a little two-yard run and he said, 'Did I hurt him? Did I hurt him?'" tackle Ted Albrecht said. "He makes two yards and wants to know if he punished the guy. That's what makes him a great back."

Payton came into the league vowing to play only three years. He was so nervous that he suffered headaches and dizziness. He gained zero yards on eight carries in his debut as he tried to score a touchdown on every play. He got better. When he extended his contract, he promised only three more years. Again, he was being elusive.

"If I'd come into the league my first or second year and said, 'I'm going to play twelve years,' all the reporters would have been looking for ways where he can't play twelve years, 'he's doing this wrong, doing that wrong.' But if I said I'm only going to play two more years, then they start looking for ways where I might play another year. And it worked. Kept you guys off of me," he said.

Payton's mother, Alyne Payton, had other plans for her son.

"I always thought he'd turn out to be a preacher," she said. "He's very serious, very religious."

Payton was a reluctant role model.

"I'm not a role model," he said once. "I'm just Walter Payton. If kids see some good in me they can utilize and emulate and make their lives better, so well and so good. But they have to realize I'm human just like anybody else. I'm capable of making mistakes. I'm capable of making the wrong decision. They should realize that. Nobody's perfect. Please don't put that on me, because I'm not perfect."

He also said, "I don't perceive myself as being better than anyone. I shovel my driveway. I go to the grocery store. I pump my own gas. Some athletes don't do that."

He did have an ego and admitted it, complaining once that former ABC commentator Simpson "doesn't even mention me when he's talking about the great running backs."

Payton didn't make a million-dollar salary until his last season in 1987. He admitted he was disappointed after his first three seasons when the Bears offered him only half of Simpson's then league-leading $733,000 salary.

After eventually signing for $400,000 in the pre–free agency era, Payton said, "The thing is, people want me to beat all of O.J.'s records. Why don't they want me to beat his salary? Tell me that."

Before his final season, in a relaxed moment at the Pro Bowl in Hawaii, Payton "practiced" a retirement speech that now serves as a fitting epitaph: "Chicago, National Football League, world: I am so proud I've had the opportunity to be a part of your lives, to bring some happiness to your lives, and express my talents on the field and off the field. And if I've done anything that has helped your lives, please use it. If I've done anything to offend you, please forgive me. I've had a ball, and now I'm bowing out."

FRIDAY, JANUARY 7, 2000

George J. Halas Sr., Seventy-Five; Sales Executive, Bears Scout

By James Janega, *Tribune* Staff Reporter

The name was a mixed blessing for George J. Halas Sr., both instant recognition and the challenge to avoid it for a man named for a legendary uncle, former Chicago Bears owner George "Papa Bear" Halas.

Yet while Halas strove throughout his life to make his own way—building a reputable career in the military and as a sales manager for Chicago-area industrial firms—the Halas name and tradition still called to him in the 1960s and

1970s, when he replaced his father, Walter, as a part-time advance scout for the Bears.

After a lifetime spent balancing his identity with his family's inevitable association with the Bears, Halas, seventy-five, died of cancer Tuesday, January 4, in his Mt. Prospect home.

A serious man with a commanding presence, Halas was a decorated warrant officer when he retired from the army reserves in 1986. He later gained recognition for marketing space-age technologies for industrial applications during his twenty years with Siemens-Furnas Controls in Batavia.

"He was an individual who could look at something new and discover new applications for anything," said his son George Jr. "He wasn't a research scientist, but once he understood what something did, he was able to apply it for uses in ways that other people had not thought of."

Drafted into the army in 1943, he chose to remain in the Army National Guard after World War II, and he served in the Korean War. During the wars, he worked in antiaircraft batteries and as an airborne artillery observer, peering out of airplanes to pick out targets on the ground.

He was awarded several commendations, including the Legion of Merit, the Bronze Star, a Meritorious Service Medal, and the Air Medal.

After the Korean War, Halas received a bachelor's degree from Northwestern University and worked in sales and marketing for Chicago-area industrial companies specializing in electric motors.

But after the 1959 death of his father, who scouted opposing teams for the Bears, Halas took over his father's role on weekends, flying around the country to observe teams the Bears would play the following week.

The late nights of paperwork at his rolltop desk began stretching into the weekends, his harsh desk lamp illuminating statistics from opposing football teams as well as sales forecasts and expense reports.

"He was, in essence, a football spy," his son said, adding that it was also a role his father felt he owed the family. "Having the name 'George Halas' in Chicago is a two-edged sword.

"I don't think my dad ever tried to avoid being involved with the Bears. He didn't try to downplay or take advantage of his name at all. But he did put a lot of effort into establishing his own separate identity."

In addition to his son, Halas is survived by his wife of fifty years, Mildred; another son, Timothy; two daughters, Anne Graham and Cynthia Dery; three grandsons; and six granddaughters.

THURSDAY, MAY 3, 2001

Ben Bentley, Eighty-One; Promoter, *Sportswriters* Mainstay

By James Janega and Ron Grossman, *Tribune* Staff Reporters

The voice was unmistakable, something like a foghorn with a Northwest Side accent. With it, Ben Bentley promoted Chicago fighters from the boxing ring, Chicago basketball in the sports offices of the city's newspapers, and sports in general from the moderator's seat of *The Sportswriters*, a television and radio show known as widely for its prolific on-air consumption of cigars as for its lucid opinions about Windy City sports teams.

Chicago already had a reputation as a tough town, a hustler's town, before Bentley made sure his name was well known in it. But from the time he began promoting its homegrown boxers in the late 1940s until *The Sportswriters* went off the air in 1995, Bentley helped cement its reputation as a brawny place in love with its sports.

The onetime comedian and master of ceremonies, occasional personal public relations man for Rocky Marciano and Sugar Ray Robinson, and first spokesman for the fledgling Chicago Bulls died Tuesday. He was eighty-one and had suffered a stroke in his Chicago home.

Mayor Richard M. Daley said Wednesday that Bentley "was a colorful character and he loved sports. He was part of Chicago's history."

The sportswriters who worked with him over four decades recalled a salesman who became the namesake for Chicago Bulls mascot Benny the Bull, a fight promoter Muhammad Ali called his "little white brother"—even after Bentley taped Ali's mouth shut during the controversy over the fighter's refusal to submit to the draft in 1966—and a prankster who once sneaked a crowd of Chicago newspapermen into a chic New York steakhouse by telling the maître d' that former Chicago American sportswriter Ed Stone was the ambassador from Peru.

"He could con the best of them," Stone said. "There have been many characters in Chicago, and sports, and in the media, but he stood out. He was one of a kind."

All agreed Bentley's greatest talent was knowing people. It was his relationship with the late Jack Brickhouse and others that helped land him a job with the Bulls in 1966, and once in the position, Bentley remained a regular in the offices of every newspaper sports section in the city, where he personally advocated—sometimes connived—for coverage of his clients.

He may have known little about basketball, but he knew everything about getting coverage in Chicago, said Bill Gleason, longtime sports journalist and founder of *The Sportswriters*.

"Ben was everywhere. He'd say 'I gotta bop. I'm boppin' around, gotta make my rounds,'" Gleason recalled. "He was probably the most publicized

Sports promoter Ben Bentley's namesake is the Chicago Bulls mascot Benny the Bull.

publicity man in the city."

Bentley grew up in Humboldt Park, where he fondly remembered getting into a lot of fights as a boy and later

told former heavyweight boxer Bobby Hitz that was where he got his start in boxing.

"He'd get a couple of kids together

for a fight in the alley," Hitz, now a boxing promoter himself, remembered Bentley saying. "He'd be the promoter, the matchmaker. He'd announce the fight, and he probably booked a few bucks on it too."

Bentley was drafted into the army in 1941 and fought in the Pacific, where he was tapped toward the end of his tour to handle visiting entertainers.

By his own admission, his postwar nightclub act borrowed liberally from their routines, and after a few years he said doing publicity work for boxing matches seemed a good way to settle down. A short, active man who both announced fights and promoted them, he started off getting publicity for fights at Marigold Arena and moved quickly to the Chicago Stadium before then promoting fights for the International Boxing Club.

When he married the former Jo Slepak in 1953, they honeymooned at Rocky Marciano's fight camp. Chicago was a fighting town, and he was the fight game's ambassador to the public.

Still, he leapt at the chance to represent Dick Klein's Chicago Bulls, the fourth NBA team to attempt putting down roots in Chicago and a tough sell to skeptical sportswriters who tended to think good college teams were all the basketball Chicago needed. After several years of that, Bentley became a long-time public relations official for the Chicago Park District.

It was in 1975 that he joined Gleason and *Tribune* sportswriters Bill Jauss and George Langford on WGN-AM for the radio debut of *The Sportswriters*. Though Bentley was originally asked to help find a good radio moderator, he produced a string of radio personalities who nevertheless knew nothing about sports; Gleason said the group ultimately decided they might as well give the post to Bentley.

In 1985 *The Sportswriters* went on television at WFLD-TV and moved shortly to SportsChannel, which then became Fox Sports Chicago, where it ran until 1997.

"He didn't pretend to be an expert," said John Roach, producer of *The Sportswriters* on TV. "He was someone who liked sports. In his own way, I think Ben added a kind of innocence to the panel."

Bentley is survived by his wife; two daughters, Iris Becker and Shelly Dreifuss; and five grandchildren.

SUNDAY, NOVEMBER 3, 2002

Edward "Moose" Cholak, Seventy-Two; Crowd Favorite on Pro Wrestling Circuit
By Rudolph Bush, *Tribune* Staff Reporter

In the old Marigold Arena on Chicago's North Side, the long, low calls would begin even before Edward Cholak entered the ring.

"Moooose. Moooose," the crowd called, until Cholak, a giant of a man at 6'4" and nearly 400 pounds, emerged, often with a real moose head propped on his shoulders.

He was known as Moose Cholak throughout a professional wrestling career that spanned four decades and took him across America. He also worked for many years as an engineer for the City of Chicago.

Cholak, seventy-two, of Chicago, died of complications from a stroke Thursday, October 31, in St. Margaret Mercy Healthcare Center in Hammond, Indiana.

He was born and raised on Chicago's Southeast Side, where his parents ran a tavern. Large and strong even as a youth, he was an all-city wrestler at Chicago Vocational High School, and he played football for a year at the University of Wisconsin before leaving to join the navy during the Korean War. Cholak received engineering training while in the service.

When he returned to Chicago in 1952, Cholak was recruited by wrestling promoter Chief Don Eagle to join the pro circuit.

Though a far cry from the outrageous antics that make up televised wrestling today, professional wrestling in those days was a show, and the wrestlers knew they were the players.

"The crowds wouldn't come just to see somebody wrestle somebody else on the mat," said Cholak's wife of forty-five years, Arlene.

And in those early days, Cholak always guaranteed a good time, donning his moose head and giving his moose call before grappling with an opponent.

Though he was well known on the U.S. circuit and went to Japan several times to wrestle, the pay didn't match his celebrity.

In the mid-1970s, Cholak joined the city's Streets and Sanitation Department, for which he worked until 1996, overseeing crews involved in street projects.

Until the mid-1980s, Cholak continued to wrestle.

Toward the end of his career, he weighed more than 400 pounds and his knees gave him trouble. Still, he loved the life under the lights and hearing the crowd rumble his name.

"Everybody called it out. He was very, very popular," his wife said.

Other survivors include a daughter, Kathleen, and a son, Steven.

Moguls and Other Big Cheeses

Chicago's executives changed the way America ate lunch, where it shopped for tools and household goods, how it defined optimism, and what the nation's businesspeople found when they traveled to conventions.

It is a city that carved statues of its most prominent industrialists and that still celebrates their business heirs' accomplishments, no matter how surprising.

SATURDAY, JANUARY 22, 2000

Roland Miller, Eighty-Three; Cheese Firm Executive

By James Janega, *Tribune* Staff Reporter

Roland E. Miller never went to engineering school, never planned to be an executive, and never planned that his first job—cleaning out cheese crocks at the Kraft Inc. plant in Freeport, Illinois—would change much of anything.

But Miller had an affinity for solving equipment problems, and his innovations catapulted him further and further up the food chain at Kraft.

One of the projects he led during his forty-five-year career with the company, which produced a contraption as big as a dump truck, revolutionized the way Americans eat lunch.

It made individually wrapped slices of cheese. Kraft patented the design, and grilled-cheese sandwiches, cheeseburgers, and after-school snacks would never be the same.

Miller, eighty-three, a gregarious man who went by "Bud" and enjoyed chatting with friends back home in Lena, Illinois, died Wednesday, January 19, in his home after apparently suffering a heart attack.

"I don't think he picked it; it picked him," his daughter, Janet Jones, said of his career. "He always loved to fix things, and he particularly liked to fix things that nobody else could fix. Toasters, anything. He liked to make parts for it, whatever it took."

Shortly after Miller was hired as an apprentice mechanic in 1935, his ingenuity became apparent, Kraft officials said. Within a short time, he was promoted to plant engineer. In 1946 the company promoted him again and moved him to its Chicago headquarters. The next year, he was promoted yet again to project engineer.

His efforts led to the development of more than twenty-seven patents for the food giant, from high-speed packaging for cream and processed cheeses to packaging for salad products.

But it was the development of the system to individually wrap slices of cheese that gained him the most acclaim. Liquid cheese entered the machine, was squirted out into ribbons, and then sliced, wrapped, and stacked.

"That type of process had significant importance to the company. It's a very public invention, and it's one that has meant a lot for the future of the company," said Moyra Knight, a spokeswoman for Kraft.

During his time in Chicago, his daughter said, Miller was nominated for the Package Engineering Hall of Fame. He retired in 1985 as Kraft's director of corporate engineering services.

But Miller still was a small-town man. He and his wife, Francis, moved to Lena, where Miller spent mornings chatting with friends at a town diner, was a member of the village board, and collected antique cars. He was well known for playing cards and hosting parties on the houseboat he and his wife kept on the Mississippi River.

One of his last "inventions" was to have his wife sew the fronts of his white, short-sleeve button-up shirts together so the lapels wouldn't pull apart between the buttons.

Other survivors include two grand-daughters and a sister. His wife died in 1999.

FRIDAY, SEPTEMBER 1, 2000

A. Dean Swift, Eighty-One; Sears CEO in 1970s
By James Janega, *Tribune* Staff Reporter

A. Dean Swift, eighty-one, president of Sears, Roebuck & Co. through the recessions and inflation of the 1970s, died Monday, August 28, in Evanston Hospital after suffering a stroke over the weekend.

He was the eleventh president of the 114-year-old company, elected to the position in 1972 at perhaps the height of Sears' national influence, and he held the post until the beginning of the massive company upheaval of the 1980s.

The size of Sears, Roebuck in 1972 is hard to imagine. Sears accounted for 1 percent of the United States' gross national product. Two out of three people had shopped at Sears within any three-month period, and half the adults in America held a Sears charge card.

But then came oil embargoes, inflation, growing unemployment, and a recession. By the end of the 1970s, Sears, like almost every other retail outlet in the United States, was struggling to regain its former footing.

Swift, who retired in 1980, was popular among Sears workers throughout his tenure.

He headed an effort to bring diversity to Sears' workforce and among its suppliers and was widely regarded as an employee-oriented humanitarian.

"If you could pick a father, it was said of Swift, it would be Dean," wrote author Donald Katz in his 1987 book *The Big Store*.

A man with an energetic, folksy manner, Swift started his career at Sears as a salesman and served in almost every other capacity after that.

Other executives said he was the kind of manager who took off his sport coat during meetings and gave impromptu speeches remembered for decades.

"He excelled at that," said Ernest Arms, a friend of Swift's and a longtime spokesman for Sears. "It was his nature, the kind of guy he was."

Swift grew up in Evanston and graduated in 1940 from the University of Illinois with a political science degree. He went to work as a salesman in the Highland Park Sears store the same year. During World War II, he was a field artillery officer in Europe, winning two Bronze Stars.

He became the Highland Park store's division manager when he returned. Until 1964, he held managerial positions in Illinois, Indiana, Missouri, and Kentucky, then was named general manager of stores in Indianapolis and later Detroit.

He became vice president of Sears' thirteen-state southern territory in 1969, serving also on the boards of Allstate Insurance, Homart Development, and Sears Roebuck Acceptance Corp. He began his term as Sears president in 1973.

Donald Deutsch, a former Sears vice president, said Swift also served on dozens of boards, ranging from Commonwealth Edison and the Chicago Board of Trade to the National Urban League, the Crusade of Mercy, and the Metropolitan Housing and Planning Council. Most of his affiliations involved people-oriented organizations, and Swift clearly got a lot of enjoyment from them, Deutsch said.

"You could just tell. It was a part of him; he had a great gift for talking to people," said Deutsch. "It was just a part of his makeup and soul."

And it played a big part in why Swift, minutes after his retirement from Sears, marched across the Loop and volunteered with the Executive Service Corps, said Dennis Zavac, president of the group in which former executives of major companies do volunteer consulting with nonprofit groups.

In twelve years as chairman of the board at Executive Service Corps, Swift increased its annual budget from $160,000 to $1.1 million and increased the number of corporate supporters tenfold, Zavac said. He accomplished it largely by persuading chief executive officers to come over for a ham sandwich, coleslaw, and a slide presentation, Zavac said.

"There was no one in town he wouldn't call, and he delivered," Zavac said. "He was a quiet man, but he threw himself into what he believed in."

Swift was still chairman of the Executive Service Corps executive committee when he died.

He is survived by his wife, Mary Lou; two sons, Dean W. and Dr. Dan; a daughter, Sara Snyder; and eight grandchildren.

THURSDAY, JANUARY 4, 2001

Harry Katz, Eighty-Two;
Business Owner Arranged Conventions in Chicago
By James Janega, *Tribune* Staff Reporter

Harry Katz, eighty-two, who became involved in the Chicago convention industry when he and his brothers founded a company to serve expositions after World War II, died from an unspecified cancer Tuesday, January 2, in his Gold Coast condominium.

Many of the trade shows and

expositions that came to Chicago starting in the 1940s turned to United Exposition Service Co. to rent equipment, set up convention floors, and negotiate with unions.

By the 1970s and 1980s, Katz was on the executive committee of the Chicago Convention Bureau, and some believed the family business had become the world's largest contracting firm serving the trade show industry.

"He knew the convention business, but he also knew the city," said his son-in-law, Jerry Pearlman. "They really brought the convention business here."

A gregarious man who hailed from an era when deals were sealed with a handshake, Katz wooed show managers and negotiated with trade and union leaders. He was soft-spoken and casual, though a regular on the black-tie circuit in the 1940s and 1950s.

A native of Atlantic City, New Jersey, Katz grew up just off the famed boardwalk. He attended the University of Pennsylvania, pursuing a degree in business, but left in 1940 to volunteer for the army.

During World War II, he was stationed at army airfields in Alabama and Texas. He married the former Mabel Crenshaw while stationed in Montgomery, Alabama.

Katz was a major when the war ended. He decided to start United Exposition with his brothers and brother-in-law in Atlantic City rather than go back to college, though he returned to finish his degree in the early 1980s. He moved to Chicago in 1947, where the company found a prominent niche in the emerging convention industry.

The company went through a public offering but was bought back by the family in 1971. Two years later, it was one of the first U.S. companies to stage a trade show in Moscow.

In the 1970s and 1980s, Katz raised Thoroughbred racehorses on a farm in Ocala, Florida. One of those horses, Hold Your Tricks, won the Cornhusker Stakes at Aksarben in Omaha.

He sold United Exposition in the mid-1980s but remained in management roles until 1990. During retirement he split his time between Chicago and Palm Beach, Florida.

Besides his son-in-law and wife, survivors include a daughter, Barbara Pearlman; a brother, Solomon; five grandchildren; and six great-grandchildren.

WEDNESDAY, SEPTEMBER 4, 2002

W. Clement Stone, 100; Positive Thinking, $100 Led to Fortune

By Pat Widder, James Janega, and Rick Pearson, *Tribune* Staff Reporters

For W. Clement Stone, who parlayed $100 and a positive mental attitude into a $2 billion insurance empire and a personal fortune once estimated at half a billion dollars, anything was possible.

The founder and chairman emeritus

Insurance mogul W. Clement Stone was as famous for giving away money as he was for making it.

of the giant Combined International Corp.—since merged with Ryan Insurance Group to form Aon Corp.— Stone was as famous for giving away money as he was for making it with his legendary "success system that never fails."

He was 100 when he died Tuesday in Evanston Hospital. What had seemed like a charmed life ended due to natural causes, according to his son Norman.

Stone's trademarks were a pencil-thin mustache, a bow tie, an endless supply of Havana cigars, an infectious optimism, and political and philanthropic donations estimated to have exceeded $275 million, not including political donations themselves worth millions. To Richard M. Nixon's campaigns alone, Stone donated more than $8 million. Stone viewed his gifts to politicians and civic causes as a way to influence events. "I have a magnificent obsession," he once said. "All I want to do is change the world, make it a better place for this and future generations."

And what seemed a large contribution to others wasn't significant to him. "What's a few million dollars?" he once asked. "Everything's relative."

But those contributions often had a profound impact on their recipients.

"Clem was one of the first influential Americans to believe that my father could make the impossible comeback to become president," said Julie Nixon Eisenhower, Nixon's daughter. "He was truly an inspiration to the president."

Mayor Richard M. Daley praised him as "an innovator" but added, "I will remember him most as a man deeply committed to the civic life of Chicago, and, in fact, the nation."

The former governor James R. Thompson, who knew Stone during his record fourteen-year tenure as Illinois' chief executive, said Stone was an active participant and "no passenger" when it came to Republican politics in Illinois.

"Clem Stone for a long time cared deeply about the party and what it represented, and its principles coincided with a lot in his life," Thompson said. "He gave generously to the party, and he gave generously to the candidates."

Stone, a staunch Republican since he chaired the Third Ward Evanston Young Republicans during the Depression, supported the GOP lavishly throughout his life, bestowing on both his time and money.

He was the largest single contributor to the coffers of Nixon during his 1968 and 1972 presidential campaigns and stood by Nixon even after he was forced to resign in 1974, predicting he would "go down in history as one of the greatest presidents by virtue of his achievements."

Nixon returned the compliment when he made a surprise visit in 1980 to a Chicago Boys Club ceremony honoring Stone as Chicagoan of the Year. "I've never known a man who gave more and asked less," Nixon said of Stone.

Born to Louis and Anna M. Stone in Chicago on May 4, 1902, Stone was not yet three when his gambler father died, leaving the family impoverished.

He began selling the *Examiner* newspaper on Chicago's South Side at the age of six while his mother worked as a dressmaker. When it was tough to compete with bigger boys on the street corners, Stone recalled in his 1962 book, *The Success System That Never Fails*, he tried to sell papers to customers inside a restaurant. The owner tossed him out after three sales. Stone went right back in and started selling again. The restaurant owner, perhaps Stone's first convert to what was to become his legendary optimism, gave in.

During summers in his early teens, Stone worked for his stepfather in a small insurance agency. At sixteen, he moved with his mother to Detroit, where he first sold insurance going office to office in the Dime Bank Building in downtown Detroit, developing and honing sales techniques and his legendary positive mental attitude—to which he attributed his fortune.

To devote more time to the insurance business, Stone dropped out of high school, though he later obtained a diploma by attending night classes at the YMCA Central High School in Chicago. At nineteen, he entered the Detroit College of Law but dropped out after a year because, he said, "I felt I couldn't make a large enough income as a lawyer until I was at least thirty-five."

He attended Northwestern University from 1930 to 1932 without graduating, though by the end of his life, he had amassed twenty honorary degrees ranging from doctor of jurisprudence from Monmouth College to doctor of public letters from the National College of Chiropractic.

At twenty, he used savings of $100 to set up his own insurance agency in Chicago. Eight years later, about one thousand agents throughout the country were selling insurance for him.

A Stone dictum holds that every adversity contains the seed of an equivalent benefit if one searches for it. He once said the Depression was the "best thing that happened" to him because "it forced me to develop good work habits."

Between 1939 and 1946 Stone built the foundation of his insurance empire. The nucleus of his Combined Insurance Co. of America was the moribund Pennsylvania Casualty Co., which Stone bought in 1946. Under his tutelage, the company grew steadily. New recruits quickly were immersed in the Stone philosophy of self-motivation. "What the mind can conceive and believe, the mind can achieve," he said.

"Think positively," he would tell anyone who would listen.

Stone's insurance empire now is encapsulated by Aon Corp., with total revenues of just over $2 billion.

"How are you feeling today?" he would ask of employees at training sessions, or of shareholders at annual meetings, or of anyone at any time. The correct and unanimous response was: "Terrrrific!" Ask Stone how he was feeling and, inevitably, he would answer, "I feel healthy. I feel happy. I feel terrific."

When Combined was reorganized in 1980 into a holding company, Combined International, and listed for trading on the New York Stock Exchange, it came as no surprise to anyone who had followed the company that the exchange symbol on the Big Board was PMA—for "Positive Mental Attitude," of course.

In 1987 shareholders approved the company's name change to Aon, at which Stone became chairman emeritus. Until recently, he went each day from his Spanish-style lakefront mansion in Winnetka to an office in Lake Forest to work on philanthropic and political activities.

He wrote or coauthored three books: *The Success System That Never Fails, Success Through a Positive Mental Attitude*, and *The Other Side of the Mind*. He also spread the PMA gospel through a magazine, *Success Unlimited*, founded in 1954 and sold in 1985.

In 1981 Stone was nominated for the Nobel Peace Prize by three U.S. senators, as well as former secretary of state Henry Kissinger. In his letter of nomination, Senate Majority Leader Howard Baker Jr. (R-Tenn.) wrote that Stone had dedicated his life to a philosophy of "that which you can share multiplies."

"Can his impact be measured? Yes and no," said Wallace Watson, president of the Boys & Girls Clubs of Chicago, which Stone was involved in for some fifty years. "He has put literally millions of dollars into Boys & Girls Clubs through the years, and those kids have been able to finish high school and go on to college and into society. They're a measurement. His life will live on here, I hope, forever."

Although his acts of generosity to prominent Republicans brought him headlines, countless civic and charitable groups (particularly those concerned with volunteerism, mental health, youth welfare, religion, and education) were quiet beneficiaries for decades of Stone's generosity.

In 1923 Stone married his high school sweetheart, Jessie Verna Tarson. They had three children: Clement, Norman, and Donna. His wife and son Norman, who serves as president of the W. Clement & Jessie V. Stone Foundation, survive him, along with twelve grandchildren and thirteen great-grandchildren.

THURSDAY, SEPTEMBER 26, 2002

William Lane III, Fifty-Nine; Expanded Lane Industries

By James Janega, *Tribune* Staff Reporter

William Lane III, fifty-nine, who built his family's office document–binding firm from what one analyst called "a nice little company sitting around" into a nearly billion-dollar office supply enterprise supplemented by ranching and hotel operations around the United States, died of cancer Friday, September 20, in his Lake Forest home.

Lane served as chairman of Northbrook-based General Binding Corp. from 1983 to 2000 and had been an officer and director of its parent company, Lane Industries, beginning in 1968. He was a blunt and worldly man with a penchant for big-game hunting in Africa and a strong desire to diversify his family's businesses.

During Lane's tenure, General Binding, which was founded by his father in the late 1940s, saw its sales grow from $105 million annually to $911 million. By the time he retired, General Binding was a dominant company in binding and laminating office documents, while Lane Industries was among the largest privately owned companies in the country.

Lane had expanded Lane Industries to include a regional security business, farming and ranching operations in New Mexico and Virginia, and hotels from the Chicago suburbs to the Caribbean.

Lane grew up in Lake Forest. He graduated from Lake Forest Academy

William Lane III liked to hunt big game in Africa and was adept at diversifying his family's business.

in 1961 and earned a bachelor's degree in economics from Princeton University in 1965 before joining the family business in 1968.

When his father died ten years later, Lane took over the document firm and continued its expansion into other businesses. The earliest venture had been banking, a business offshoot begun in the late 1960s that went public in 1986. In 1988 Lane Financial was sold to ABN/LaSalle, the North American banking network of Algemene Bank Nederland, LaSalle National Bank's Dutch parent.

Around the same time, Lane began acquiring hotels and, in 1994, Protection Service Industries, a small security firm that eventually went on to become a regional venture with clients in three western states.

Lane Industries also bought several radio stations around the country, selling them all a few years later.

The pace of acquisitions grew so great that former General Binding chief executive Govi Reddy told the *Tribune* in 1996, "We didn't plan acquisitions; we kind of bumped into them."

"There were opportunities that were becoming available," Reddy said Wednesday.

"He really understood the business, and he really cared about people," Reddy said. "Bill Lane was a humble man—enormously successful but very humble. Everybody felt special, and he made everybody feel important."

Survivors include his wife, Mary, and son, Carl.

XII

Labor Leaders

One Chicago teamster rose from a truck driver's helper to a local leader, had two bronze busts cast in his likeness and apparently forgot about them, shot and killed his own son in self-defense, and was stripped of ties to the union for embezzling money. Another went from a beer-truck driver to a leader with a quiet style and a redeeming influence in a culture battling with corruption.

Chicago is the city that works, and its workers' lives told the tale behind that often turbulent identity.

SUNDAY, DECEMBER 12, 1999

Daniel Ligurotis, Seventy-Two; Teamsters Leader

By James Janega, *Tribune* Staff Reporter

There were his years as a power broker, as the handpicked leader of the sixteen thousand–member Teamsters Local 705, one of the union's largest and most influential locals.

There was the pair of bronze busts made in his likeness, which together cost $14,000, found in 1993 in the basement of the Teamster City office complex on West Jackson Boulevard after then Teamsters president Ron Carey took over the local and vowed to reform the union.

And there was the story of how Daniel C. Ligurotis, the onetime truck driver's helper who rose to become secretary-treasurer of Local 705 and president of Teamsters Joint Council 25, shot and killed his son and namesake in self-defense in the basement of the local's headquarters.

Two months after he was acquitted of second-degree murder, a court-appointed administrator stripped him of all ties to the Teamsters after finding he embezzled money from the union and put three felons on its payroll.

Ligurotis, seventy-two, died in his Westchester home Wednesday after a lengthy battle with cancer, ending a lifetime that paralleled the often violent struggle of Chicago's labor movement in the latter half of the twentieth century.

A high school dropout who grew up in Cicero, Ligurotis was the son of a professional boxer. As a teen, he followed his father and uncle into the truck-driving business. He joined the Teamsters in 1947 and began working for Local 705 in 1966.

He carried the iron-fisted union dealings of his predecessor into the 1980s, fighting dwindling union membership, factory closings, and a tough, Reagan-era business climate along the way. At the peak of his career in 1990, he made hundreds of thousands of dollars a year, wielded tremendous political clout, and held the respect of many within the Teamsters International Brotherhood hierarchy.

But he was portrayed by friends and associates as a visionary who walked a tightrope between maintaining traditional labor values and being progressive enough to win benefits for members without constantly asking for employer concessions.

"He spent all his life trying to figure out how to do something good for members of his union. For a short while, he was able to do a lot of things. That and his own family were what really mattered to him," said Rory McGinty, a former legislative representative for Joint Council 25 and a personal friend to Ligurotis.

"He was the kind of guy that you won't see another like," McGinty said.

Ligurotis' influence declined rapidly with the reform efforts of the early

1990s. The professional losses were magnified in 1991 when his son, Daniel Ligurotis Jr., then thirty-six and a trustee in the union, struggled with drug use and threatened his father's life.

The elder Ligurotis testified that at the culmination of his efforts to get his son off drugs, the younger man pulled a gun and held it to his father's head. Ligurotis said he disarmed his son before firing a single, fatal shot in self-defense.

"It wasn't my son. It was cocaine," a saddened Ligurotis later told reporters.

Ligurotis is survived by his wife, Vasila "Betty" Ligurotis; a brother, Peter; and two grandsons, Daniel III and Michael.

WEDNESDAY, NOVEMBER 8, 2000

Raymond Schoessling, Ninety-Three; Ex-Teamsters Boss
By James Janega, *Tribune* Staff Reporter

It was said that City Hall observers often mistook the unassuming, quiet man visiting the late mayor Richard J. Daley's fifth-floor offices as a corporate executive, perhaps a physician or banker. Few who didn't know Raymond Schoessling guessed he was a beer-truck driver.

A member of the Keg Beer Drivers Union beginning in the 1920s, he was a high-ranking member of the Teamsters union in Chicago by the 1950s. He was named general secretary-treasurer of the Teamsters International Union in 1976, holding the union's number two post until retiring in 1984.

Schoessling, at age ninety-three, died Friday, November 3, in Little Falls, Minnesota, where he had been living in retirement.

He kept a low profile, though Teamster insiders said he could be a rugged infighter when it was called for.

And in a labor organization investigated almost continuously by federal authorities in the 1970s and 1980s, Schoessling maintained a reputation as a redeeming influence on the corruption-riddled union.

Born in Des Plaines, he grew up in Chicago near Damen and Chicago Avenues. After graduation from Lane Tech High School, he landed a 25¢-per-hour job as a railyard worker.

He joined the AFL Keg Beer Drivers Union in 1926, delivering nonalcoholic beer during Prohibition. His career as a labor leader began when he became president of Chicago's Brewery Workers Local 344 in 1938. Two years later, he merged the brewery local into Teamsters Local 744.

The president of Teamsters Joint Council 25 from 1951 until 1973, he became an international vice president with the Teamsters in 1967 and director of the Central Conference of Teamsters in 1973. Already the longtime president of Local 744 by 1975, he ascended to the highest levels of the international

Teamsters boss Raymond Schoessling could be a rugged infighter.

union when he became general secretary-treasurer in 1976.

He also served in the 1970s as chairman of the Metropolitan Pier and Exposition Authority and on the Chicago Police Board.

Though less controversial than other Teamsters leaders, Schoessling had a career that was hardly uneventful, though at its most exciting, he denied it had anything to do with labor matters.

When a bomb destroyed his son's car in the driveway of Schoessling's former house in Glenview, Teamster sources told the *Tribune* the blast, which caused no injuries, was intended as a warning to Schoessling.

Schoessling denied it.

He is survived by his son, James; four daughters, Joan Carlson, Janet Lyter, Peggy Hoffman, and Susan Frank; twenty grandchildren; and twenty-five great-grandchildren.

TUESDAY, NOVEMBER 14, 2000

Elcosie Gresham, Seventy-Four; CTA Bus Union President

By James Janega, *Tribune* Staff Reporter

Elcosie Gresham, seventy-four, a one-time Chicago Transit Authority (CTA) streetcar driver who became the head of Amalgamated Transit Union Local 241, the union representing bus drivers in Chicago, died Thursday, November 9, in his Southeast Side home of cancer.

"He truly loved working with the union, just serving and working hard for them," said his daughter Denise Gresham-Knox, adding that her father felt his role was to open doors for future workers. "He knew when they were not being treated fairly, and he went to work on it. He knew how to negotiate."

His career drove him through the officer ranks of Local 241, taking him to the local's top position in 1984, when as a first vice president he narrowly defeated John Weatherspoon in a runoff by campaigning for a pay increase.

The president of Local 241 for the next six years, Gresham consolidated support in the occasionally fractious local, cementing a reputation as a principled man who promoted unity.

Loyal to the membership of his union, he was both a formidable and genteel rival across the negotiation table, said James Daley, a partner with the law firm of Bell, Boyd & Lloyd who at one time represented the CTA in labor talks with Local 241.

"He represented his members very well, was a gentleman to negotiate with, and was a worthy adversary in the labor arena for any management lawyer," Daley said.

Gresham was born in Carbondale, though his family moved to Chicago when he was young. He attended Crane High School, where he was a standout

CTA bus union president Elcosie Gresham had a reputation for being a principled man who promoted unity.

track student until volunteering for the U.S. Navy during World War II. After being discharged in 1946, he earned his diploma by taking night classes at Englewood High School.

Chicago neighborhoods once were connected by streetcars and elevated trains, and in 1951 Gresham was hired as a conductor on electrically powered streetcars, later moving to buses as the CTA converted.

In the early 1960s, he worked out of the Seventy-seventh Street Station, making his way onto the Local 241

executive board, on which he served for nine years in the 1970s. A union officer since 1972, he was elected second vice president in 1975 and first vice president in 1978.

Outside of his Local 241 activities, Gresham served on numerous boards, including the Federation of Labor and Amalgamated Bank. His involvement in community organizations included stints with the Hyde Park Community Conference, the South Shore Commission, and the South Shore Garden Betterment Association. He served as a member and later chairman of the Consuella York Alternative High School local school council.

His family said he made a point of being fair and honest when it came to labor matters. Those who knew him recalled a man with a witty sense of humor and a love of golf and cooking.

In addition to his daughter, Gresham is survived by his wife, Marilyn; another daughter, Sandra Gresham-Rawls; and three granddaughters.

WEDNESDAY, NOVEMBER 29, 2000

John "Tim" Phelan, Fifty-Six; Engineers Union Chief
By James Janega, *Tribune* Staff Reporter

Operating Engineers leader John J. "Tim" Phelan was fiercely loyal, had a reputation for tenacity at the bargaining table, and was said to be able to tell when he could push for a sweeter contract.

The president and business manager of Operating Engineers Local 399, which represents building engineers throughout Illinois and Northern Indiana, Phelan, fifty-six, died Monday, November 27, in Rush-Presbyterian-St. Luke's Medical Center after suffering a heart attack in his South Loop home.

"John was a great labor leader, a steadfast supporter of Chicago, and a friend to all working men and women," Mayor Richard M. Daley said in a statement. "His death is a great loss to Chicago's organized labor movement and to the city as a whole. I am proud to have also been a personal friend of his."

Phelan's temperament and personal contacts in the business and political world made him one of the most successful labor negotiators in the city, said Brian E. Hickey, recording corresponding secretary of Local 399.

In Phelan's seven years as president, he brought Local 399 members broad increases in pay and benefits, their first statewide contract for Illinois secretary of state workers, and a jump in membership to 9,000 from 6,500, Hickey said.

"We've achieved some of the best contracts in the history of the local in the last five years," Hickey added, attributing it to Phelan's negotiating ability. "If things didn't go right, he'd come charging."

Tough even as a boy, Phelan had literally grown up around Local 399 negotiations, said Bernard Riordan, who traced a lifelong friendship with Phelan to a Southeast Side playground fight they had when they were thirteen.

"He was the first person you would want as a friend and the last person you would want as an enemy," said Bill Widmer, a friend and attorney for Local 399.

The son of a Chicago operating engineer who also negotiated pay and benefits matters for the union, Phelan often was dragged by his father to contract talks as a teen. That was partly to keep the spirited youth out of trouble, Riordan said, and partly for backup if things got dicey. "Those conversations could get pretty heated," Riordan recalled.

By the time Phelan graduated from the old Mendell Catholic High School in 1962, he went straight into Local 399, working for a time as a building engineer before becoming heavily involved in union matters by the late 1960s. The local's membership elected him secretary in 1972, business agent in 1982, and president in 1993.

As his reputation grew, so did his influence outside the local. When Service Employee International Union (SEIU) Local 1 janitors threatened a job action in the Loop in April, Phelan was among the first labor leaders SEIU officials sought for support, Hickey said.

Little of that maneuvering made the news, but those who knew Phelan said it was the kind of arena in which he thrived.

"He wasn't a guy who liked preaching," Hickey said. "He'd rather stand in the background, do his homework, and decide how the deal would get done."

It was an approach that impressed even management, said Building Owners and Managers Association executive vice president John Burns.

"He was very well respected by those that knew him, whether you were across the table from him or not," Burns said.

Also the president of the AFL-CIO's Chicago Port Council, Phelan was a general vice president in the International Union of Operating Engineers and served on the boards of directors of the Metropolitan Pier and Exposition Authority, the Chicago Convention and Tourism Bureau, and the Illinois Port Authority.

In 1997 he became the first labor leader appointed to Cook County's Economic Development Advisory Committee.

He is survived by his wife, Karen; daughters Nora Clifford and Nellie Wilson; sons Joseph and Ryan; three sisters, Kathleen Griffin, Norine Byrne, and Eileen O'Connor; and two grandsons.

XIII

Lawyers

The man who overturned Jack Ruby's murder conviction and gained parole for Nathan Leopold was Chicago attorney Elmer Gertz. Another Chicago lawyer pioneered advertising for clients. Still another was a former prizefighter who hobnobbed with political celebrities and journalists. Chicago's legal bar was open to all.

FRIDAY, APRIL 28, 2000

Elmer Gertz, Ninety-Three;
Civil Rights Champion, Defender of Underdog

By James Janega and Maurice Possley, *Tribune* Staff Reporters

Elmer Gertz, a civil rights attorney, overturned Jack Ruby's murder conviction.

Chicago civil rights attorney Elmer Gertz, a passionate litigator who gained parole for Nathan Leopold, overturned Jack Ruby's murder conviction, and rescued Henry Miller's racy *Tropic of Cancer* from government censorship, died Thursday. He was ninety-three.

The cause of death was pneumonia, his family said, a complication of open-heart surgery he underwent in January.

His legal career spanned seven decades and included a landmark case he argued before the U.S. Supreme Court that prevented judges from excluding individuals opposed to the death penalty from serving on juries.

But he also made his mark with a case he brought against the John Birch Society that redefined libel law. Gertz's lawsuit resulted in a decision by the U.S. Supreme Court that made it easier for some public figures to claim libel. The ruling became a staple of journalism school classes.

"He was a creative, dynamic, forceful advocate," said Harvey Grossman, legal director of the American Civil Liberties Union of Illinois. "Institutionally, we simply regarded him as truly the symbol of a civil libertarian, an icon."

A gregarious man with a literary bent, Gertz chaired the fractious Bill of Rights Committee during the 1970 revision of the Illinois Constitution. During his career, he published more than a dozen books and scores of articles on both the law and literature.

But beyond his legal and publishing accomplishments, Gertz provided a living link with a different era in American law, a single degree of separation for modern Chicagoans to crime fighter Eliot Ness, attorney Clarence Darrow, and author Carl Sandburg, whom he counted among his acquaintances.

"He was, in a sense, a link to a certain colorful past," said Chicago author Studs Terkel. "He was a solid lawyer who represented what was decent, hardworking. I suppose if you were looking for a lawyer, he wouldn't be a bad guy to have around at all."

"Longevity was a factor, but a minor factor. It was his scholarship—he did his homework," said former U.S. senator Paul Simon, who once praised Gertz for "standing like the Rock of Gibraltar on behalf of civil rights and civil liberties."

Senior U.S. District Judge Abraham Lincoln Marovitz called him courageous.

"Where angels feared to tread, he would go," said Marovitz, a friend to Gertz for decades. "He will be missed by guys like me who had a lot of respect for his independence and his honesty."

Gertz was born on the West Side into a family with six children. His mother died when he was nine, and Gertz and a brother were sent to live in a series of orphanages because their father could not afford to raise them.

Gertz later described the orphanages as a world of warm companionship and endless learning possibilities. He never harbored bitterness over the separation. Instead, he attributed his lifelong love of literature to the books he found.

By the time he graduated from Crane Tech High School and the University of Chicago, he said writing had become instinctive.

While at the university, Gertz took a course from then-renowned writing teacher Teddy Linn. On the top of his first paper, he said he found Linn's distinctive scrawl: "I'll be dog-goned. Let me take a look at you."

But Gertz, despite having always appreciated the praise of others, had two other collegiate experiences that tipped his life permanently on the course of legal study and civil justice.

He was arrested on suspicion of forging the endorsement on a savings bond given to him as a gift but was released without being charged.

Around the same time, he was outraged by the 1927 robbery-slaying case against Nicola Sacco and Bartolomeo Vanzetti, believing they were innocent. The two events convinced him to pursue a career in law.

Family influence landed Gertz a $15-a-week position at McInerny, Epstein &

Arvey, the politically connected law firm of Jacob M. Arvey, Democratic ward boss and later head of the Cook County Democratic Party. At Arvey's insistence, Gertz did nothing but practice law, despite the younger lawyer's frequent offers to help out during election times.

Gertz didn't reach widespread prominence until he took over representation of Nathan Leopold in the 1950s. In a case considered by many lawyers to be a lost cause, Gertz succeeded the late Clarence Darrow, who had saved Leopold and Richard Loeb from execution. Gertz won parole for Leopold in 1958 and full freedom in 1963, arguing the inmate had been fully rehabilitated.

It was his best and worst year: shortly after winning Leopold's parole, Gertz's wife, Ceretta, was seriously injured in a car accident. The woman with whom he had been in love since his first legal job died in May of that year after an accidental overdose of painkillers. He remarried the next year to the former Mamie Friedman, who died in 1997.

In 1964 he joined in defending Jack Ruby, who had been convicted of killing Lee Harvey Oswald, setting off conspiracy theories over the assassination of President John F. Kennedy. Gertz got Ruby's conviction overturned on grounds that too much publicity had surrounded his first trial. Ruby died in jail of natural causes as he awaited retrial.

Around that time, Gertz also fought several cases involving obscenity, including Henry Miller's fight against censorship when *Tropic of Cancer* was banned in Chicago on morality grounds.

In 1968 a landmark case was decided in Gertz's favor, the Supreme Court holding that excluding potential jurors because they had objections to capital punishment violated the Constitution. It was perhaps his most lasting contribution to the American legal system, said Northwestern University journalism professor David Protess.

"He was the forerunner of the modern movement to abolish capital punishment, both as a lawyer as well as an activist who had a lifelong dream of ending the death penalty," Protess said.

His writing paralleled his legal career. He authored a series of tomes that included *Censored: Books and Their Right to Live* in 1965, *Charter for a New Age: An Inside View of the Sixth Illinois Constitutional Convention* in 1980, and in 1990, the second edition of *To Life: The Story of a Chicago Lawyer*, his memoirs.

Survivors include a son, Theodore; a daughter, Margery Hechtman; two brothers, Robert and Dr. George; six grandchildren; and five great-grandchildren.

WEDNESDAY, JUNE 7, 2000

Lawrence Raphael, Fifty-Three; Adoption Lawyer
By James Janega, *Tribune* Staff Reporter

His newspaper advertisements—reading "Pregnant? Scared? Are you ready to be a single parent?" and referring those who were not ready to an 800 number—said much about the high emotions and intensely personal field of law in which Chicago adoption attorney Lawrence Raphael practiced.

A pioneer in the practice of advertising for adoptions, Raphael offered hope in the most desperate of situations for would-be adoptive parents who were not at the top of adoption agency selection lists, including interracial, handicapped, remarried, gay, or older couples. He could deliver when the established adoption system had failed.

But to the adoption establishment, including many fellow adoption attorneys, Raphael's approach was considered at best to be overly aggressive, and his practices led ultimately to his disbarment in 1997.

Raphael, fifty-three, an upbeat, active man who worked his way through law school night classes after the deaths of his parents and who raised two adoptive children of his own, died of cancer Monday, June 5, in a family member's Northbrook home.

Raphael was only one of many attorneys who had begun advising clients on how to advertise for potential birth mothers and also acted as go-betweens for pregnant women and prospective parents.

But Raphael became noteworthy for his consistent successes and high profile in the emerging, controversial subpractice of private adoption in Chicago. His many clients included some of the city's most prominent personalities, said his brother, Arthur.

"The difficult part for many of these people is that they can't go through private agencies," his brother said. "He helped a lot of people with getting children who had a lot of trouble getting children."

Born in Chicago and raised in the Galewood neighborhood, Raphael graduated from Steinmetz High School in 1964. He had an active interest in sports and, said his brother, built up an extensive collection of baseball and football cards in his youth, memorizing many of the statistics on the backs of them. "It was incredible," his brother said, "he should have been a sports broadcaster or commentator."

Graduating instead with a bachelor's degree in business from DePaul University in 1968, he went on to attend the Chicago-Kent School of Law and obtained his law license in 1973. He opened his own practice in the Loop, sharing office space with an uncle and a cousin who were also attorneys, and his early practice was filled with the typical routine of general-practice lawyers.

But in the mid-1970s, a friend came

to Raphael looking for legal assistance because local adoption agencies would not allow her to adopt a child. He suggested taking out an ad in the newspaper so pregnant women could contact her directly. The idea worked and was the beginning of Raphael's private-adoption career.

His practice became well known in the 1980s, enough so that his photograph appeared on the cover of *Time* magazine in 1989 as part of an article highlighting the changes in adoption practices nationwide. He continued practicing law in Chicago, while at the same time running a confectionery store with his wife at O'Hare International Airport.

But the marriage, and his legal career, dissolved in the late 1990s when he was disbarred amid allegations that he failed to place advertisements paid for by his clients, among other accusations. He was never charged with criminal wrongdoing.

He also is survived by two daughters, Alexis Esther and Sabrena; and a son, Paul.

FRIDAY, DECEMBER 1, 2000

Louis Biro, Eighty-One; Headed Law School's Trustees
By James Janega, *Tribune* Staff Reporter

Louis L. Biro, eighty-one, a prominent liquor licensing attorney who waited tables while attending John Marshall Law School and then led the school for three decades, insisting it keep the legal profession open to people from all walks of life, died Wednesday, November 29, in his Near North Side home. He had been battling cancer, the school said.

The president of John Marshall's board of trustees since 1968, Biro resigned from his duties last month because of his worsening health. The day before he died, the school named its law library in his honor.

"I have watched the law school grow, change, and evolve," he wrote to John Marshall's students and faculty when he retired, "and I take pride in being, in some small way, part of that growth, change, and evolution."

A well-dressed man with a sophisticated knowledge of the law, Biro had a very populist view of who should practice it.

"He was a passionate believer in the mission of John Marshall, particularly providing an opportunity for people to go to law school who might not otherwise have had the opportunity," said Jordan H. Peters, an alumnus and a member of the John Marshall board of trustees. "During all the things he did for the school, I think he always had an eye on that goal."

During Biro's tenure at John Marshall, he insisted the school maintain its night classes so people working full time could pursue a law degree. He meanwhile added new courses to the curriculum, developed a now nationally recognized legal writing program, and started masters programs in specialty areas of the law.

At the same time, Biro worked to increase classroom, library, and office space for the once-cramped law school, and he recently took part in a capital campaign that also provided for scholarships to help underwrite the cost of a legal education.

Raised in Chicago, he had started law school when World War II broke out. He enlisted in the army and fought in the Pacific, and on returning to Chicago, he got married and took a job waiting tables at Binyon's in the South Loop.

After a short time, he started taking night classes at John Marshall and graduated in 1948.

In the early 1950s, he served as secretary and the first technical adviser to the Illinois Liquor Control Commission, reorganizing its renewal system so license holders could renew state liquor licenses throughout the year. (Previously, all licenses were renewed on the same day.)

Later, his practice on North LaSalle Street represented clients that included the Wirtz Corp. Liquor Division, Paterno Imports, Old Style Beer distributors, Joseph E. Seagram & Sons, and others before federal, city, and state licensing bodies.

"He used to tell me that the only reason I knew more [about state liquor law] than he was because I had to read the current stuff," said John Stanton, chief legal counsel for the state Liquor Control Commission and a graduate of John Marshall who often consulted with Biro on historical matters.

"Given all those years, he forgot more than most people know," Stanton added.

Biro is survived by his wife, Irene; a son, Richard; two stepdaughters, Linda Eve Parker and Karin Lea Rosedale; a stepson, Dr. Ronald Rosedale; a sister, Pauline Wasserman; and five grandchildren.

SUNDAY, MARCH 18, 2001

Abraham Marovitz, Ninety-Five; Veteran Jurist Beloved for Feisty Spirit, Compassion

By Rick Kogan and Noah Isackson, *Tribune* Staff Reporters. *Tribune* Staff Reporters Joseph Sjostrom and Ron Grossman contributed to this report.

Abraham Lincoln Marovitz, a hustling West Side street kid and prizefighter, rose from grinding poverty to become Illinois' first Jewish state senator and a U.S. District Court judge who swore in Mayor Richard M. Daley and his father, Richard J.

Marovitz was a pal of countless celebrities and politicians, a lifelong habitué of Chicago's nightlife scene, and a raconteur who often peppered his speech with his mother's teachings, Talmudic

Abraham Marovitz (center), Illinois' first Jewish state senator and a longtime federal judge, swears in Mayor Richard J. Daley (left) in 1955.

aphorisms, and four-letter words.

"The whole town was his," said longtime friend and *Sun-Times* columnist Irv Kupcinet.

Marovitz, ninety-five, died Saturday, March 17, of kidney failure in his North Side home.

The judge's distinguished legal career began with his graduation from law school twenty months before he was old enough to take the state bar examination, which he passed on his first attempt. Marovitz became a Cook County judge in 1950 and a federal judge in 1963.

Since his seventieth birthday in 1975, Marovitz had been on senior status with the federal court. But until about four months ago, he still went to his chambers in Chicago's Dirksen Federal Building bright and early.

Some days, he would swear in a federal officeholder or a group of new citizens. Mostly, he answered and placed a constant round of telephone calls.

Some calls were from the rich and

famous, but most were from lesser lights, many phoning to ask a favor. Maybe the child of an old political buddy was down on his luck and needed a job. Or someone caught in a legal scrap was seeking a lawyer who could wait for his fee.

"When we were kids, my mother used to ask, 'Have you done your mitzvah, your good deed, for the day?'" Marovitz said in one interview. "Besides, if I hadn't been extended a helping hand, I'd have wound up a punch-drunk prizefighter instead of a federal judge."

Marovitz's kindness came mixed with a powerful charm, and few moments emphasized the combined effect like his ninetieth birthday party in 1995. The celebration drew about 1,700 well-wishers to the Chicago Hilton and Towers.

"To be in his presence was to be engulfed by his abundant warmth and generosity of spirit," said Richard Hirschhaut, Chicago regional director for the Anti-Defamation League. "So many lives have been enriched by Judge Abe."

"He was close with Frank Sinatra, Bob Hope, and Jimmy Durante, but he was just as comfortable sitting down and having a cup of coffee with a workman in the building or a police officer on the beat," said U.S. District Chief Judge Marvin Aspen.

A young, aggressive assistant state's attorney from 1927 to 1932, Marovitz prosecuted hoodlums of the type who later were among his clients.

A change of political administrations forced Marovitz out of the prosecutor's office and into private practice with his two brothers. Harold, the oldest, had worked for years to save money for law school; then he and Abraham paid the tuition for Sydney, who joined the firm in 1936.

Some of their clients were the minor-league mafiosi who ran the city's nightspots, which is how Abraham Marovitz started meeting the showbiz types whose photographs would later line his chambers. Unions and union officials, including some who would become nationally known, also became his clients.

After coming to the attention of Jacob Arvey, then alderman of the West Side's Twenty-Fourth Ward, he moved into the ward, became a Democratic precinct captain, and soon was tapped by Arvey as a candidate for the Illinois Senate, to which he was elected in 1938.

Marovitz went to Springfield as the state's first Jewish senator, a milestone a fellow legislator noted via an anti-Semitic remark. Marovitz refused to let it pass and confronted the man in a statehouse hallway.

"Judge Abe fought anti-Semitism when it still manifested itself in very overt and crude terms, and he would not stand for it," Hirschhaut said.

In the general assembly, Marovitz was no less tenacious, brokering deals between Democrats and Republicans but usually standing by his original plans.

"He was courageous," said George Dunne, former Cook County board president. "He had his opinions, and he stuck by them."

In 1943 Marovitz waived senatorial deferment to enlist as a private in the

Marine Corps. He was assigned to non-combat duties because, it has been variously reported, he was thirty-eight years old or he was color-blind. Mike Fritzel, who ran Fritzel's restaurant and the Chez Paree nightclub, mailed him care packages.

"Mike was sending me tomato soup cans," Marovitz said, "filled with excellent Scotch."

Marovitz, though, wanted to get into combat and started pulling political strings. But his commanding officer, who also itched to see action, resented Marovitz for his big-shot friends. He swore never to sign Marovitz's transfer orders while he himself was stuck behind a desk.

"So we got to Adlai Stevenson, who was then special assistant to the secretary of the navy, and he arranged for my commanding officer and me to get combat duty," Marovitz said. "Adlai said, 'Abe, your mother's never going to forgive me for this.'"

When an attempt was made to declare his state senate seat vacant because he was in the marines, another senator, Richard J. Daley, promised Marovitz in a letter that he would see it did not happen.

Marovitz's path and Daley's had first crossed in 1939, during Marovitz's first term in the senate, and were to intersect many times later.

In 1950 Daley, as Cook County clerk, swore in Marovitz as a judge of the Cook County Superior Court. That same year, Marovitz swore in Daley as the elected county clerk. Daley's previous tenure had been by appointment of the Cook County Board.

Marovitz later swore in Daley six times as mayor of Chicago. He also swore in Daley's son, Richard M., for all of his terms as mayor.

"Abraham Lincoln Marovitz was a fine jurist, a well-known personality, and a personal friend," the mayor said Saturday. "He lived a long, full life, and no one who knew him will ever forget him."

Marovitz was, in a way, responsible for Stevenson's becoming governor of Illinois and, later, a Democratic candidate for president. During the World Series in New York City in 1947, he took Stevenson to Gotham Hotel to introduce him to Arvey, another returning veteran who was then Cook County Democratic chairman and was to become a Democratic committeeman from Illinois.

"This man may be a terrific vote-getter," Marovitz said in presenting Stevenson to Arvey, who in less than a year made Stevenson the Democratic candidate for governor in the 1948 election.

After Marovitz became a judge and Daley became mayor, there were rumblings that Daley might have Marovitz run for governor.

Marovitz said, however, that he had promised his mother, Rachel, that he would not leave the bench. To her, being a judge, or a "law giver" as she called it, was the highest honor that could come to her son.

His mother died in 1957 at age eighty-three, and when Marovitz was sworn in as a U.S. district judge in 1963, he said his greatest regret was that she was not there for the ceremony.

Marovitz was born in Oshkosh, Wisconsin, where his Orthodox Jewish parents, both immigrants from Lithuania, were trying to make a living after having been married in Chicago.

Marovitz explained how he got the name Abraham Lincoln: "My mother, God rest her, was a poor immigrant who discovered that in this country, high-class Jews went to temple, not synagogue. She heard Lincoln was shot in the temple and saw pictures of him with a beard, so she figured she was naming a son for a great Jewish hero."

The family returned to Chicago in 1910. Marovitz, his parents, brothers Harold and Sydney, and sisters Jeanette and Bess lived in three rooms behind a penny-candy store his mother ran at Laflin and Fillmore Streets. Young Marovitz sold newspapers on the streets, delivered groceries and telegrams, and was a fair club prizefighter.

His nephew James Marovitz said Saturday that the judge constantly spoke of his mother and father.

"He had tremendous love and respect for them," James Marovitz said.

As a judge, Marovitz cherished citizenship ceremonies because they reminded him of his parents' journey to America. He liked to show the citizenship certificate of his father, Joseph, to the crowd.

Joseph Marovitz was a tailor with pride in his skills and a short fuse. Whenever a customer or a boss questioned his craftsmanship, he'd curse him and stomp off the job. Relatives said his last words to his son Abraham were, "Don't hurt the name."

As a kind of genetic birthright, that don't-take-no-guff personality passed on to the judge. Marovitz said his own instinct was always to put up his dukes first and weigh the odds afterward.

A few years ago, he was having a cup of coffee in a Loop restaurant when a gun-waving robber accosted the cashier. Marovitz wrestled the weapon away and held the robber until the police came.

"It was strictly automatic response," Marovitz said, "reflexes honed in a boxing ring, years ago."

As a teenager, Marovitz's boxing ability earned him a few bucks, with a little help from his dramatic talents. In the 1920s, Marovitz and a buddy would make the rounds of the stag nights and men's smokers, then staples of neighborhood social life. They'd box a few rounds, having previously decided who'd win and agreeing nobody would get hurt. The purses helped make ends meet for Marovitz, whose day job was as an office boy for a law firm.

One evening, they were on a card presided over by a professional referee who, guessing their scam, separated Marovitz and his buddy, matching each with a different opponent. Marovitz was knocked down six times in the first round.

The next morning, as Marovitz told it, he was summoned to the office of Alfred Austrian, head of the law firm. Unbeknownst to Marovitz, a couple of junior partners had been ringside.

"Do you intend to become a professional boxer, young man?" Austrian asked.

Hanging his head to hide a black eye and cut lip, Marovitz stammered, "No, sir."

"Good, because from what I hear you'd get yourself killed," Austrian said. "Now I want you to go over to Kent College of Law and register for night school."

Marovitz, who had just graduated from high school, tried to argue that he couldn't afford it. Waving off the objection, Austrian summoned his secretary and told her to issue a check for the tuition.

"In those days, you didn't need a college degree to go to law school," Marovitz explained. "So that's how I wound up the only sitting federal judge who never went to college."

After graduating at nineteen, he had to wait almost two years to be eligible to take the bar exam.

Some years ago, in acknowledging "the great number of true friends who gave me a push upward, a word of help along the way," Marovitz said: "It is my credo that there are no self-made men. The only thing a fellow can do by himself is fail."

"He was a politician with a small *p*; he truly loved people, and he wanted to help them," Aspen said.

Marovitz was a widely known collector of busts, pictures, and other memorabilia relating to Abraham Lincoln. He once said his one remaining ambition was "to leave behind an honored name."

His suite of offices was covered with photos of celebrities and politicians. Next to Abraham Lincoln, Jimmy Durante appeared the most.

Though considered by many law-enforcement officers to be a judge who was soft on defendants, Marovitz once said: "In my simple way of thinking, law means justice. If following a particular law would do an injustice, I try to find some way within the framework of the law to circumvent it and do what I think is right."

Marovitz lived on North Lake Shore Drive, where he maintained the strictly kosher household that his mother had kept in the years she lived with him.

He is survived by five nieces and nephews: Adrienne Garman, Sanford, James, Robert, and William, a former state senator.

"I don't think you can tell the story of twentieth-century Chicago without talking about Abe Marovitz; he had a remarkable life," Aspen said. "He was a beloved fixture, and he influenced a lot of people's lives."

FRIDAY, AUGUST 31, 2001

John G. Phillips, Eighty-Two;
Personal-Injury Attorney Helped Aspiring Lawyers
By William P. Bohlen, *Tribune* Staff Reporter

America was a dream for Felipe Giovanni Giangrosso when he was a young boy in Bagheria, Sicily. Years later, as John Phillips, he worked as a lawyer specializing in medical-malpractice and personal-injury litigation, a calling that helped him live out his American dream.

John G. Phillips, eighty-two, of Chicago, died of a heart attack Monday, August 27, at Loyola University Medical Center, Maywood.

Friends and family said he remained active, working at his law firm and writing legal articles, doting on his grandchildren, and enjoying his custom-built yacht, *Illusion*.

According to friends in the profession, Phillips, who opened his practice in 1949, was a tough adversary inside the courtroom but a gentleman and philanthropist outside of it.

"He was really a watchdog for the underdog," said son Stephen D. Phillips, who became his law partner.

"I would be on the other side of cases from John," said John Bell, a Chicago lawyer. "Here's one of the premier plaintiff's attorneys; you respected him, and yet John would talk with you."

Through the Justinian Society, a group for lawyers of Italian descent, Phillips established a scholarship fund for law students of Italian heritage and often personally assisted applicants.

"John would say, 'I can't decide which three of the fifteen should get the scholarships . . . I'm going to give them all a scholarship,'" said Enrico Mirabelli, former president of the society. "We knew that if you applied, John was going to help you out."

His family moved from Italy to Buffalo when he was nine. A year later, the family moved to Chicago, where Phillips lived the rest of his life, attending school at Illinois Wesleyan, DePaul, and Harvard.

"He wanted to Anglicize his name before law school, because he knew he would be at a disadvantage as a lawyer of Italian descent," his son said.

He took the bar exam while on weekend leave from the navy, which he joined during World War II, Stephen Phillips said. Phillips married Nancy Zelken in 1957, and they divorced in 1964.

Other survivors include another son, John C.; a sister, Theresa Proietto; and two grandchildren.

SATURDAY, NOVEMBER 2, 2002

Nicholas J. Bua, Seventy-Seven; Judge Issued Shakman Order
By Rudolph Bush, *Tribune* Staff Reporter

U.S. District Judge Nicholas J. Bua, seventy-seven, a son of Italian immigrants who rose to sit on the federal bench and issued the ruling that limited the system of politically motivated hiring in Cook County and Chicago government, died of leukemia Friday, November 1, in Gottlieb Memorial Hospital, Melrose Park.

Raised in Chicago during the Depression, Judge Bua knew he wanted to be a federal judge at age twelve, when

Federal judge Nicholas J. Bua signed off on the Shakman Order to curb politically motivated hiring practices in Chicago and Cook County government.

he attended his mother's naturalization ceremony.

"He went down to the federal courthouse and he saw the power of a judge to make a person a citizen of this country, and that inspired him," said his son-in-law, Scott Krinch.

Bua's success did not come easily. His father died when he was six, and he later had to leave high school to care for his ailing mother and younger brother and sister.

At the outbreak of World War II, Bua joined the army, serving as an infantryman and completing his high school equivalency degree.

When he returned, he enrolled in DePaul University on the GI Bill. Because the army would pay for only four years of school, he went year-round, completing college and law school in that time.

After practicing law for eleven years, Bua was elected village court judge in Melrose Park in 1963. Thirteen years later, he was elected to the Illinois Appellate Court, receiving an unprecedented total of 1,139,183 votes in Cook County.

In 1977 President Jimmy Carter nominated him to the federal bench, where Bua would develop a reputation as an efficient and fair jurist who also treated everyone in his courtroom with respect.

"Our court has never had a better colleague. Whenever anybody needed help with their calendar or in settling cases, Nick was the first one there," said U.S. District Chief Judge Charles P. Kocoras.

In the mid-1970s Bua was assigned a lawsuit filed by attorney Michael Shakman, who challenged the patronage hiring system of the Democratic Party machine in Chicago.

In 1979 Judge Bua entered a summary judgment that the city's patronage hiring practices violated civil and voting rights. In 1983 he entered a consent judgment that effectively blocked the city and county from hiring most employees for political reasons.

"He was a skillful judge, and he appreciated the great public importance of the case," Shakman said.

Bua, a longtime Melrose Park resident, retired from the bench in 1991 to pursue private practice. He joined the law firm of Burke, Weaver, & Prell and in 2000 became a counsel at the law firm of Holland & Knight.

A man with deep respect and love of the law, Bua often said, "I apply the law whether or not I agree with the law."

He is survived by his wife of fifty-eight years, Camille; a daughter, Lisa Bua-Krinch; and two grandchildren.

SECTION
XIV

Chicago's Jazz, Seen

Swing stylings crawled their way up the Mississippi and west from New York, dropped down in Chicago, and were changed here forever—for the better. Jazz music pounded in corner bars and flowered in sleek clubs. Fat hands pounded on piano keyboards, and fingers floated over trumpets and saxophones, together beating out an urban rhythm as stirring as anything else, anywhere else. The players who made their art in the Midwest had a sound all their own, a culture that invited description and demanded attention.

THURSDAY, MARCH 14, 1991

Jimmy McPartland, Eighty-Three; Chicago Jazz Pioneer

By Howard Reich, *Tribune* Arts Critic

Jimmy McPartland, a brilliant cornetist and a critical link to the birth of Chicago jazz in the Roaring Twenties, died early Wednesday, two days short of his eighty-fourth birthday.

McPartland, who made his final local appearance last October at the University of Chicago's Mandel Hall, died in Long Island, New York, of lung cancer.

"Jimmy wasn't aware of it, but I knew that the Mandel Hall concert would be his last back home in Chicago," said Marian McPartland, the distinguished jazz pianist who married McPartland in 1945. Though the McPartlands divorced in 1970, they remained close friends and neighbors on Long Island, recently remarrying.

"Last night, a few hours before he died, I played some of his old records for him," added Marian McPartland. "He smiled at hearing the old music."

Those late 1920s recordings by McPartland and colleagues helped define Chicago jazz at its inception.

"The Chicago style, which put equal emphasis on solo and ensemble playing, and which reflected the fast dance tempos of the day, was something Jimmy helped create," said Dick Wang, of the Chicago Jazz Archives at the University of Chicago.

"Jimmy also proved that there was a lot more to be done on cornet, and later on trumpet, than what Louis Armstrong had done in the 1920s. It was Jimmy who explored the middle and lower registers of the instrument as no one had done before."

Born James Dugald McPartland on March 15, 1907, McPartland grew up in Chicago. As a teen, he founded and led the fabled Austin High Gang, a pack of rough-and-tumble, self-taught players smitten by the music of black New Orleans musicians who had migrated to Chicago.

"Most of us actually had started playing violin or piano when we were little kids," recalled McPartland during an interview with the *Tribune* late last year.

"But we got excited about [black] jazz music because it was swinging, the rhythm was great, and the harmonies these guys were improvising were incredible. King Oliver, Bix [Beiderbecke], Louis Armstrong—they inspired us."

McPartland and his young cohorts learned the new sound the hard way: "We took the music right off the records by the New Orleans Rhythm Kings, Bix and the Wolverines," McPartland recalled. "We'd listen to two bars, repeat it on our instruments, then move on to the next two bars."

That drill produced an astonishing group of young virtuosos, including McPartland, guitarist Dick McPartland (the cornetist's brother), bassist Jim Lanigan, saxophonist Bud Freeman, reed player Frank Teschemacher, pianist Dave North, and drummer Dave Tough (the latter two from other high schools). Now, only Freeman survives among the Austin High players, and in recent months he has been ailing.

"After about six months, word got around that you ought to go see these Austin High guys," McPartland recalled. "And if you didn't like us, it was a good idea not to say anything, because I was an amateur boxer, and if anyone told me we stunk, I'd punch them right in the puss."

Even amid this high-powered group, McPartland's contributions stood out, for he, more than anyone in jazz, carried forth the melting lyric tone of Beiderbecke's cornet.

"You could hear Bix in Jimmy's tone," said Chicago pianist Art Hodes, who, at eighty-five, holds vivid memories of McPartland in the 1920s. "You could hear Bix in the way they both would bend a note, and in the sweetness and softness of their sound."

Beiderbecke paid McPartland the ultimate compliment when he handpicked McPartland as his successor in the Wolverines; McPartland was seventeen.

"When the Wolverines were auditioning me, they said, 'Which of our numbers do you know?'" recalled McPartland. "I said, 'Anything you've recorded; I know them all in the right key.'

"After they hired me, I roomed with Bix, and he taught me all the rest of the band's repertoire."

Thereafter, McPartland came to epitomize the sound and style of vintage Chicago jazz. After fighting in the Battle of the Bulge in World War II, McPartland met the British pianist Marian Turner in Belgium, and they were married at the end of the war.

During his October concert in Mandel Hall, McPartland sang but did not play his instrument. "I hate practicing," he quipped. The event marked the McPartlands' donation of their memorabilia to the Chicago Jazz Archives.

Looking back on the rambunctious early days of the Austin High Gang, McPartland said, "I guess it worked out fine. The music kept us out of jail."

McPartland is survived by his wife, grandson, granddaughter, and twin great-grandsons.

SUNDAY, MARCH 17, 1991

Lawrence "Bud" Freeman, Eighty-Four; Chicago-Style Jazz Legend
By R. Bruce Dold and Jerry Crimmins, *Tribune* Staff Reporters

Lawrence "Bud" Freeman, eighty-four, the last living member of the fabled band the Austin High Gang, and one of the earliest jazz musicians to play tenor saxophone, died of cancer Friday in the Warren Barr Pavilion nursing home.

Freeman was a leader of the "Chicago style" of jazz that embodied the rough-and-tumble spirit of the music and the city in the 1920s.

He was a student at Austin High School on the West Side when he met the group of young musicians, including Jimmy and Dick McPartland, who would become renowned as the Austin High Gang.

Inspired by the music of Louis Armstrong and Joseph "King" Oliver, they studied traditional jazz styles and, through several different bands, popularized the tenor saxophone in jazz and created one of the links between traditional jazz and the "swing" jazz that was to come.

"He was a pioneer," said author Studs Terkel. "Bud was a precursor of Lester Young in a way, with that cool, economic style. With Bud, it was cool and crisp.

"He was very gentle; he was very elegant in his manner of walking and talking. And there was a generosity of spirit for others."

Freeman had many friends among authors and actors. John O'Hara wrote a short story called "The Flatted Saxophone" in which the protagonist says, "If I want to hear a good saxophone, I'll find out where Bud Freeman is playing."

When asked to assess his contributions to music, Freeman often demurred.

"There are a lot of egomaniacs, big names who thought they were the whole show," he said in an interview with the *Tribune* last April. "What's the difference as long as you play? I wasn't trying to do anything other than play well."

Freeman was widely known in jazz circles for his dapper manner and dress, and he was admired for his crediting black musicians for the development of jazz.

"I used to go to the black churches to hear the singing and to hear the most wonderful beat in music, the most inspired jazz I've ever heard. That is where jazz, I think, really came from— from the black churches and from black tap dancing," he wrote in his 1989 book, *Crazeology: The Autobiography of a Chicago Jazzman.*

In 1928 he moved to New York and worked for some of the most famous orchestra leaders of the time, including Benny Goodman, Tommy Dorsey, and Paul Whiteman.

Later in his career, he led his own small groups and took his bands to Brazil, Chile, and Peru.

During World War II Freeman served in the army in the Aleutians, where one of his buddies was the famous author, Sgt. Dashiell Hammett.

Freeman later lived for a while in London until he was invited to appear at the Chicago Jazz Festival in 1980.

One night after that festival, he went to a party and met Lenore Gibbs, the daughter of one of the Austin High Gang, Dick McPartland. She was divorced, and so was Freeman. "He said, 'Can I take you out to dinner?'" she recalled Friday.

Pretty soon, "He canceled his ticket back and decided to stay here in Chicago," Gibbs said. "We were best of friends. I would call him every night to see how his day was and see how he was . . . He was a gentle person and a gentle man."

Because he stayed in Chicago,

Freeman became a fixture in Chicago jazz clubs again until poor health forced him to retire from playing in 1989.

His last concert was in the Field Museum in the fall of 1989.

Cornetist Jimmy McPartland died Wednesday in Long Island, New York. The other members of the "gang" were Dick McPartland on guitar; bassist Jim Lanigan; reed player Frank Teschemacher; pianist Dave North; and drummer Dave Tough.

Art Hodes, a Chicago pianist who played with Freeman when "we were both kids," said of Freeman: "He left his mark and played his tenor saxophone in a different way from anyone I know. What came out of the saxophone, his tone, his ideas, were his own."

"I've had a rich life, a good life," Freeman said last year. "I played around the world for sixty-five years, virtually every place that had an interest in American music. . . . And I had a lot of fun."

Freeman is survived by a sister, Florence Charles.

TUESDAY, MARCH 9, 1993

Art Hodes, Eighty-Eight; Legendary Jazz Pianist
By Howard Reich, *Tribune* Arts Critic

Art Hodes—a legendary jazz-blues pianist who was born in Russia, made a name in 1920s Chicago, and rubbed elbows with Louis Armstrong, Gene Krupa, Benny Goodman, Bix Beiderbecke, and Bud Freeman—died Thursday morning at Ingalls Memorial Hospital in Harvey. He was eighty-eight.

"Art Hodes was a beautiful man and the best blues piano player I ever heard," said Chicago jazz drummer Barrett Deems, who knew Hodes since the 1940s.

"It's hard to say exactly what made him so great at the piano, except that you really felt the music and the blues he was trying to express."

Born in Nikoliev, Russia, Hodes never knew his exact birth date, for family records did not survive the family's move to New York, when Hodes was six months old. He later settled on November 14, 1904, as his birthday. By the time he was ten, the family had moved to Chicago's West Roosevelt Road.

"Coming to Chicago was a lucky break for me," Hodes recently recalled in a *Tribune* interview. "See, the neighborhood we lived in was right between the blacks and the whites. So I could go to a theater and hear the greatest jazz and blues musicians alive. . . .

"It was an era. New Orleans players were coming up the river; everyone was here. Bix, Louis, [drummer] Baby Dodds, [reed player] Jimmie Noone—Chicago was the place."

For tenement kids like Hodes, there also was Jane Addams' Hull House, which served as an oasis amid the rough-and-tumble streets of the West Side. Music lessons there were cheap and opportunities plentiful, with Hodes jamming alongside other gifted youngsters such as clarinetist Benny Goodman.

By the time Hodes reached Crane High School, "I started ditching classes so I could sneak into theaters like the State and Lake, where I could get real close to this incredible music," he said in the *Tribune* interview.

Of all the musicians Hodes heard, none left a deeper impression than Armstrong.

"I hung out with Louis every day for years on the the South Side," said Hodes, "and he opened all the doors for me. When he found out how I felt about the blues, he started showing me where to go to hear the real blues.

"He taught me a lot," Hodes said, "like his incredible joy in playing and his humor and, I hope, his humility, because he carried himself very easily. He didn't act like he was a king or anything. His attitude was: 'Hey, you're one of the guys, come on in and partake.'"

Hodes did, club hopping with Armstrong, chatting with King Oliver, jamming with Beiderbecke. "It was almost like being born to the purple," Hodes later said.

After Armstrong, the foremost influence on Hodes was blues singer Bessie Smith.

"There were many other singers at the time, and they could sing the words," Hodes recalled. "They could go over the song, but with much less meaning. . . . When Bessie came to town, the lesser lights were in the audience."

From these musical influences, Hodes formed a pianistic style of his own, merging the intensely lyric approach of 1920s blues with the free-wheeling improvisation of jazz.

Like most any jazz musician, though, Hodes saw hard times too. By the late 1930s, he had moved with his wife to New York; but when bebop became the new sound, some listeners dismissed Hodes.

"The critics started rapping us," Hodes later said. "These writers decided that our music should go out with high-button shoes, and that included Louis Armstrong. . . .

"That was their right and their privilege, but at the time it was very painful. It hurt me, but I'm a survivor."

Indeed, Hodes simply fought that much harder, establishing his own record label, Jazz Record; editing a magazine of the same name; and taking to the airwaves as jazz deejay, all in 1940s New York.

By 1950 he had moved back home to Chicago, performing here and around the world until a year and a half ago, when multiple strokes left him unable to play.

"Chicago in the 1920s was an age that was here and gone," Hodes said in 1992. "I'm lucky I heard it."

Hodes is survived by his second wife, Jan; five children, Janet Gordley, Karen Sullivan, Margaret Figueroa, Robert W., and Daniel R. Hodes; twelve grandchildren; and two great-grandchildren.

FRIDAY, MARCH 5, 1993

Art Hodes, Eighty-Eight;
Music Cannot Mourn Legacy Left by Hodes
By Howard Reich, *Tribune* Arts Critic

With horns blowing, rhythms swinging, and hands clapping, Chicago bid farewell to one of its most enduring jazz artists.

Calvary United Protestant Church in Park Forest was filled to overflowing with performers, fans, and friends paying tribute to pianist Art Hodes, the eighty-eight-year-old jazz-blues master who died Thursday in Ingalls Memorial Hospital.

"It's a little hard to talk on an occasion like this, but I've got to say that Art really was an inspiration to so many musicians," said Chicago trombonist Jim Beebe, one of many who stood up to reminisce before a rapt audience.

"When I was a kid," continued Beebe, "one of the first records I ever heard was a Blue Note seventy-eight featuring the Art Hodes Band. I still remember every note of that recording.

"Then I remember the first time I went to this restaurant on the North Side to hear Art play. I think that was the night I realized I was going to learn to play that kind of music."

Indeed, Beebe and uncounted others studied the elements of early Chicago jazz and blues by listening to Hodes, who had come up during the first great heyday of the music in Chicago—the 1920s. Because Hodes had befriended the likes of Louis Armstrong, Bix Beiderbecke, and King Oliver, among others, he had come to epitomize a glorious musical era now preserved mostly in history books, vintage recordings, and repertory bands.

"I first met Art Hodes in 1950 in my old hometown of Oshkosh [Wisconsin]," Chicago trumpeter Bobby Lewis told the crowd, "and little did I know that when I settled in Chicago in 1961 that I'd be playing with him for thirty-two years after that.

"I can only tell you that he was always a marvel, not only to play with but to listen to. And believe me when I say that never, in those thirty-two years, never did I hear him play a wrong note."

Others spoke of the "radiance" of Hodes' tone and the "joy" in his playing, no doubt referring to the fervently melodic nature of his music as well as its rhythmic buoyancy. Though any number of today's piano-pounders claim to play early jazz and blues styles, Hodes represented the real thing. The complex, contrapuntal nature of his playing and the exquisite ornamentation of his lines were genuine throwbacks to an earlier era.

As if to underscore the point, Monday's services were punctuated by ebullient performances from a jazz band playing in the 1920s tradition. Most of the players—including Beebe, Lewis, and Franz Jackson—had worked with Hodes for decades.

"Black and Blue," "My Blue Heaven," "When the Saints Go Marching In"— each tune unfolded exuberantly, as if this event were more a celebration of Hodes' life than a mourning over his death.

"I'll tell you one thing about Art Hodes," said Jackson, himself an octogenarian. "Back then, there was one musicians union for blacks and one for whites.

"But Art Hodes wouldn't have any of that. He said he knew all about persecution, and he went ahead and played with whoever he wanted, white or black."

Rev. Lorenz DeVries added, "Art always considered his move to Chicago [from New York when he was ten] a lucky break."

In many ways, it was a lucky break for Chicago, too.

THURSDAY, MAY 21, 1998

Dorothy Donegan, Seventy-Six; Chicago Jazz Pianist
By Howard Reich, *Tribune* Arts Critic

Dorothy Donegan, the flamboyant and often-brilliant jazz pianist indelibly linked with the South Side of Chicago, died Tuesday night in her Los Angeles home. She was seventy-six.

She had been fighting colon cancer and had hoped to rejuvenate her ties to her hometown.

"I talked to Dorothy just three weeks ago, when she was in Tijuana [Mexico] to get some holistic treatment, and she was determined to be a part of the Chicago Jazz Museum," said Geraldine de Haas, a Chicago jazz singer who is heading a plan to build the institution.

"Dorothy said to me, 'You save some space in that museum for me, because I want to teach there.' She wanted to be a mentor to kids who came from the same place she did."

Though trained as a classical pianist, Donegan realized early on that the world's symphony halls were not likely to embrace a black woman as a concert soloist.

"I started taking lessons on the South Side of Chicago when I was eight, and it was classical all the way," she said in a 1993 *Tribune* interview. "But there were [racial and gender] barriers back then, you know? I mean, I wasn't going to make any money at classical, and you have to eat."

To her good fortune, she was enrolled at DuSable High School, which produced jazz stars such as Nat "King" Cole and Johnny Griffin. Donegan quickly blossomed as a jazz improviser.

"I was studying piano at the same time, and she made me look like I was standing still," remembered Chicago author Dempsey Travis, who graduated from DuSable in 1939, the same year as Donegan. "That girl was a magic piano player. She had incredible technique."

Donegan studied music at the

Chicago Conservatory, the Chicago Musical College, and the University of Southern California. For all her talent and training, though, Donegan found the going rough. The lean times persuaded her to transform herself once again, this time from jazz virtuoso to stage entertainer.

"It was at the Latin Quarter that I learned larceny—in other words, my show business," she said in the *Tribune* interview. "You've got to learn tricks, like the gestures, how to walk out on stage, how to play to the audiences. . . ."

The stage shtick made Donegan a headliner.

Donegan appeared on film in *Sensations of 1945* and, the same year, she performed in the production *Star Time* on Broadway.

Donegan was married and divorced three times and had two children.

THURSDAY, JULY 2, 1998

Lucy Reed, Seventy-Seven; Sang Jazz in Top Chicago Clubs
By Howard Reich, *Tribune* Arts Critic

Lucy Reed, one of Chicago's most admired jazz singers and a former vocalist with Woody Herman's sextet and Charlie Ventura's big band, died Wednesday in her North Side home, at age seventy-seven.

Though Reed performed infrequently in recent years, in her prime she played some of the most prestigious clubs and showrooms in the country, including Mister Kelly's in Chicago and the Village Vanguard in New York.

Her first recording, *The Singing Reed* (on Fantasy, 1957), was notable not only for her interpretive savvy but for the work of a young pianist named Bill Evans, who would go on to become one of the most influential jazz keyboardists of the postwar years.

Yet Reed, who was born in Marshfield, Wisconsin, launched her professional career without much forethought and out of tragic circumstances.

"I started out singing on KSTP radio in St. Paul, where I was in a group of four girls, and we got paid $5 a week," Reed told the *Tribune* in 1992. "But I never really thought about singing professionally until my husband [drummer Joey DeRidder] was killed in World War II, and that's when I decided I had to decide to do something or other with my life."

In just a few years, Reed had risen to the top of Chicago's jazz-cabaret scene, her sensitive vocals and obvious musicianship placing her in the company of such estimable singers as Audrey Morris and Lurlean Hunter.

"I first met Lucy when she was at the Lei Aloha Club, performing with Dick Marx and Johnny Frigo, and they were the hottest thing in town at the time," recalled singer Frank D'Rone, referring to a fabled early 1950s engagement at the North Side club.

"I was working in Kankakee at the time and I heard about it out there, and everything people were saying about that act was true."

Sophisticated songs performed with subtlety and refinement were Reed's stock-in-trade. When Fantasy decided to record her in the mid-1950s, she insisted on using Evans on some tracks, though he was barely known to general audiences.

The critical acclaim of *The Singing Reed* inspired a follow-up on Fantasy, *This Is Lucy Reed*, which also featured Evans.

Like many women in jazz, Reed ultimately decided to devote most of her energies to her growing family rather than to her career. After her marriage to Serge Seymour, in 1957, she often turned down opportunities that might have increased her fame.

Nevertheless, "I can't say I've been frustrated," she said in the *Tribune*

interview. "I've got the records now, and whenever I want to sing I seem to make it happen.

"I've always wanted to be in Chicago. In fact, I was offered a chance to work with Duke Ellington, but I was never tuned into becoming a star.

"Sure, I wonder what might have happened if I had done this or that, but life really has been happy for me, because I've been around to see my kids have kids, and that meant a lot."

On Tuesday, the day before she died, Chicago jazz singers such as Morris, D'Rone, and Buddy Charles visited Reed in her home and performed for her.

"We had a music party, and it was a wonderful last day," said her son, Ted Seymour.

Survivors include three sons: Jeff DeRidder, Steve Seymour, and Ted Seymour; seven grandchildren; and four great-grandchildren.

WEDNESDAY, SEPTEMBER 16, 1998

Barrett Deems, Eighty-Five; Chicago Jazz Fixture
By Howard Reich, *Tribune* Arts Critic

Barrett Deems, eighty-five, a virtuoso drummer and one of the most colorful characters in Chicago jazz, died Tuesday morning in Columbia Grant Hospital in Chicago of pneumonia.

Deems, known throughout jazz as "the world's fastest drummer," made fans through the brilliance of his technique, the unmistakable joy of his playing, and his ebullient personality.

Though Deems circled the globe many times with Louis Armstrong and other stars, the Springfield-born drummer was based in Chicago during most of his career.

"You just never thought that he would ever die—he was like the Buckingham Fountain, just a fixture here," said Paul Wertico, a noted Chicago drummer who counted Deems

Barrett Deems was known in the jazz world as "the world's fastest drummer."

as a mentor. "His playing had irony and humor—it was a direct extension of who he was."

A performance by Deems typically was part music, part comedy. In introducing an eightieth birthday performance at Andy's, on East Hubbard Street, announcer Dick Buckley remarked, "Boy, you're sure getting up there in years, Barrett. You're pushing the outside of the envelope."

To which Deems responded, "Yeah, but I've still got plenty of glue left."

Indeed, despite various health problems, Deems refused to cut down his performance schedule, playing several nights a week in Chicago clubs and touring periodically.

His abilities never flagged. During his last recording session, in March at Chicago's Delmark Records, Deems set vigorous tempos and unleashed hard-driving and complex solos, often tossing a drumstick in the air between downbeats, catching it in the nick of time.

"The first thing that goes are the feet and hands, which is why most drummers don't last as long as I have," he said.

"You want to know why I've been able to keep going? It's no big secret: I never took drugs or got into booze. The stuff didn't interest me."

Music did, from the time he was five

years old and began pounding on a small bucket with a pair of sticks. Deems, who never considered himself a very good reader of music, realized as a teenager that the freewheeling world of jazz better suited his temperament. He began playing for bandleader Paul Ash at age fifteen, and in Chicago, he came under the spell of such drummers as Gene Krupa, Dave Tough, and Baby Dodds.

"There was a real Chicago style of drumming then—tough sound, everything on the snare drums," said Deems. "Not like today, where everyone concentrates on the cymbals."

Deems emulated the hard-hitting style but also refined it with the sheer speed, dexterity, and crisp attacks that were his signature. He quickly found himself keeping time for the likes of Armstrong, Joe Venuti, Jimmy Dorsey, Buck Clayton, Roy Eldridge, Benny Goodman, Muggsy Spanier, Jack Teagarden, Art Hodes, Benny Carter, and other jazz royalty.

Touring with Armstrong in the 1950s and backing him in the film *High Society* (1956) extended Deems' fame. "Barrett Deems," Armstrong famously said, "makes coffee nervous."

Deems is survived by his wife, Jane Johnson; a daughter from an earlier marriage, Mary Jane Serene; and two grandchildren.

WEDNESDAY, MARCH 31, 1999

Joe Williams, Eighty; Legendary South Side Jazz Singer

By Howard Reich, *Tribune* Arts Critic

During the first half of the century, the South Side of Chicago produced such defining jazz singers as Nat "King" Cole, Johnny Hartman, and Dinah Washington.

On Monday afternoon, the last of them, Joe Williams, died in Las Vegas at age eighty.

Williams' death silences a generation of major South Side vocalists and removes from the world stage a charismatic ambassador of Chicago jazz. In clubs and on television, where he played Grandpa Al on *The Cosby Show* in the 1980s, Williams spoke poetically about his youth in Chicago.

He was admitted last week to Sunrise Hospital in Las Vegas, where he lived, to be treated for emphysema. On Monday, he left the hospital (without checking out), walking several miles before collapsing a few blocks from his home, the Associated Press reported.

Williams last sang publicly two weeks ago in a Seattle jazz club, "and he was sounding as good as always," manager John Levy said.

Indeed, Williams was unusual among jazz singers in that his instrument never lost its range, plushness, or dexterity. He proved the point last summer at the Ravinia Festival in Highland Park.

Perhaps more important than the crushed-velvet quality of his bass-baritone was the way he used it, effectively summing up—as well as modernizing—the sound of traditional South Side jazz and blues.

Asked in a 1991 *Tribune* interview to name his source of musical inspiration, Williams said simply, "Chicago."

Williams was born Joseph Goreed in Cordele, Georgia, but moved north with his family when he was four. "When I was a kid here [in the 1920s], Chicago already was one of the most exciting places in the world, especially where music was concerned," he said. "I remember that as a kid I'd go to the Vendome Theater to hear people like Louis Armstrong, Earl Hines, Jimmie Noone. Then I'd hear the broadcasts on the radio. Art Tatum from the Blackhawk, Roy Eldridge from the Three Deuces, sets from the Aragon."

"He'd always be singing, even on the baseball diamond," remembered Chicago saxophonist Eddie Johnson, who attended Englewood High School with Williams. "When he started playing in South Side ballrooms with Johnny Lang's band in the late 1930s, he already was very meticulous about his sound and his enunciation."

But Williams faced a long struggle in attaining recognition. He toiled as a bathroom porter in South Side clubs and as a backstage doorman at the Regal Theater, singing low-paying gigs at roller-skating rinks. He couldn't find work because "my skin was too shady," or black, he said in Dempsey J. Travis'

An Autobiography of Black Jazz.

"Nat 'King' Cole, who was blacker than I, struck it big nationally through his recordings before most people outside the black community knew he was black," added Williams, who credited Cole for opening doors.

Williams' growing reputation around Chicago eventually earned him touring dates with Coleman Hawkins, Lionel Hampton, and Andy Kirk, as well as engagements with Red Saunders' band at Club DeLisa.

But it wasn't until he teamed with a down-on-his-luck Count Basie—first in 1950 at Chicago's Brass Rail, then again in 1954—that both artists attained new acclaim. Williams' version of "Every Day I Have the Blues," with Basie, made him a star in 1955.

"Joe brought a new modernism to the blues," said Chicago singer Geraldine de Haas, referring to his urbane style.

"He could sing blues, ballads, just about everything with Basie, and he was being backed by great new arrangements from Frank Foster and Ernie Wilkins," said Jeff Lindberg, music director of the Jazz Members Big Band, which toured with Williams for the past decade.

Though Williams performed widely on the strength of such recordings as "Goin' to Chicago" and "Smack Dab in the Middle," he maintained close ties to Chicago. He was to appear with the Jazz Members at the Harold Washington Library Center on May 16 and at the Chicago Jazz Festival in Grant Park in September.

In addition to his wife, Jillean, Williams is survived by a son, Joe, and a daughter, Anne.

TUESDAY, JANUARY 4, 2000

Wilbur Campbell, Seventy-Three; Jazz Drummer
By Howard Reich, *Tribune* Arts Critic

In the often insular world of jazz, some musicians acquire exalted status among colleagues but remain virtually unknown to the general public.

Chicago jazz drummer Wilbur Campbell, seventy-three, who died Thursday, December 30, at his South Side home of complications from liver disease, belonged to this select category of jazz legends.

"He was one of the great drummers of the world, even though a lot of people don't know it," said drummer Jack DeJohnette, a revered player who considered Campbell a mentor. "When I first started getting into jazz, in Chicago, Wilbur used to take me by his house, and we'd play piano together.

"When he'd play drums, he would fill up his solos like somebody that was packing a suitcase with as much as he could."

Known among friends and colleagues as "the Chief," for his preeminence among Chicago drummers, Campbell was a product of a celebrated training ground for jazz musicians: DuSable High School on the South Side of Chicago. There, Campbell studied with Capt. Walter Dyett, who nurtured such rising jazz stars as Dorothy Donegan, Gene Ammons, Von Freeman, and Eddie Harris.

"Wilbur came up with all these incredible musicians, and I think he benefited greatly from that," said Chicago pianist Stu Katz. "He wasn't just a drummer; he was an accomplished musician who understood song construction and the theory behind the music he was playing."

Because Campbell played vibes and piano, he comprehended the subtle harmonic underpinnings of the music he was playing, as is apparent even on such early recordings as "Blue Stroll" (on the Delmark label), with Ira Sullivan and Johnny Griffin, and "Nicky's Tune" (Delmark), also with Sullivan.

Yet Campbell did much more than keep time. Steeped in the bebop vocabulary of drummers such as Kenny Clarke and Art Blakey, he thrived on playing off the beat. The "bombs," or syncopated eruptions of sound, that were essential to bebop percussion played an important role in Campbell's accompaniments. But Campbell's blasts never interfered with the work of a band's frontline soloist.

"He may have been called 'the Chief,' but he never played like he was trying to be in charge," said Chicago drummer Robert Shy. "He was always listening to what someone else was doing."

DeJohnette considered Campbell's work "good, solid, soulful swinging that could be precise and sloppy at the same time," while Chicago bassist Larry Gray placed him in a league with some of the leading drum innovators of the post–World War II era.

Campbell rarely traveled, however, and his day job as a substance-abuse-prevention counselor may have prevented him from developing a bigger career.

Nevertheless, "He was the hometown drummer who every cat wanted to play with," said Chicago drummer Paul Wertico.

Campbell is survived by his wife, Valarie; five daughters, Deborah, Bessie, Osceola, Paris, and Coco; three sons, Olafemi, Wilbur Jr., and Cosala; a stepson, Martin; eighteen grandchildren; and six great-grandchildren.

FRIDAY, JUNE 9, 2000

John Steiner, Ninety-One; Chicago Jazz Expert
By Howard Reich, *Tribune* Arts Critic

John Steiner, ninety-one, widely regarded as the world's foremost authority on early Chicago jazz, died Saturday, June 3, in Milwaukee.

Steiner, who was smitten with the music during its first great blossoming in Chicago in the 1920s, built a unique personal collection of about thirty-five thousand recordings, plus sheet music, newspaper articles, and related ephemera. The collection will be housed in the Chicago Jazz Archive of the University of Chicago Library, which had received several boxes of Steiner's papers in 1998.

"It's one of the top collections in the country, and it would be impossible for anyone to put it together today," said Deborah L. Gillaspie, curator of the Chicago Jazz Archive. "It exists only because John Steiner knew to collect these materials when they were available."

Born in Milwaukee and trained as a chemist at the University of Wisconsin in Madison, Steiner nourished his emerging passion for jazz by spending weekends in the nightspots of Chicago's South Side. Early on he came to know key figures such as pianist Earl Hines and drummer Baby Dodds, and he befriended members of the fabled Austin High Gang (including cornetist Jimmy McPartland and saxophonist Bud Freeman).

"He would take the train down from Milwaukee or Madison and make it a weekend in Chicago, absorb as much of the club scene as he could, then sleep in the train station," recalled Richard Wang, professor of music at the University of Illinois at Chicago.

"It was through his contacts with so many musicians that he was able to begin to build his collection, and he was doing it in the 1930s, when most people weren't interested in this music and its history in Chicago," added Wang.

"Without his research and appetite for Chicago music, we would be bereft of information upon which future histories of this music will be based. He was the seminal figure in documenting the history of Chicago jazz."

Though Steiner worked full time as a research chemist and, in the 1960s and 1970s, taught at UIC, he used his off-hours to document music in Chicago. In 1946 he dragged a portable recording machine to the Civic Opera House, climbed onto the catwalk above the stage, dangled a microphone below, and captured the Duke Ellington Orchestra on recordings that would not have existed without such efforts.

As a self-styled oral historian, he taped hundreds of hours of interviews with notable musicians, but the exact contents of this cache will not be known for years, because University of Chicago archivists will have to catalog two truckloads of material. "It's a treasure trove," said curator Gillaspie, "but it's also a preservation nightmare."

In the 1940s, Steiner promoted concerts featuring McPartland and Freeman, among others, and with Hugh Davis started S&D Records to issue Chicago jazz recordings. By leasing and, in 1949, purchasing the catalog of the old Paramount record label, Steiner was able to reissue historic recordings of Jelly Roll Morton, King Oliver, Bessie Smith, Ma Rainey, and Blind Lemon Jefferson, among others.

Steiner, a founding member of the nonprofit Jazz Institute of Chicago, also held considerable stature as a jazz scholar. His articles in collectors' magazines and contributions to jazz history books brought authoritative information to a field often shrouded in myth and stereotype. "He was incredibly curious, spoke several languages, and had an extremely fine mind, which made him a great researcher," said Charles A. Sengstock

Jr., who collaborated with Steiner on a bibliography of newspaper coverage of Chicago jazz.

Steiner is survived by his wife, Nina, and a stepson, William Davis.

FRIDAY, SEPTEMBER 15, 2000

R. H. Harris, Eighty-Four; Singer Fueled Gospel Sound
By Vanessa Gezari, *Tribune* Staff Reporter

R. H. Harris, eighty-four, the legendary gospel singer and former Soul Stirrers front man who profoundly influenced the sound of gospel and soul music in the second half of the twentieth century, died of a stroke Sunday, September 3, in Holy Cross Hospital in Chicago.

As the Soul Stirrers' lead singer, Harris helped transform the sound and structure of gospel music, trading the simple harmonies of the Jubilee style for blues-influenced melodies sung by two lead vocalists instead of one.

His singing was characterized by bluesy moans reminiscent of early African-American church music, cowboy yodels, and a soaring falsetto with "the epicene purity of an Irish tenor," said Anthony Heilbut, author of *The Gospel Sound: Good News and Bad Times* (Limelight Editions) and a producer of several Harris albums.

Known in gospel circles as Old Pop Harris, he left his mark on generations of gospel and soul singers, including the man who replaced him as lead singer for the Soul Stirrers, Sam Cooke.

He always said his technique, particularly his falsetto, was derived from birds.

"He had a very wide range," Heilbut said. "As late as 1978, he was able to howl in yodeling style to C sharp, two octaves above middle C. That's extremely high for a man."

Born in Trinity, Texas, Harris started singing when he was a boy and joined the Soul Stirrers as a teenager in the 1930s. The quartet moved to Chicago permanently in 1937.

In 1931 one of the group's singers got sick and another man was hired to temporarily replace him, Harris told the *Tribune* in 1997. When the first singer recovered, the second one stayed on, leaving the Soul Stirrers with two lead vocalists and an innovative sound.

"Never before had churchgoers in Chicago—or anywhere else—heard religious music so rhythmically seductive and melodically enthralling," *Tribune* arts critic Howard Reich wrote.

"Never again would gospel quartets be content to offer a lone melody line backed by static chords, all delivered at a somewhat lugubrious tempo."

Harris was modest, but "he knew what he had done within the gospel field and he understood his influence," Heilbut said.

"Every quartet, all the quartets, turned to the style and the sound—to the best that they could—of the Soul Stirrers," Harris said in 1997.

"But we didn't mind, because we were all young Christian men, and we were glad that we were able to produce something that someone else would want to do."

In 1947 Harris and other singers formed the National Singing Quartet Union of America. He served as its president for fifty-three years.

He left the Soul Stirrers in 1950 and recorded with the Christland Singers, another Chicago group, on the Peacock and Nashboro labels. He sang with the Gospel Paraders, whose music was recorded by Sam Cooke on his SAR label.

Harris recorded "The Father of Them All," accompanied by the Masonic Quintet, in 1975 and joined the Masonic Quintet on one other recording, "Because He Lives," on the RHJC label in 1978. It was his last record.

Although his sound found its way into soul and rock, Harris was emphatically a gospel singer.

"It was a point of pride for him that he never 'sold out,'" Heilbut said.

"Sam Cooke and Johnnie Taylor and all these others were singing soul music, love lyrics, and Harris never did that."

A distinguished-looking man with a sober temperament, Harris worked several day jobs after leaving the Soul Stirrers. He sometimes spoke in a cryptic, country style and favored parables, Heilbut said.

In 1986 he began working at Gatlings Chapel, a South Side funeral home with a recording studio. He helped coordinate Sunday gospel music broadcasts and counseled singers with the Soul Stirrers and other music groups.

"He was a matter-of-fact man and he didn't bite his tongue, yet he was very gentle, very wise," said Princella Hudson-Gilliam, general manager of True Gospel Productions Inc., a concert production company owned by Gatlings.

"He's really been a blessing to a lot of people."

Survivors include his wife, Mary; three daughters, Jackie, Sheila, and Cheryl; three sons, Greg, James, and Tray Lee; three stepsons, James Parker, Gus Jefferson, and Bill Butts; a stepdaughter, Felicia Wilson; a sister, O'Verna H. Jolly; and twelve grandchildren.

TUESDAY, JUNE 11, 2002

Charles V. "Truck" Parham, Ninety-One; Influential Jazz Bass Player Known for "Chicago Style"

By James Janega, *Tribune* Staff Reporter

Charles V. "Truck" Parham, ninety-one, who along with the late Chicago jazz bass legend Milt Hinton was regarded as one of the most influential bass players on the Chicago jazz scene, died Wednesday, June 5, in Michael Reese Hospital of respiratory illness and complications from kidney disease.

Parham's sound fit into what was regarded as the "Chicago style" of bass playing, a distinctive but wide-ranging style at once dark-toned and compulsively swinging.

But while Hinton was acclaimed for performing with Cab Calloway and working widely in New York recording sessions, Parham remained for the most part in Chicago, in a career noted for his collaborations with trumpeter Roy Eldridge and pianist Earl Hines.

Growing up in "the Flats," a South Side neighborhood known for its music in the 1920s, Parham sold newspapers across the street from the Dreamland Cafe, a club headlined by such musicians as King Oliver and Darnell Howard.

Within a few years, he was doing Saturday chores for Louis Armstrong as a way to listen to Armstrong play duets with his piano-playing wife, Parham told the *Tribune* in 1985.

He lived upstairs from Freddie Keppard, a New Orleans musician known both for his trumpet playing and late-night Saturday night parties that were part after-hours jam session, part beer bash. Parham's job, he said, was supplying the beer.

"Keppard would hit on the radiator with his mouthpiece. This was the signal for me to come downstairs, get the beer buckets, go down in the saloon for the beer," Parham told the *Tribune* years later. "So I'd go down, get the beer, drink some foam off it, then come up the stairs. He'd say, 'Boy! What you doin' drinkin' that beer?' 'I didn't have any.' 'I see that foam all over your mouth.' I was there settin' up all night waitin' for the cats to hit on that thing."

Parham began his professional career after graduating from Hyde Park High School in 1928, when he played tuba in a band led by Albert Ammons. He later switched to bass—some accounts have it at the advice of Sy Oliver—and sang with a band on a Cincinnati radio station from 1932 to 1934. Around the same time, he also tried his hand at playing football with the Chicago Negro All-Stars, and he stepped briefly into the ring as an amateur boxer.

It wasn't until Parham moved back to Chicago in the mid-1930s that he began working with jazz groups that would later become famous, including one led by Zutty Singleton and later fronted by Eldridge.

From 1936 to 1938 Parham collaborated with Eldridge and pianist Art Tatum at the Three Deuces club in Chicago. He became an important name by 1942, when he started regular associations with Hines and bandleader Jimmy Lunceford.

In the early and mid-1950s, he played with swing band front man Muggsy Spanier, followed by a stretch in drummer Louis Bellson's quartet and numerous other collaborations.

A regular performer at jazz festivals around the country, he was somewhat of a headline act himself by the mid-1980s, and he toured Europe with a group of other jazz all-stars as recently as 1998. Parhams's family said he kept playing until he couldn't lift his bass anymore.

"That was his thing, just being with his buddies, playing for people who enjoyed what they were playing. He seemed to love it all," said his daughter Lynn Shelton.

In 1937 Parham married Treopia Wilkes, whom he had met when both were teens. His wife died in 1998, his daughter Nona Briggs in 1989. Besides Shelton, Parham is also survived by another daughter, Rita Parham Banks, and three granddaughters.

SECTION

XV

Classical Musicians

As Chicago grew, so did its musical sophistication. The twentieth century brought concert halls; the halls brought directors, composers, and musicians; and the musicians brought renown to their city.

The notables included Sir Georg Solti, the Hungarian-born music director of the Chicago Symphony Orchestra; Thomas Peck and Margaret Hillis, two of the nation's leading choral masters; and others who conferred on the residents of America's second city the refinement they knew to be in their souls.

THURSDAY, JUNE 9, 1994

Thomas Peck, Fifty-Six; Grant Park Chorus Founder

By John Von Rhein, *Tribune* Music Critic

Thomas Peck, fifty-six, founder and director of Chicago's Grant Park Symphony Chorus for more than three decades and one of the nation's leading choral directors, died Tuesday in his home in St. Louis. He died of complications from AIDS.

Along with his Chicago affiliation, Peck directed the St. Louis Symphony Chorus, an organization he had created eighteen years ago at the invitation of music director Leonard Slatkin. It was at Grant Park where Slatkin first became aware of Peck's abilities as a chorus master.

"His unfailing musicianship, humanity, and grace touched us all," said Slatkin in a statement. The conductor will dedicate his program with the Grant Park Symphony Orchestra and Chorus, June 19 at the Petrillo Music Shell, to the memory of Peck.

From 1975 to 1978 Peck also served as chorus director of the Cincinnati May Festival, where he prepared choruses for such conductors as James Levine and Thomas Schippers.

Born in Chicago and raised in Berwyn, he joined the then fledgling Chicago Symphony Chorus under its founder/director, Margaret Hillis, in 1957 when he was a college sophomore. The following year he formed his own ensemble, the Thomas Peck Singers, under the auspices of the Young Artists Foundation of Chicago.

Thomas Peck built the Grant Park Symphony Chorus from volunteers into one of the nation's most respected choral groups.

The group lasted only a few seasons, but Hillis was sufficiently impressed with Peck's abilities that she invited him to conduct a CSO Chorus rehearsal on his twenty-first birthday.

But it was the Grant Park Symphony Chorus that claimed his attention and affections the longest.

In 1962 the Chicago Park District was looking for a musician qualified to organize a high-caliber resident chorus for the lakefront concert series. Edward Gordon, then assistant manager of Grant Park Concerts (he later became the

Ravinia Festival's executive director), recommended Peck for the post.

The chorus' calling-card performance was a Gilbert and Sullivan evening starring Martyn Green, using a small vocal group that numbered no more than ten professional singers.

From those beginnings, Peck built the Grant Park Symphony Chorus from an essentially volunteer group into one of the most respected professional choral organizations in the nation. Over the years he prepared virtually all the major choral repertory for the guest conductors who appeared at Grant Park each summer.

In 1983, after directing public concerts with the Grant Park Symphony, he confessed to a *Tribune* interviewer that it had taken him almost twenty-five years to feel comfortable conducting an orchestra, despite his proven expertise in the rehearsal room.

Peck's work is represented on nine recordings, seven made with the St. Louis Symphony Orchestra and Chorus, several of them nominated for Grammys.

Peck left no survivors.

THURSDAY, SEPTEMBER 29, 1994

"Zina" Aleskow, Ninety-Three; Pianist, Friend of Musicians
By Kenan Heise, *Tribune* Staff Reporter

Zinaida "Zina" Joelson Aleskow, ninety-three, a retired concert pianist, was noted for cohosting with her late husband, Gregory, dinners and evenings of conversation and music for many of the leading musicians of the world. She died September 6 at home.

At the time of her husband's death in 1982, the *Tribune's* Alan Artner wrote: "He and his wife, Zina, re-created the world that they knew—a world of culture and refinement that harkened to the salon of pre-Revolutionary Russia. For a half century the North Side Aleskow apartments were open to a staggering number of great musicians. The atmosphere was relaxed, the food exquisite, and the music, in the hands of Zina and guests, predictably fine."

Among those great musicians were Ignaz Friedman, Mstislav Rostropovich, Leonard Slatkin, and Jennie Tourel.

Aleskow was a native of Russia. On the occasion of the 300th anniversary of the Romanov dynasty, she was chosen to curtsy and present a bouquet to the tsarina.

She immigrated to the United States eight years later. She subsequently gave piano recitals and coached some of the great musicians in Russian music.

Aleskow was honored last May for her many years as patron of the Chicago Symphony Orchestra.

Survivors include a son, Richard, and two sisters.

A memorial service for Aleskow was held in Chicago. At its close, musician friends played Franz Schubert's "Death and the Maiden."

FRIDAY, MARCH 14, 1997

Hugo Weisgall, Eighty-Four; Lyric Opera Adviser
By John Von Rhein, *Tribune* Music Critic

Hugo Weisgall, the composer, conductor, teacher, and adviser to Lyric Opera of Chicago's composer-in-residence program, was one of America's most widely respected, if not always widely performed, composers of operas and vocal music.

He died Tuesday of complications from a fall suffered the previous day in his New York home. He was eighty-four.

Although he had a large catalog of orchestral and instrumental works and song cycles to his credit, it was in the realm of opera that Weisgall achieved his most lasting success.

The opera that first brought him international attention was *Six Characters in Search of an Author*, with a libretto by Denis Johnston based on the Luigi Pirandello play.

The fifth of Weisgall's eleven operas, it was first presented in New York in 1959. The opera was given a major production by the Lyric Opera Center for American Artists here in 1990. A recording of the production was issued on compact disc by New World Records.

Weisgall's musical idiom, blending elements of tonality, atonality, and twelve-tone composition, was difficult to categorize. Still, he insisted his works could be easily performed by well-trained musicians. In answer to the charge that most modern operas are unsingable, he said, "If I can't sing 'em, I don't write 'em."

His vocal style and keen sense of theater recommended him to Lyric Opera, which in 1986 engaged him as adviser to its Brena and Lee Freeman Sr. Composer-in-Residence Program, a position he held for eleven years.

Three of his former composition students—Lee Goldstein, Bright Sheng, and Bruce Saylor—wrote new operas for the Lyric under the terms of their Chicago residencies.

Late in life, Weisgall won widespread critical praise for his final opera, *Esther*, a grand biblical spectacular commissioned, but never performed, by the San Francisco Opera. The work had its premiere by the New York City Opera in 1993.

That production is scheduled for revival by City Opera this autumn, opening October 12, the day before what would have been the composer's eighty-fifth birthday. A Lyric Opera production originally scheduled for the 1998–1999 season has been postponed until after the year 2000.

His other operas include *The Tenor; The Stronger; Nine Rivers from Jordan; Jenny, or The Hundred Nights;* and *The Gardens of Adonis*.

Born in Ivancice, Moravia (Czech Republic), Weisgall immigrated with his parents to the United States in 1920. He studied piano, harmony, and composition at Peabody Conservatory in Baltimore, composition with Roger

Sessions, and conducting with Fritz Reiner and Rosario Scalero at the Curtis Institute of Music in Philadelphia, where he earned diplomas in conducting and composition.

He taught composition for twenty-three years at the City University of New York and at Queens College, New York. He also served as president of the American Academy and Institute of Arts and Letters. Until recently, he was faculty chairman of the Cantors' Institute of the Jewish Theological Seminary in Manhattan.

Weisgall is survived by his wife, Nathalie, and a son and daughter.

SATURDAY, SEPTEMBER 6, 1997

Georg Solti, Eighty-Four;
Chicago Symphony's Music Director Laureate
By John Von Rhein, *Tribune* Music Critic

Conductor Georg Solti won 32 Grammy Awards and turned the Chicago Symphony Orchestra into a world-class ensemble.

Georg Solti, age eighty-four, the Hungarian-born music director laureate of the Chicago Symphony Orchestra (CSO) and one of the world's most eminent conductors, died Friday while visiting Antibes, France.

His twenty-two seasons as music director of the CSO, which began in

1969 and ended with his retirement in 1991, marked the pinnacle of his distinguished career and carried the orchestra to new heights of artistic achievement and international celebrity.

In addition to his Chicago post, Solti was music director of the Royal Opera, Covent Garden, in London, for a decade starting in 1961; chief conductor of L'Orchestre de Paris from 1970 to 1975; principal conductor of the London Philharmonic from 1979 to 1983 (he subsequently held the title conductor emeritus); and director of the Salzburg Easter Festival starting in 1992.

Sir Georg was made a Knight Commander of the British Empire in 1972 for his contributions to British music.

Solti had been scheduled to return to the CSO podium October 25 in a special celebration concert at Orchestra Hall honoring his eighty-fifth birthday on October 21 and his one-thousandth concert with the orchestra he once boasted was "the greatest in the world."

By anyone's reckoning, Solti and the Chicago Symphony were one of the great conductor-orchestra partnerships of the century, perhaps of all time.

Older generations had Leopold Stokowski and the Philadelphia Orchestra, Arturo Toscanini and the NBC Symphony, Serge Koussevitzky and the Boston Symphony, George Szell and the Cleveland Orchestra, and Frederick Stock and Fritz Reiner with the Chicago Orchestra. Solti and his Chicago Symphony earned their membership in that musical elite.

When Solti came to the CSO as its chief conductor (he had made his CSO debut at Ravinia in 1954), he found a technically superior orchestra that during the post-Reiner years of Jean Martinon had lost the spark of inspiration. The orchestra had no world reputation to speak of, and its numerous visits to New York under Martinon had created no ripples in the vast pond of Manhattan's musical life.

Solti immediately began changing all that. His muscular, whiplash style of conducting, which led one critic to compare him to a beleaguered tennis player, did wonders to rejuvenate the orchestra and restore the player morale that had sagged during the Martinon years.

The musical and technical improvement brought about under Solti was astounding. The "Solti sound" had enormous power, precision, and intensity, with a lean, hard brilliance and a dynamic scale wide enough to embrace the wispiest pianissimo up to fortissimos so saturated with glorious brass sonority (Solti's Chicago trademark) that they all but melted the organ pipes framing the Orchestra Hall stage.

By spring 1970, the Solti-CSO juggernaut had begun its conquest of New York City with a celebrated performance of Mahler's Fifth Symphony. In 1971 came the orchestra's first European tour, with a triumphant parade down State Street upon its return.

Two years later, the "Fastest Baton in the West" had been given the ultimate media accolade, a *Time* magazine cover. The national and international acclaim for the orchestra grew. Solti and the Chicagoans became known as the finest conductor and the greatest orchestra active in America. On the

Continent, as Solti never tired of pointing out, only his archrival Herbert von Karajan and the Berlin Philharmonic presented serious competition.

And with that outside attention came a dramatic increase in the CSO's artistic esteem and financial strength in its own city. Solti and the orchestra became a source as well as symbol of civic pride, representing the finest product of Chicago's cultural traditions.

As part of his wedding "dowry," Solti brought with him a contract with London/Decca that over the coming two decades would make him and the Chicago Symphony the best-selling team on the American orchestral recording scene. Their recordings earned them a score of international awards and included a remarkably wide range of orchestral, vocal, and operatic works.

He won thirty-two Grammy Awards, more than any other musician, classical or popular. His most recent Grammy was a lifetime achievement award in 1996.

But none of Solti's Chicago recordings could equal the musical and historic impact of the complete Wagner *Ring* he made over eight years' time with the Vienna Philharmonic. Due for reissue on compact disc next month, it was the first integral recording of Wagner's masterpiece. It featured the leading Wagnerian singers of its day, and it brought a theatrical dimension to the recording art that had not been heard before or, many believe, since.

At times, his conducting could produce music that sounded dry, overly calculated, strenuous, or curiously enervated, with little or no inner repose or spirituality evident in the aural product. A warm, unforced lyrical flow was not invariably Solti's to command, despite his technical expertise and his long operatic experience. In later years, however, a mellowness crept into his conducting, with the result that a new depth and feeling were evident in his interpretations.

At the summit of his international fame, in the 1970s and 1980s, Solti was one of the handful of top conductors whose role was that of a freewheeling power broker in the high-risk world of symphony and opera.

It was his finest role, and he played it to the hilt, with the easy assurance of a multinational corporation president who has clawed his way up from the bottom of the ladder and remembers every painful detail of the rise.

Early on, Solti had by his own admission a big talent coupled with "an unshakeable belief in [myself] and [my] ability." But he soon realized that talent and ambition and self-assurance were not enough. Luck had to figure somewhere in the grand equation.

Solti's road to musical eminence began at an apparent dead end and proceeded from one apparent failure to the next. Born in Budapest, Hungary, in 1912, he was quickly recognized by a doting Jewish mother as a possible child piano prodigy. His incipient virtuoso talents were nurtured at the Liszt Conservatory, where his teachers included Bela Bartok, Zoltan Kodaly, and Erno Dohnanyi. Those years marked the end of his formal education.

The pianist who wanted to be a conductor was put to work in the dusty backstage studios of the Budapest Opera, coaching singers in their roles. Two events relieved the tedium of that period.

In 1936 he was chosen as an assistant to conductor Erich Leinsdorf, who was then assisting Toscanini at the Salzburg Festival. (In a celebrated "pirate" recording of Mozart's *The Magic Flute* from the 1937 festival, Solti can be heard playing the glockenspiel for Papageno.)

The following year, when he was twenty-five, Solti was allowed to conduct his first opera, Mozart's *The Marriage of Figaro*.

It was to be his last operatic conducting for more than eight years. On that very day—March 11, 1938—Hitler's troops marched into Austria. While Solti was in Lucerne, Switzerland, World War II broke out. His mother sent him a telegram warning him not to return. Penniless and jobless, Solti had to shelve his fierce musical ambitions as he pondered an even fiercer question: survival.

Unable to gain a work permit as a conductor in Switzerland, he returned to the piano and won the 1942 Geneva International Piano Competition. The prize gave him enough money on which to live for five months.

In 1946 he was invited by the U.S. military authorities to conduct Beethoven's *Fidelio* in Munich. Solti had recently acquired a Swiss wife, Hedi (the marriage ended in 1966), and he was impatient to conduct again, although he realized his experience was practically nil.

Nevertheless, his will to succeed led to his appointment as music director of the Bavarian State Opera, where he remained for six years, laying the foundation of the company's postwar reputation and repertory. Solti made his first records in 1947, as pianist for the violinist Georg Kulenkampff and as conductor with the Zurich Tonhalle Orchestra.

In 1952 Solti moved to Frankfurt, West Germany, as Generalmusikdirektor, directing the city concerts as well as opera. For the first time, the opera conductor began to consider himself a symphony conductor as well.

A Lyric Opera engagement in 1956 carried with it the promise of a major staff position, but Solti's Chicago reviews were not auspicious and the arrangement was canceled in 1957. Nor did he generate much enthusiasm with a series of Metropolitan Opera appearances in the early 1960s.

The turning point in Solti's rise came in 1961, when he was named music director of London's Royal Opera, Covent Garden. He announced his intention of making Covent Garden "quite simply, the best opera house in the world," and in the opinion of many, he succeeded. For his efforts, he was rewarded with a knighthood on taking British nationality in 1972.

Solti's coming to the Chicago Symphony overlapped with his Covent Garden responsibilities, which he finally relinquished in 1971. But Solti saw his chance to do his competitor one better that year when Karajan stepped down as conductor of L'Orchestre de Paris. But even Solti could do little with the notoriously undisciplined French musicians. In 1979 he firmed up his close affiliation with the London Philharmonic by consenting to be that orchestra's principal conductor, a post he gave up in 1982.

All his life, Solti seemed driven by a

single desire: to make an indelible, unmistakable impact upon the symphonic and operatic music of our time. He succeeded, perhaps better than the far-from-modest maestro ever would have imagined.

He is survived by his wife, Valerie, and two daughters, Gabrielle and Claudia.

THURSDAY, FEBRUARY 5, 1998

Margaret Hillis, Seventy-Six; Chicago Loses Its Giant in World of Choral Music
By John Von Rhein, Tribune Music Critic

Margaret Hillis , founder and director of the Chicago Symphony Chorus, was known as "Mama Chorus."

Margaret Hillis, one of the nation's foremost chorus masters, who achieved widespread and lasting recognition as founder and director of the Chicago Symphony Chorus for nearly four decades, died Wednesday in Evanston Hospital. She was seventy-six.

Her family said the cause of death was lung cancer. A heavy smoker for much of her life, Hillis, of Wilmette, recently had undergone surgery to remove a section of one lung and was breathing with the help of an oxygen tank, according to Cathy Duke, a friend who sings with the chorus.

It is no exaggeration to say that Hillis, along with her former teacher Robert Shaw, transformed the performance of choral music in the United States.

She formed the chorus in 1957 at the request of Chicago Symphony Orchestra music director Fritz Reiner, leading it for thirty-seven of its forty years. Its flexibility, discipline, and warm, expressive, unforced, impeccably blended sound became a model for many other choral organizations. It became a catalyst for the growth of other choral ensembles in the Chicago area and across the nation. By the late 1960s, more symphony orchestras had resident choruses than ever before.

With Hillis as director, the Chicago Symphony Chorus appeared with the orchestra nearly 600 times, recorded forty-five works, won nine Grammy awards between 1977 and 1993, and accompanied the CSO on domestic and foreign tours, including the chorus' successful European debut in 1989 in London and Salzburg.

Although she announced her retirement as chorus director in 1991, she continued to work until Duain Wolfe succeeded her in June 1994.

"She was an extraordinarily beneficent influence in American choral music, in both performance and scholarship," said Shaw, conductor laureate of the Atlanta Symphony. "Her Chicago Symphony Chorus was one of the finest in the world, and her analytical studies of the choral repertoire have been very helpful. In addition, she was a strong and lovely human being."

"She was greatly respected by the major conductors of the world and greatly revered by the singers she directed," said Wolfe. "I appreciated her trust and support as a colleague and especially her warmth as a friend."

A conductor and educator in addition to her choral work, Hillis made national headlines in 1977 when she substituted for an ailing Georg Solti in a CSO performance of Mahler's massive Eighth Symphony in New York's Carnegie Hall. Leading more than 400 singers and instrumentalists, she won a standing ovation.

When Reiner charged Hillis with organizing a resident symphony chorus in Chicago in 1957, he wanted a chorus worthy of sharing the stage with his orchestra. Hillis, then director of the American Concert Choir in New York, was the right person to turn to because she was dedicated to the same level of quality. She built the Chicago Symphony Chorus into a formidable instrument in its own right.

Rare is the American choral director who was not to some degree influenced by Hillis' methods or the sound she achieved with her choruses. John Oliver, founding director of the Boston Symphony's Tanglewood Festival Chorus, has said the rich, full Hillis sound is something he carries around with him in his ear.

The Chicago Symphony Chorus is made up of more than 136 professional and volunteer singers, all of whom Hillis required to audition each year, regardless of how long they had been singing in the ensemble, a tradition that has survived her.

At the same time, the relationship between the CSO and its chorus is not typical. Most American orchestras use community or amateur choirs or contract with independent professional choruses for choral programs. Few can afford to maintain a paid, professional chorus as do the Chicago, Cleveland, Boston, San Francisco, and Atlanta orchestras, among others. Most members of the CSO chorus are professionals.

Like Solti, Hillis was a rigorous perfectionist who knew how to transfer her zeal to those under her. Her tenacious dedication, combined with a strongly maternal regard for her charges, earned her the nickname "Mama Chorus."

A Hillis rehearsal was all efficiency and organization—serious work. Some choristers found her insistence on long and meticulous preparation counterproductive, but most came to appreciate the difference this made in the finished performance.

"When I began in Chicago, I never looked down the line and imagined we would one day have this great choral organization," she told the *Tribune* in 1987. "I was just looking at the next musical project that had to be done."

Along with the great choral works of Bach, Handel, Mozart, Haydn, Beethoven, Mendelssohn, Brahms, and Mahler, the chorus has explored an impressive range of contemporary works by such composers as Stravinsky, Schoenberg, Bartok, Hindemith, Roberto Gerhard, Ned Rorem, Ezra Laderman, Roger Sessions, Alan Stout, and Martin

David Levy.

The chorus most recently sang in performances of Ravel's *Daphnis et Chloe* under Pierre Boulez in November.

In her various capacities as a member of the advisory council to the National Endowment for the Arts (NEA) and the Association of Professional Vocal Ensembles (which she helped found in 1977), Hillis was a tireless fighter for the professional dignity of choral singers.

During contract negotiations in 1984, when rumors were flying of possible cutbacks or elimination of the CSO chorus, she got up at a union meeting and presented an eloquent defense of the chorus and its importance to Chicago.

Years later, when an NEA cultural report carried nary a mention of choruses or choral music in America, she angrily confronted NEA chairman Frank Hodsoll. "We've been overlooked too long," she told the embarrassed arts chief, all but flattening him with her baritonal voice.

Along with her CSO duties, Hillis was for several seasons a member of the conducting staff of the Civic Orchestra of Chicago.

She also had held positions as choral director of the Cleveland and San Francisco orchestras and as music director of the Elgin and Kenosha Symphonies.

That she never achieved success as an orchestral conductor anywhere near what she achieved as a chorus director remained a nagging disappointment to her, friends said. But if she believed she was the victim of sexist prejudice, she kept her feelings well hidden behind a hearty façade.

Born into a well-to-do family in Kokomo, Indiana, she learned to play the horn, piano, trumpet, saxophone, and string bass, and she toted a tuba in her high school marching band. By the age of eight, she knew she wanted to conduct an orchestra.

But other pursuits intervened. At twenty she was a junior golf champion, able to drive the ball 250 yards. Men would come up to her and say, "That's pretty good—for a girl."

That infuriated her, but it wasn't until she was in college, at Indiana University and the Juilliard School of Music in New York, that she came face to face with music's glass ceiling.

One of the teachers who recognized her talent, as well as the obstacles, advised her to get into choral conducting "through the back door," because there were no jobs available for women conductors. She accepted his advice and went on to study choral conducting with Shaw.

At first Hillis was frustrated by the fact that choruses, their ranks generally filled out with nonprofessional singers, needed more rehearsing than orchestras. But she persisted in her conducting objectives, and over the next fifteen years she succeeded in making a name for herself in New York musical circles.

When she arrived in Chicago, the city had no professional choral activity whatsoever. Whenever the CSO wished to present a big choral work, it hired a local university chorus or an amateur group. The only other American orchestra with a resident chorus at that time was the Cleveland Orchestra. Hillis found her first years in Chicago a constant struggle—for singers, for funding, for recognition. But the tenacious Hoosier made it happen.

The debut performance of the CSO Chorus—March 13, 1958—was the Mozart Requiem conducted by Bruno Walter.

Apparently no one thought it odd that a choral group flushed with youthful promise should announce itself to the world with Mozart's dying valedictory to earthly things.

For the chorus' first five seasons, Hillis led the hectic life of a commuting musician. The young conductor who imagined she would stay just long enough to get the chorus established found her guidance so badly needed that eventually she shifted her home base to Chicago.

Hillis recently donated her scores, books, papers, and other memorabilia to the CSO archives.

She never married. Survivors include three brothers: Elwood, Robert, and Joseph.

XVI

The Musicians We Knew

Sing "Ol' Man River" to yourself. The voice you hear in your head, that booming baritone, was William Warfield of Chicago. Think of Chicago's ethnic bands, and your mind's eye will re-create a man like Stanley Lyskawa, master of the bouncing polka genre. Picture Chicago's most famous blues musicians, and your memory will be looking through the lens of Ray Flerlage, whose photographs of the city's 1960s blues scene became iconic. In Chicago, the musicians were like weather: inescapable, inimitable.

TUESDAY, AUGUST 27, 2002

William Warfield, Eighty-Two; Pioneering Bass-Baritone Defined "Ol' Man River"

By John Von Rhein, *Tribune* Music Critic. *Tribune* Theater Critic Michael Phillips and *Tribune* News Services contributed to this report.

William Warfield, the velvet-voiced American bass-baritone who died Sunday in the Rehabilitation Institute of Chicago where he had been recovering from a fall, was a shining example of the human spirit's refusal to bow to the physical challenges of old age.

Warfield, eighty-two, sang his final performance little more than a month ago in Cambridge, Massachusetts, where he brought down the house with "Ol' Man River," the Jerome Kern and Oscar Hammerstein song that was his signature.

In Warfield's big, still-imposing voice, the line "I'm tired of living and scared of dying" carried an especially poignant resonance. At the time of the concert, he was quoted as saying, "Music will always be a healing refuge, a refuge to which man retreats whenever he needs something beyond himself."

He was closely associated with George Gershwin's *Porgy and Bess* (in which he portrayed Porgy opposite Leontyne Price, to whom he was married) and famously sang "Ol' Man River" in the 1951 MGM film version of *Show Boat*. A respected voice teacher later in life, he was chairman of the Voice Department at the University of Illinois before joining the Northwestern University School of Music faculty in 1984 as a part-time voice professor.

But even more remarkable was Warfield's success in carving out the beginnings of a notable career at a time when there were relatively few opportunities for African American singers in classical music.

His many accomplishments made him a role model for aspiring black classical musicians.

"He was truly devoted to sharing with others what music gave him throughout his life," said Bernard Dobroski, dean of the Northwestern School of Music, where Warfield was due to resume teaching next month.

"He was a wonderful man, a wonderful singer and artist," said soprano Camilla Williams, a close friend. "We came along at a time when it wasn't so easy. But he at least had the chance to sing what he sang." With the film version of *Show Boat*, Williams said, "People were grateful to hear him sing, whether it was 'real' opera or not."

Martina Arroyo, another friend and colleague, recalled that her church group made the trip from 154th Street to Midtown in Manhattan to see *Show Boat*. When Warfield's rich, roaring rendition of "Ol' Man River" ended, the operatic soprano-to-be said, "It was the first time I'd ever seen an audience stand up and applaud after a number in a movie. The people actually began applauding and standing up."

Warfield broke his neck during a fall late last month outside his South Side home. His condition had been improving, and he was moved last week from Northwestern Memorial Hospital to the Rehabilitation Institute, said his brother Thaddeus. The cause of death had not been determined, his brother said.

In a January 2000 interview with the *Tribune*, Warfield made no secret of the fact that he loved the attention he was getting at an age when most singers have long since retired.

"Why should I quit the stage, anyway? Age has nothing to do with anything. As long as this old voice holds out and I still enjoy it, I'll never stop singing," he said, in that deep oratorical voice that put him in high demand as a narrator for Aaron Copland's *A Lincoln Portrait*.

During his career, which began more than fifty years ago with his triumphant debut recital in New York's Town Hall, Warfield covered the show business waterfront—from stints in churches and nightclubs to performances on stage and screen.

In 1952 Warfield performed opposite Price in *Porgy and Bess* during a tour of Europe sponsored by the U.S. State Department. After they married in 1952, they found that the demands of two careers left them little time together. They divorced in 1972.

In a television interview, he recalled, "There was a time when a black artist thought very seriously as to whether or not he or she should perform in *Porgy* or *Show Boat*." He said that black groups had misgivings that Russia would use the touring *Porgy* produc-

tion as propaganda to highlight the problem of racism in the United States.

"Leontyne and I both had to search our hearts before we decided to do the tour," he said. "But I have to tell you, the tour produced absolutely the opposite reaction. What the foreign press saw and reported, including the Russians, was a group of gifted artists performing an exciting work in an exciting manner."

In 1975 Warfield gave a sold-out concert in Carnegie Hall, marking the twenty-fifth anniversary of his New York debut, and in 1984 he received a Grammy Award.

As his trademark, "Ol' Man River" was the song he most often sang.

"It's different every time, and that's what keeps it fresh for me," the singer told the *Tribune*. "I adapt it to what is on my mind in the course of the day I'm performing. Sometimes there's a sadness to it, sometimes it's really laid-back, and sometimes it's even angry. The most difficult time I had with it was singing it just four days after Martin Luther King's assassination. It was a Sunday matinee in a small Midwestern town. I had to hold back my emotion somewhat to keep from breaking down altogether."

Warfield's original goal was to become a music teacher, not a singer. Born the son of a Baptist preacher in Arkansas and raised in Rochester, New York, he was awarded a scholarship to the Eastman School of Music and interrupted his studies to serve four years in the Military Intelligence Division of the army.

Warfield is survived by two brothers and numerous nieces and nephews.

THURSDAY, OCTOBER 3, 2002

Stanley Lyskawa, Eighty-Two; "Wesoly Stas," Comical Polka Band Leader

By James Janega, *Tribune* Staff Reporter

There were moments in the Polonia Ballroom, in the Glendora House, or at one of the other half dozen dance floors on the Southwest Side when a police siren would cut through an accordion solo and flashing blue strobes would light up.

That was Stanley Lyskawa in an expansive mood.

"Jolly Stan," or "Wesoly Stas" in Polish, a longtime Chicago polka band leader, kept the police lights and siren on his drum set for special occasions. He played standing up so the audience could see him singing.

Lyskawa and his wife, Irene, died Saturday, September 28, after being hit by a sport-utility vehicle as they crossed Ninety-fifth Street in Hickory Hills.

Mr. Lyskawa was eighty-two, and Mrs. Lyskawa was eighty-one.

Both died of multiple injuries from the accident, said a spokeswoman for the Cook County medical examiner's office.

The Lyskawas were an amusing contrast, said Eddie Blazonczyk, leader of Eddie Blazonczyk's Versatones and a polka music disc jockey on Chicago radio. Mrs. Lyskawa was quiet and a little shy, Blazonczyk said. Mr. Lyskawa was anything but.

"He was well known," Blazonczyk said. Mrs. Lyskawa was also familiar to audiences as she was frequently in the wings during performances.

"He was a great musician, a great drummer. And he sang. He was known also as a comedian. A lot of the lyrics in his songs were comical," Blazonczyk said.

For instance, in one song with Polish lyrics, "He tells the story of how this woman buys a rooster, and then has to stick the rooster in her shoe."

Lyskawa wrote the words for many of the songs he played, Blazonczyk said.

"Stanley was one of the most entertaining performers on the polka stage," reporter Patrick Henry wrote in the *Polish American Journal* this week. "There wasn't a prop or bit that he wouldn't use to excite his audience."

The most famous, said Henry, was the police siren, but Lyskawa kept a box full of other gags beside his drum set. He joined Chicago's bustling polka scene in the 1950s and continued playing weddings and special events until just a few years ago, Blazonczyk said.

Lyskawa was a drummer for the Joe Pat Orchestra in the 1950s and brought his own band, the Stan Lee Orchestra, to regular performances on the Chet Schafer Stage Show through the 1970s.

Two of his recordings, *Sing Along with Stas*, Volume 1 and Volume 2, were recently rereleased.

The Stan Lee Orchestra gained national acclaim in the 1950s, appearing on radio and television stations from Connecticut to Nebraska.

Lyskawa was nominated to the Polka Music Hall of Fame, said chairman Leon Kozicki, a clarinet and saxophone player who shared a stage with him.

"He would know when to get the excitement of people to the highest point, to get them in the swing of things," Kozicki said. "You knew that if you were going to work with him that it was going to be a satisfying job."

Lyskawa and his wife, the former Irene Majewski, are survived by three children, Barbara Scott, Lorri Roe, and Stanley S. Lyskawa.

FRIDAY, OCTOBER 4, 2002

Raeburn "Ray" Flerlage, Eighty-Seven; Photographer of 1960s Blues Scene
By James Janega and Donna Freedman, *Tribune* Staff Reporters

Raeburn "Ray" Flerlage, eighty-seven, whose pictures showed Howlin' Wolf howling and Muddy Waters at his moody best and brought innumerable Chicago blues halls to pounding life in glossy images snapped during the blues heyday of the 1960s, died Saturday, September 28, in the University of Chicago Hospitals.

Flerlage died of complications from an infection, said Chuck Cowdery, a blues author and former collaborator.

"He was a form of rapid transportation to that period for anyone who saw his work," said Shirli Dixon, executive director of Willie Dixon's Blues Heaven Foundation. "He wasn't a singer, but he certainly was a bluesman."

She said his pictures captured moments as diverse as bass player Willie Dixon deep in concentration at a recording session and a group of women—dressed in white and wearing hats and high heels as if they were going to the opera—at a blues bar in 1965.

Flerlage's photos appeared in Cowdery's 1995 book, *Blues Legends*, and his own 2000 book, *Chicago Blues as Seen from the Inside*. The collection of backstage images captured musical life in the Trianon Ballroom and the Fickle Pickle, Mandel Hall, Smitty's bar, Robert's Show Lounge, and some two dozen other Chicago blues hubs of the 1960s.

"The pictures take your breath away," Cowdery said.

Val Wilmer, a photojournalist at *DownBeat* magazine, wrote years later of Flerlage's "moody action shots" that were "so full of atmosphere and so full of the blues."

Flerlage joked with Cowdery that the atmosphere largely was smoke from the musicians' cigarettes.

"He once made a crack to me that he wouldn't be any good anymore because people don't smoke enough anymore," Cowdery said.

Flerlage often felt that success late in his career was a fluke in a life lived on the brink of failure.

He was born in Cincinnati and grew up listening to his parents' records. He counted a professor's gift of seventy-eight-rpm orchestra records among the greatest things to have happened to him while at the University of Cincinnati, and his later career veered in and out of writing music reviews, lecturing on folk music, and running album distributorships.

From time to time, he took pictures for album covers and music magazines. He was often on the verge of bankruptcy.

"The record business supported me and, in the end, almost ruined me," he wrote in the foreword to *Chicago Blues.*

But photography often paid less, he wrote. The irony that he would be remembered for pictures taken when most professional Chicago photographers were too busy to cover the city's blues scene was not lost on him.

He had moved to Chicago in 1944 to sell auto insurance and lecture on folk music and later returned to record distributing. He didn't take on his first professional photo assignment until 1959.

Though he retired from distributing records in 1984, Flerlage always regarded his time photographing blues musicians as the most productive portion of his career.

"I am most grateful," he wrote in his book. "I was lucky in the long run."

Flerlage is survived by his wife of thirty-six years, Luise; four daughters, Kristin Laxar-Landell, Karen Parker, Linda Davidson, and Ty Reynolds; two sons, Anthony Nichols and William; twenty-five grandchildren; twelve great-grandchildren; and three great-great-grandchildren.

XVII

Dancers

With the music in place, the dancers were inevitable. Dance halls boomed, and dance troupes thrived. But it was the personalities of Chicago's dancers that we remembered, the thoughts traced in the air, thumped into the floor, and left to echo in our minds.

SATURDAY, NOVEMBER 18, 2000

Jimmy Payne Sr., Ninety-Five; Master of Tap Dancing
By James Janega, *Tribune* Staff Reporter

Jimmy Payne Sr., ninety-five, a master Chicago tap dancer whose precise steps, shuffle-hops, and flaps could electrify and mesmerize, whose expertise was sought by the city's top hoofers, and whose sense of rhythm could thrill a skilled Afro-Cuban drummer, died of natural causes Monday, November 13, in Trinity Hospital.

His strength was his precision: where other tap dancers would leap or flip, Payne directed his energy into the floor.

"He didn't want sloppy steps. If you had to do a shuffle-hop, step, flap, you had to do a shuffle-hop, step, flap," said his son Mark. "If there was a shuffle-hop, step to be done, he did it precisely."

When Payne danced, the onetime Afro-Cuban drummer sounded like a drum himself.

"Badda-doom-BOP, ba-doot doom-BOP! That's where he got the rhythms," said Jimmy Payne Jr., who followed his father into the dance business. "A lot of people had the showiness to them, but my dad, he was more of a rhythm dancer. Every step he did, he said, 'Make sure that means something.'"

That mastery of rhythm and technique, combined with the elder Payne's cheerful forbearance, was a passport to top-drawer access in Brooklyn even before he moved to Chicago and a studio career here in the 1940s. Lena Horne, June Allyson, Gregory Hines, Bob Fosse, and Jane Goldberg all either worked with him or studied under him.

An old-time performer who saw dancing as a polished combination of flawless steps, immaculate appearance, and not a little versatility, his teaching style was decidedly grounded in the basics: he boiled down every bit of tap dancing he knew into three exercises, his sons said. After that, he figured a student could pretty much do the rest on their own.

The son of a Cuban mother and Barbadian father, Payne grew up in the Panama Canal Zone and moved to New York City in 1917. Already an accomplished drummer, he studied tap, jazz, and modern dance with Billy Pierce, Edith la Sylphe, and Hemsly Winfield, and started performing and teaching himself by the nineties.

Married briefly in the 1940s, he came to Chicago in 1947, bringing the then wildly popular stylings of African and Afro-Cuban drumming and dancing with him. From the 1950s into the 1970s, he taught from a series of dance studios in the Loop and then continued to teach many of the city's most accomplished dancers until a series of strokes slowed him down in his early nineties.

"He was it for Chicago, basically. It seemed like he had just been around forever," said Nila Barnes, representative for the International Tap Association. Everyone, she said, seemed to have studied with him at one point or another.

"He spent his lifetime teaching and tapping and passing it on," said Gail Kalver, executive director of the Hubbard Street Dance Co. "Even tap dancers who were working in town would go see him to tap with him, or else ask him to guest star with them."

A patient perfectionist, Payne tried to spread his love of dance to anyone willing to take up the challenge of rehearsing the same step over and over until it was flawless—and then accept his call to find a new way to do it. Payne felt everybody needed their own style,

his sons said.

And Payne could hardly have had it any other way, said Jimmy Payne Jr.: dancing to him was just about the same as talking.

"You felt that every step he did had a meaning," the son said. "People could feel it and understand it."

Payne is also survived by his second wife, Elnada; two other sons, Jeff and Byron; seven daughters, Michelle, Bonita, Sandy, Tammy, Patricia, Colette, and Sara; a brother, Merrold; and two sisters, Olga Stewart and Olive Elliston.

OCTOBER 26, 2004

Patrick J. Roche, Ninety-Nine; "Put Irish Dancing on the Map"
By Barbara Sherlock, *Tribune* Staff Reporter

Patrick J. Roche's story has all the romance hoped for in any Irish tale.

It is of a boy raised with his nine siblings in a thatched cottage in a small Irish village who meets an Irish dance master, serves with the Irish Republican Army, then—wearing a new suit and carrying his meager savings—comes to America, where he becomes a legend.

"Pat Roche is the single most influential person in Irish dancing in this country," said Mark Howard, founder of the Trinity Dance Co. and the Trinity Academy of Irish Dance, a Chicago school that is the largest of its kind in the world. "Everything stems from him . . . he is the Christopher Columbus of Irish dancing."

Roche, ninety-nine, died of complications from pneumonia Sunday,

October 24, in the Glenview Terrace Nursing Center in Glenview. The former Chicago resident was dance master, founder, and president of the Roche School of Irish Dancing; host of an Irish radio show; and former editor of the *American Gael* newspaper.

"No matter where I travel his name is the most frequently uttered name in Irish dancing, and he appears to have taught everybody and their grandchildren," said Howard. His teachers, Marge and Dennis Dennehy, were Roche's students. They also taught Michael Flatley.

When Roche was seven, traveling dance master Michael Hennessy visited his small farming village of Doonaha.

Roche became his student. And over two years inside a defunct creamery, he learned every jig, reel, and hornpipe

Hennessy knew. Roche eventually developed his own signature style of dancing and teaching that relied on a system in which steps were counted as in a musical score.

During Ireland's war of independence, fought in the 1920s, Roche served as a dispatcher for the Irish Republican Army.

In 1925 he immigrated to New York, and then five years later he moved to Chicago where for three years he ran a grocery business selling eggs and butter door-to-door. At the same time, he opened his school, teaching Irish dance at numerous venues throughout the city.

For Chicago's World's Fair in 1933 and 1934, Roche organized shows of Irish music and dance and founded the Harp and Shamrock Ceili Band, the first ceili, or dance, band in the country.

"And the rest was history," said his daughter Peggy Boyle, who, like her father, is a dance master certified by the An Coimisiun Le Rinci Gaelacha in Dublin.

Decca Records approached Roche's band to make a record. With a microphone at his feet, he performed the set dances "Blackbird" and "Garden of Daisies" on a table as the band performed. It was the first recording of an Irish dancer.

"My father put Irish dancing on the map here," Boyle said. In 1945 he introduced the first Irish dance competition, called a feis, to the Midwest. Three years ago, Howard began a Pat Roche Feis in his honor.

While running his school, Roche held two full-time jobs as an operating engineer, one at Cook County Hospital, the other with the Chicago Board of Education. He also had a radio show.

His first wife, Kathleen, died in 1948. The following year he married his second wife, Grace.

Besides his daughter, he is survived by his wife; three other daughters, Kathleen McDonnell, Mary Pat Kulak, and Colette McGrath; four sons, Patrick Jr., John, Kevin, and Michael; twenty-six grandchildren; and fourteen great-grandchildren.

XVIII

Restaurateurs

In Chicago, dining could be like theater. It was home to Chez Paul, where maitre d' Jean-Pierre Sire embodied tuxedoed regality. And to MaeJuel Riley Riccardo Allen, a newspaper columnist who married two of Chicago's most famous restaurateurs. (Ric Riccardo claimed to have invented Chicago-style pizza; Bill Allen ran a nightclub so small it had to be exclusive.)

Were it not for a bad batch of cantaloupes at Eli Schulman's restaurant in 1977, Schulman might not have experimented with the dessert recipe that gave the world Eli's Cheesecake.

Over the years, the city's contributions to cuisine have become world-renowned because of the characters who created them.

SUNDAY, MAY 8, 1988

Eli Schulman, Seventy-Eight; Chicago Restaurateur

By Rick Kogan, *Tribune* Staff Reporter

Eli Schulman, a poor West Side kid who became one of the city's most colorful and influential personalities, died Saturday morning in his Near North Side apartment, apparently of a heart attack. He was seventy-eight.

To most, he was known as a restaurateur. But Eli's The Place for Steak on East Chicago Avenue was no ordinary restaurant. It was a gathering place for luminaries from the worlds of sports, show business, and politics—especially politics—drawn as much by the food as by the personality of the owner.

He was no ordinary man. A high-school dropout, he gave lectures in finance at DePaul University and large amounts of money to such organizations as the Community Assistance for Secondary Education, which provides scholarships for Israeli students, and the Juvenile Diabetes Foundation. A former Democratic precinct captain, he helped elect a Republican governor.

Equally conversant with machine politics or the vagaries of the ponies, he was an enthralling storyteller. Though the center of a star-studded milieu, he clung firmly to the simple values of friendship and honesty. He was a Chicago original.

"He is the nicest man to walk the face of this earth," said U.S. Atty. Anton Valukas.

"To know this man is to love him," said Chicago Bears coach and restaurant owner Mike Ditka.

But even those who did not know him personally knew his name, thanks to the success of Eli's Chicago's Finest Cheesecake, a dessert he invented a decade ago and one that has grown into an $8 million company that spreads his name into more than thirty states.

The man who proudly wore a watch given to him by Frank Sinatra and who could count such people as Jack Brickhouse, Irv Kupcinet, George Dunne, Ingrid Bergman, Joe DiMaggio, and virtually every Chicago "name" among his friends and admirers was born in Chicago in 1910 and reared in the Greater Lawndale area on the city's West Side.

His father, who owned a bakery on Roosevelt Road, died in 1927, and Schulman was forced to leave Marshall High School. He sold newspapers and delivered packages, hawked 10¢ windup toys on street corners in the winter, and sold scorecards and seat cushions at the ballparks in the summer. He was the manager of a shoe store. He sold women's dresses.

In 1934 he became a precinct captain in the Twenty-Second Ward, a job he compared to that of a "social worker . . . And on election days I used to climb so many stairs I thought I'd get to shake hands with God." He was a precinct captain for twenty-five years and was deputy coroner from 1948 to 1952.

"I never thought of politics as a career," Schulman said. "I wanted to be a businessman, like Hershey or Wrigley. Politics was just a hobby."

Schulman entered the restaurant business—"I'd never cracked an egg in my life"—shortly before World War II, opening the Ogden Huddle, at Ogden and Kedzie Avenues.

Schulman's charitable ways began in earnest on Pearl Harbor Day, when he put a pair of signs in his window: "25 percent discount for men in uniform," and "If you are hungry and don't have any money, come in and we'll feed you free."

He served in the army as a mess sergeant, and shortly after his return he married the former Esther Nettis and opened a grill at Sheridan Road and Argyle Street. In 1958 he opened Eli's Stage Deli on Oak Street, and it became a favorite haunt of both the Rush Street crowd and the Lake Shore Drive set. But even with the success of the Stage Deli, Schulman longed to be something more than "a salami surgeon . . . I wanted a white-tablecloth place."

In 1966 he got it, opening his current establishment in what was then a luxury hotel called the Carriage House.

From the beginning, Eli's was a mandatory stop for visiting stars such as Sinatra and Sammy Davis Jr. (who posed for photos with Eli on a recent visit), sports heroes such as Gale Sayers, and political powerhouses such as Dunne. Part of the reason was the food: a no-nonsense meat-and-potatoes menu, including the famous calf's liver, which came smothered in onions and green peppers.

And Schulman was always around, moving from table to table, chatting, joking, making friends. He took a special liking to a young federal attorney named Jim Thompson. He introduced the young lawyer to his powerful friends and prodded him to run for political office, even printing and distributing buttons that said, "Big Jim Can Get the Job Done."

"Eli is the man more responsible than any other for convincing me that I could be governor of this state," Thompson said at Schulman's seventy-sixth birthday.

It was in 1977 that Schulman came upon the idea that would bring him his greatest fame. It happened when a customer complained that the cantaloupe he had been served at Eli's "tasted like a potato." After weeks of experimentation, Schulman developed a recipe for a dessert that pleased everyone.

Eli's Chicago's Finest Cheesecake was the hit of the first and subsequent Tastes of Chicago, and was soon being produced for other restaurants and retail outlets. In 1984 his only son, Marc, left a career as a historic-preservation attorney to become president of the operation, housed in a North Side plant, and sales have grown steadily since.

Marc Schulman plans to continue with the operation of both the restaurant and the cheesecake company.

At the time of his death, Schulman was spending many late afternoons at the restaurant, reminiscing and philosophizing for a writer who was putting together a book about his life. A couple of months ago the writer asked Eli if he was amazed by how far he'd come.

"It's been the best and the worst. I've met so many people, made so many friends. But as you get older you start to see them drop off, like leaves from a tree, and it breaks your heart," he said. "But to have come from where I came from, to have known the people I've known . . . I'd have to say that I'm the luckiest man in the world."

In oberservance of his death, both Eli's The Place For Steak and the cheesecake plant closed for one day.

In addition to his son, Schulman is survived by his wife, Esther; two sisters, Bertha and Florence; and two granddaughters.

FRIDAY, MARCH 3, 2000

Jean-Pierre Sire, Fifty-Eight; Maître D'

By James Janega, *Tribune* Staff Reporter

Jean-Pierre Sire, the sandy-haired, genial maître d' of Chicago's Chez Paul restaurant for more than twenty-five years, who instructed a generation of the city's best waiters on how to serve and recommend food in a way that made patrons feel pampered, died Friday, February 25, in St. Francis Hospital in Evanston.

Sire, fifty-eight, of Edgewater, had been suffering from lung disease.

He grew up in Paris and Tours, working in restaurants owned by his parents and close family members. He was still working in restaurants as recently as two weeks ago, and his wife and friends said that when he socialized, it was usually at a bistro or café owned by one of his many friends in the business.

"He liked to eat," chuckled a friend, Joe Lane, who remembered Sire in an open-collared shirt and sport jacket.

"He liked the contact with people," said Sire's wife, Mocky.

Despite a penchant for casual conversation, travel, and occasionally competitive tennis and backgammon, at work Sire—tall, tuxedoed, and refined—cut the quintessential image of a French head waiter.

Even so, he strove to make dining out a relaxed experience, his wife said.

"He tried to get away from the stuffy maître d' approach," she said. "He was very easy-going, a very gentle man."

Still, he was unflappable in the often hectic atmosphere of popular, high-class eating places. Behind the scenes, he gently but carefully instructed waiters and captains in his charge on the preparation of dishes, which wines best complemented them, and how to answer questions from patrons unfamiliar with formal dining.

Five nights a week, often for ten hours or more, Sire smoothly set the example he wanted his staff to follow, friends said.

"He not only preached the walk, he

walked the walk. He was not a phony," said Christian Zeiger, a longtime friend and restaurant owner. "He had class, you know? He was soft-spoken but never looked down on people."

Sire was born in Paris in 1941. For two years in the early 1960s, he served as a radio operator for the French army in Algeria. Arriving in Chicago in 1965, he worked in a series of French restaurants here, including Chez Paul, where he headed the restaurant's dining rooms from 1970 until 1996. He was maître d' at the Everest Room downtown for the last three years.

In addition to his wife, Sire is survived by a son, Christian, and a daughter, Nicole.

MONDAY, FEBRUARY 12, 2001

Bill Allen, Seventy-Eight; Pallbearers Include a Grieving Bag Boy
By Bob Greene, *Tribune* Staff Reporter

Bill Allen had no college degrees in marketing, but on an August afternoon in 1976 I found out just how smart his promotional instincts were.

Allen—who died last week at seventy-eight—was a cofounder of the Treasure Island supermarket chain and went on to own the Gold Star Sardine Bar nightclub. It was in his role as a grocer that we met.

In the summer of 1976, Paul Galloway and I—then at the *Sun-Times*—decided to write a fictional serial for the paper. I made up a character whom I called Mike Holiday—a twenty-six-year-old graduate of the University of Illinois who decided to reject the success track and to work instead as a grocery store bag boy.

We called the serial "Bagtime" and populated it with real-life Chicagoans. The initial episodes of "Bagtime" concerned Mike's angst about his ex-wife's involvement in a bisexual thrill cult involving the Bears, the White Sox, and the waitresses from R.J. Grunts. (As you may have surmised, this was a somewhat different Chicago newspaper era.)

We had to have Mike Holiday work somewhere specific—so we said he was a bag boy at the Treasure Island supermarket on North Wells Street. We chose that grocery because it was where Galloway always shopped; Galloway lived in an apartment above That Steak Joynt, which was across the street from the Treasure Island, so we had Mike Holiday live there, too.

We didn't tell anyone at the Treasure Island that we were saying Mike Holiday worked there. We just wrote the first episode. This is how it began:

High noon Saturday, the Treasure Island on Wells Street. There's a line four-deep at the check-cashing machine, and a carton of raspberries has tipped over and turned one of the aisles bright red. We're busy. Which means I'm busy. I'm Mike Holiday. I'm a bag boy.

Some of the real-life Chicago celebrities who were featured in the first episodes of "Bagtime" called the paper to complain and say they didn't understand what this was all about. And Galloway and I wondered how long it would take for the owners of the Treasure Island to either protest or demand an explanation.

On the afternoon of the second day that "Bagtime" appeared, and we still had not heard a peep from the Treasure Island, Galloway called the store and, without identifying himself, said, "Is Mike Holiday there?"

The person who answered said, "Yes, he is."

This threw us. There was no Mike Holiday; we'd made him up.

Galloway said, "He's there?"

The person said, "Yes."

Galloway said, "Could I talk to him?"

The person said, "He's out on the floor right now. If you'd like to talk to him, come on in."

We sent a copyboy up to Wells Street. He came back to the city room laughing out loud.

Every bag boy at the Treasure Island was wearing a T-shirt that read: "I May Be Mike Holiday."

Bill Allen, whom we'd never heard of, had done it; he wasn't going to ask any questions about what this was about, and he certainly wasn't going to complain. He was going to ride this thing as far as it might take him. He had instructed all his employees to say that Mike Holiday was on the premises. He'd had the T-shirts rush-produced.

It was the start of some great times for the Treasure Island, and for us. Bill was smart enough to understand that when good luck blindsides you, run with it; he didn't know where this Mike Holiday had come from, but he was going to hop on board. We'd chosen his store on a whim; he was going to hitch his star to a bag boy who didn't really exist.

Last year I was in an airport in Ohio, and a man came up to me, introduced himself, and said he was an attorney. He said he wanted to thank me for some of the best times of his life.

"When I was younger, I worked as a bag boy at the Treasure Island," he said. "All these women would come in looking for Mike Holiday. They'd ask me if I knew Mike. And I'd say, 'I am Mike Holiday.' Boy, did I have some great dates."

I wish Bill Allen could have hung on a little longer. Out of nowhere this winter, Galloway and I got a call saying that the executive producer of *The Drew Carey Show* has decided to shoot a pilot for a new half-hour comedy based on . . .

Yep. "Bagtime." All these years later, Mike Holiday lives. We don't know what's going to happen with this whole thing, but it would have been nice to hear Bill's laughter at the absurdity of it all. He knew it from the beginning: you can't keep a good bag boy down.

WEDNESDAY, OCTOBER 31, 2001

Bill Charuchas, Seventy-Five; Popular Short-Order Cook at Billy Goat's

By James Janega, *Tribune* Staff Reporter

Bill Charuchas, seventy-five, who flipped cheeseburgers, drank beer, and flirted with girls for thirty-seven years at the Billy Goat Tavern & Grille on Lower Michigan Avenue, died Tuesday, October 23, in his onetime hometown in Greece.

He had been visiting family members and died of a gallbladder infection, said his longtime friend Sam Sianis, who owns the tavern.

Charuchas had as much to do with the Billy Goat's mystique as his more famous compatriots in the Sianis family. Though the tavern was owned by the late William "Billy Goat" Sianis and then his nephew Sam, Charuchas "was not like a worker—it's like he owned the place," Sam Sianis said.

Though the tavern's "Cheezborger, cheezborger! No fries, cheeps!" refrain was famous, Sianis said Charuchas coined the no-less-frequently shouted suggestion: "Try the double-cheese! It's the best!"

Among the people who sampled Charuchas' cheeseburgers and double-cheeseburgers were Illinois governors James Thompson, Jim Edgar, and George Ryan; former president George H. W. Bush; Chicago mayors Richard J. and Richard M. Daley; several visiting movie stars; and innumerable patrons eager to buy into what had become a Chicago legend.

From behind his linoleum counter, Charuchas shouted out orders and sped them off the grill so quickly that he usually had time to visit the Billy Goat's patrons before they finished their meals.

At a tavern that boasts a family atmosphere, Charuchas ensured the lunchtime throngs were not disappointed. He doled out free bags of potato chips to children and paper hats to young women and visiting police officers, danced with whomever would let him, and opened thousands of conversations by asking, "Where from?"

"He enjoyed being here all those hours—not only because he was a good worker, but because he liked the people," Sianis said. "He had a lot of fun. He was always telling me about the people who came from other states."

Charuchas left his family's farm in Greece for the United States in 1954 and worked for the next ten years at a small hamburger stand on Lower Michigan Avenue across the street from the Billy Goat's current location.

He went to work for William "Billy Goat" Sianis in 1964 and became a day-shift fixture at his bar, usually working six or seven days a week.

In the course of his tenure at the Billy Goat, Sianis figured Charuchas had served more than 3 million customers. According to another calculation—this one done by a group of young female patrons—Charuchas had consumed more than one hundred thousand beers at the Billy Goat, a figure of which Charuchas was proud, Sianis said.

"All of a sudden, the girls pick him up on their shoulders and are shouting 'He's the champion! He's the champion!'

Billy drank more beers than anyone else they knew," Sianis said. "He was the champion. He was the champion of everything."

Charuchas is survived by his wife, Joan; a sister, Georgia Kostopoulos; and two brothers, George and Gus.

FRIDAY, JUNE 7, 2002

MaeJuel Riley Riccardo Allen, Eighty-Six; Adventure Lover Kept Sharp Wit, Kind Heart
By Rick Kogan, *Tribune* Staff Reporter

A legendary wit and beauty, MaeJuel Riley Riccardo Allen, who was always referred to as Jill, was a personality big enough to hold her own as the wife of two of Chicago's most flamboyant and charismatic characters: the late restaurateur Ric Riccardo Sr. and businessman–nightclub impresario Bill Allen.

A lifelong resident of the Chicago area, Allen, eighty-six, died Sunday, June 2, in Lexington, Kentucky, after a series of strokes.

The daughter of the late Clyde Whitcomb and Mable Reed Riley, Allen grew up on Lake Shore Drive and attended the Starrett School. She was married four times and had successful careers as an interior decorator and syndicated newspaper columnist.

"She was an awesome woman," said her daughter, Jill Riccardo Begley. "She loved to hunt, to have fun, to experience all of life's adventures. She was so often referred to as the wife of two famous men, but she was certainly their

equal and their better in many ways."

She first met Riccardo in 1940 when she walked in the door of his Riccardo's Restaurant & Gallery at Rush and Hubbard Streets.

"Where do I sit?" she asked.

"On the floor!" said Riccardo, who opened the restaurant in 1934.

They were married a year later, and in attendance were the sixty-four waiters and waitresses, cooks, and bartenders who worked at the restaurant. The couple had a daughter in 1943 and named her Russia. (One of their dogs was named Stalin.)

"The countries were allies then, but by the time I was about seven, I decided to change my name and took my mother's name as my own," Begley said.

After divorcing Riccardo in 1949, Allen remained a frequent visitor to the restaurant. Indeed, on the night it closed in 1995 (it has since reopened as Phil Stefani's 437 Rush), she sat in one of the booths with friends and recalled games played on the boccie court that was once in the basement, lion steaks served for selected friends after she and Riccardo returned from a safari, and a private room just off the main entrance called The Padded Cell.

Allen married William J. Allen in 1964, around the time he was cofounding the Treasure Island chain of grocery stores. From 1983 to 1997 he ran the Gold Star Sardine Bar on Lake Shore Drive, a sliver of a saloon that he made world famous by hiring such big-room acts as Liza Minnelli, Tony Bennett, and Bobby Short to perform there. One of the place's special features was a small private box, and it was there that one would often see Mrs. Allen sitting alone, luminous into the late musical nights.

After her husband died in 1997, Allen continued to live in their Lake Forest home until ill health necessitated her move to a Lexington hospice near her daughter and family.

In addition to her daughter, survivors include a grandson.

XIX

They Broadened Our Minds

Hans Guterbock's life's work comprised nearly all of modern man's knowledge of Hittite life. Wallace Bacon managed to bring Shakespeare's work to life for students on the stage. Chicago scholars opened schools and opened the world's eyes, whether they worked with Hittite texts, Eskimo hunters, or Shakespearean tomes.

SATURDAY, APRIL 1, 2000

Hans Gustav Guterbock, Ninety-One; Hittite Society Scholar
By James Janega, *Tribune* Staff Reporter

Hans Gustav Guterbock, ninety-one, the University of Chicago Oriental Institute scholar whose life's work comprised nearly the entirety of modern knowledge of Hittite society, language, and culture, died Wednesday, March 29, after collapsing in his Hyde Park home.

Just hours before he died, Guterbock had been consulting with a colleague on the translation of two troublesome Hittite phrases.

The colleague, Harry Hoffner, coedited with Guterbock *The Hittite Dictionary of the Oriental Institute*, a more than twenty-five-year collaboration containing comprehensive contextual and social meanings of Hittite words and phrases. The book was the capstone of Guterbock's lifelong study of Hittite culture.

His interest began in Germany in the 1930s and included twelve years as a professor of Hittitology in Turkey, the homeland of the Hittites around 1600 BC, a period coinciding with nearby civilizations in Assyria, Babylonia, and Egypt.

But since 1949 Guterbock worked and published at the Oriental Institute, bringing a holistic approach to his study that is rare in academia.

"To him, it was the whole gamut, and he wanted to pursue the evidence for that wherever it was," said Gene Gragg, director of the Oriental Institute.

Rather than concentrate on the minutiae of a single field, Guterbock let his mind romp through the disciplines of archaeology, philology, and art history, translating his findings into a remarkably complete picture of Hittite civilization.

"Nobody else will ever quite replicate that," said Gragg.

His interests came forth in his writings: "The Vocative in Hittite," "Musical Notation in Ugarit," "Hittite Hieroglyphic Seal Impressions," and "Sargon of Akkad Mentioned by Hattusili I of Hatti." There were at least 112 publications in all.

"That was his first love. It was work, work, work. Hittite, Hittite," said his wife of sixty years, Frances.

He was a formal man who wore dark suits and tailored shirts, omitting a tie from his ensemble only while at home. He wrapped himself in intellectual ardor like a cloak and was someone whose anger flared to life when confronted by foolishness.

"He didn't suffer fools lightly," his wife said.

But his mind was exhaustive, said colleagues, a veritable library that Guterbock drew upon even though eye problems left him almost blind for the last fifteen years.

"From memory, he would be able to tell colleagues reading to him which citations were not as good as others," Gragg said.

Guterbock was born into the Jewish elite in Berlin. His father was the secretary of a noted German archeological society, and his mother was a novelist.

He pursued Near Eastern studies at his father's urging, and, unable to find an academic position in Germany under Hitler's anti-Jewish laws, was persuaded by Turkish acquaintances to seek a university teaching position in Ankara.

From 1936 until 1948, he was a professor of Hittitology in Turkey at what would become Ankara University. Following a stint as a guest lecturer in Sweden, he arrived at the Oriental Institute in 1949, attained a full professorship in 1956, and was named Tiffany and Margaret Blake Distinguished Service Professor in 1969. He had been a professor emeritus since 1976.

Though his interests in the Hittites were broad, his most ambitious work was the dictionary, a project still unfinished. With Hoffner, Guterbock reconstructed everyday life from formal documents, slowly making sense of a language not heard for 3,500 years.

Besides his wife, Guterbock is survived by two sons, Thomas and Walter; five grandchildren; and a great-granddaughter.

WEDNESDAY, SEPTEMBER 6, 2000

Sister Candida Lund, Seventy-Nine; College Chancellor
By James Janega, *Tribune* Staff Reporter

Sister Candida Lund, seventy-nine, the chancellor of Dominican University and a giant in the local arts community whose influence brought luminaries from Jessye Norman to Sherrill Milnes to perform in concerts at the university's River Forest campus, died of cancer Monday, September 4, in Northwestern Memorial Hospital.

Sister Candida traveled the world, met heads of state, and could call on dozens of artists, musicians, and writers as friends. She often lunched with Lady Valerie Solti, widow of the Chicago Symphony Orchestra's Sir Georg; on visits to Ireland, she spent time with the family of Irish playwright Brian Friel. The Lyric Opera's Danny Newman called her "a real impresario," while *Ebony* editor Lerone Bennett Jr. once called her a national treasure.

She also held a Ph.D. in political science from the University of Chicago and could boast an impressive list of accomplishments as head of Dominican University. But she was perhaps best known for spearheading the university's annual Trustee Benefit Concert, which brought some of the world's best performers to an intimate setting unequaled anywhere else.

"I personally do not see a call to religious life excluding any activity that helps to promote a love of the arts, an elevation of the mind, an elevation of the soul," she told the *Tribune* in 1997.

Still, she said her mother cried when the twenty-three-year-old graduate of Rosary College pronounced over lunch in the Walnut Room at Marshall Field's that she was going to become a Dominican nun.

Raised in Hyde Park, Sister Candida graduated from Rosary College with a bachelor's in political science in 1942 (it was renamed Dominican University two years ago) and spent the next two years working for then treasury secretary Henry Morgenthau. After joining the Sinsinawa Dominican order in 1944, she received a master's degree in political science from Catholic University in Washington, D.C.

Though the early years of her religious vocation saw her teaching social studies in a Sioux Falls, South Dakota, high school, Sister Candida returned to Rosary College as dean of students in 1955. She became a professor and later chair of the Political Science Department, was appointed president in 1964, and became chancellor in 1981.

She instituted a sabbatical program for faculty, stepped up minority recruitment, and oversaw Rosary College's transition into a coed institution in 1970. When the nation wrestled with the Equal Rights Amendment, Sister Candida could be found promoting women's rights as a member of the Illinois Commission for the Status of Women. Numerous societies and fellowships have honored her achievements.

"She was really an extraordinary woman for her time, and our time," said Donna Carroll, president of Dominican University. "She was at once a very vital presence, and at the same time, she was a very humble woman true to her vocation. It was that ability to blend those two identities that gave her this extraordinary quality."

Tribune columnist Ann Landers called her life "exemplary."

"She was a delight to be with, had a wonderful sense of humor, and always managed to see the sunny side of life," said Landers. "She was just absolutely a pro in every sense of the word. She was always poised, but she was always very kind. That was Candy."

Intelligent and articulate, Sister Candida likewise cut a dignified figure and possessed a whimsical, creative appearance more typical of the divas and sculptors she knew than women of religious orders.

Last March, she told the *Tribune* she may have been better than anyone else in the world at "reaching for life with both hands." Earlier she described the greatest lesson of her life as "a constantly increased appreciation for life and its good things, and a steady appreciation of God's good gifts and the wonders of his world."

She said she counted friendship among them.

She is survived by a sister, Eleanor Lund Spitzig.

FRIDAY, FEBRUARY 16, 2001

Wallace A. Bacon, Eighty-Seven; Northwestern University Professor

By James Janega, *Tribune* Staff Reporter

Wallace A. Bacon, eighty-seven, a soft-spoken literary scholar who breathed life into Shakespearean characters and taught thousands of Northwestern University theater students how to face the slings and arrows of interpreting fictional characters for performance, died Saturday, February 10, in his Des Montes, New Mexico, home, of liver cancer.

Bacon founded what is now the Department of Performance Studies at Northwestern in 1955 and was an eminent interpreter of Shakespeare's writings.

He led what, for years, was one of the most sought-after courses in the university's theater curriculum. Formally titled "Interpretation of Shakespeare," it was better known to students as "Shake and Bake," in homage to the subject and instructor.

Unless performing, Bacon taught in a mesmerizing whisper, and his sympathetic personality attracted as many students as the course's ambitious target of reading and performing all of Shakespeare's plays in a year.

As a teacher, he seemed to have as much compassion for his legions of students as he did for the woeful and heroic characters in the plays he taught.

"He believed the study of literature drew one out of oneself, and that what you gained by acting in plays was a sense of the 'other,'" said Chicago stage director and former student Frank Galati. "You found out what it was like to stand in somebody else's shoes."

And Shakespeare, as Bacon often said, offered the best opportunities to do that.

"He held firm," said Chicago Shakespeare Theater artistic director Barbara Gaines, another former student, "that Shakespeare was the greatest humanist there ever was."

Born in Bad Axe, Michigan, and raised in Detroit, Bacon devoted his entire life to the study and teaching of literature, earning his bachelor's degree from Albion College and doctorate from the University of Michigan.

Already accustomed to deciphering literature, he proved adept at decoding Japanese communiqués for army intelligence during World War II. He was awarded the Legion of Merit for those efforts and returned to academia in 1946.

The next year, he was recruited by Northwestern, where the English department was looking for a scholar to lead graduate studies in a new area, still in the concept stage, to be called the Department of Interpretation. It was under way by 1955 and Bacon, a dignified man with an erect bearing, served as its chairman until retiring in 1977.

During that time, he wrote numerous

articles and well-received plays, as well as two oft-used texts: *Literature as Experience*, coauthored with Robert Breen in 1959, and the seminal *The Art of Interpretation*, published in 1966.

The national president of the Speech Communication Association in 1977, he took part in research and lecturing fellowships abroad, chiefly in Japan and the Philippines. His students include actress Laura Innes and Steppenwolf artistic director Martha Lavey.

"He set the intellectual tone for an entire generation of undergraduates and graduates," said Galati. "His students not only became actors and interpreters of the classics, but also professors of literature and poetry. It's almost impossible to imagine the reach of his spirit."

A world traveler fascinated in particular with the American Southwest, Bacon retired to New Mexico, where he lived in a stately adobe house nestled among pine trees.

Native American baskets and pottery battled for space in rooms lined with bookshelves that spilled into short stacks on every surface. His niece, Patricia Ziegele, said Bacon received a steady stream of former students in his retirement.

"The most important thing he was, was a humanist," said Gaines. "He was a curious man, insatiably curious. He tried to understand the human condition."

Bacon is also survived by a brother, Robert, and five other nieces and nephews.

TUESDAY, MARCH 6, 2001

James VanStone, Seventy-Five; Ex-Curator Was Expert on Arctic Cultures
By James Janega, *Tribune* Staff Reporter

Rarely in this modern era can someone make a career of trailing arctic explorers, living among Eskimos, and assiduously recording their tribal tattoos, clothing, and native history, and it was with a certain sense of getting away with something that James W. VanStone, a former curator of the Field Museum, applied his craft.

A past chairman of the museum's anthropology department and an authority on arctic and subarctic native cultures, VanStone, seventy-five, died of heart failure Wednesday, February 28, in Evanston Hospital.

VanStone, a self-deprecating and contemplative man with a dry sense of humor, wrote more than 140 publications, including forty books and monographs, detailing North American life near the Arctic Circle. He offered glimpses of this frigid world to visitors of the Maritime People of the Arctic and Northwest Coast exhibit at the Field Museum and lectured on it in Chicago and elsewhere.

"Most people have a very poor notion of what the North is like," he

James VanStone, a former curator of the Field Museum, was one of the first arctic researchers to combine ethnology, the study of living cultures, with archaeology.

explained during a panel discussion at the Newberry Library in October of 2000. "They think of it as a dark, dismal place covered with ice."

For VanStone, the region was filled with eggshell-colored plains breathtaking in their austerity, towering dark cliffs, and native people who could get so chatty sometimes, "I almost couldn't get my work done."

"He really was solidly devoted to his subject, kind of one of your classic, old-fashioned academics," said Ben Bronson, curator of Asian anthropology at the Field Museum. "Even his private life was pretty much focused on his work."

Born in Chicago, VanStone grew up in Cleveland and attended Oberlin College. Smitten with archaeology as a teen, he pursued it as diligently as a student could at Oberlin, a small school with only one archaeology professor at the time. In a lonely course of study that may have prepared him well for the months of solitary research above the Arctic Circle later in his career, VanStone graduated in 1948, though his bachelor's degree was in art history, the closest major to archaeology offered at Oberlin then.

He did his graduate work in archaeology at the University of Pennsylvania and focused on ancient arctic and subarctic cultures in Alaska. By the time he completed his doctorate work in 1954, he had already spent a handful of years on the faculty of the University of Alaska. He had also changed the direction of his study.

"When he went to Alaska, he realized the people who were living there had the same traditions they'd had for thousands of years," said Jessica Rooney, who, with Field Museum associate curator Chapurukha Kusimba, is writing a biography of VanStone. "He realized you could learn a lot both by the way people are now and from their remains and artifacts."

Remaining in Alaska until 1958, he was one of the first arctic researchers to combine ethnology—the study of living cultures—with archaeology. Most of the others were prospecting around the Bering Strait, searching for archaeological evidence of human migration into North America via the former Bering land bridge, a recently proven concept.

VanStone taught at the University of Toronto from 1959 to 1966, when he joined the Field Museum as an associate curator of North American archaeology and ethnology. Later named a full curator, he held the title until his retirement in 1993. He was chairman of the museum's anthropology department from 1971 to 1974 and taught courses at Northwestern University and the University of Chicago.

He was a prolific and self-critical writer who was never satisfied with the amount of work he released into the flow of scholarly information, Rooney said. Nevertheless, his writings, which were uncommonly detailed and sympathetic to their subjects, were so well regarded that they were kept as reference books by academics and Native American authorities, Bronson said.

"There's probably no other writer in modern times who has written as much or as authoritatively," he said.

Since the 1950s VanStone's articles have cataloged, among other things, the distinctiveness of Athapaskan clothing, the coastal Alaskan explorations of Russian explorers, the material culture of Alaskan Eskimos, and the social history of remote places such as the Nushagak and Yukon River regions and the Davis Inlet.

The associate editor of *Arctic Anthropology* from 1961 to 1989, VanStone also founded *Anthropological Papers of the University of Alaska* in 1952, served as the journal's editor until 1957, and remained a consulting editor until 1967. At the Field Museum, he was the scientific editor of *Fieldiana*, the museum's scientific publication. He had published more than half a dozen articles in his retirement and was working on another manuscript when he died, Rooney said.

VanStone is survived by a sister, Suzanne VanStone Stambaugh; two nephews, Russell J. Stambaugh Jr. and Michael N. Stambaugh; and two nieces, Deborah S. Steinmeyer and Jennifer Voorhees.

Witnesses to Chicago History

Meet the batboy at the first All-Star Game, who died at age 84. And the vegetable vendor whose truck was the last thing standing after race riots left the West Side smoldering in 1968. And the young woman who witnessed the sinking of the steamship *Eastland* in the Chicago River in 1915 (she died at age 106 in 1999). And the man who helped to create the modern suburb, the state of Israel, and the idea of public housing.

History, it seems, was lived one life at a time.

SUNDAY, OCTOBER 11, 1998

John McBride, Eighty-Four; Batboy at the First All-Star Game

By Meg McSherry Breslin, *Tribune* Staff Reporter

John McBride, a White Sox batboy who was possibly the last living member from the game's first All-Star team in 1933, died Thursday following a heart attack in Memorial Medical Center in Woodstock. McBride, eighty-four, lived in Woodstock and was a former resident of Chicago and Evergreen Park.

While a young boy growing up just a few blocks from Comiskey Park, McBride would collect discarded bottles at the park in exchange for entry to the next day's game. By age ten, he sold seat cushions and, as he recalled, shamed plenty of men into buying them for their dates.

By the time McBride reached fourteen, the White Sox clubhouse manager knew him well enough to ask him to be a batboy. McBride was thrilled at the opportunity, even though the job wasn't salaried. Instead, his payment was a ball that had been played that day, which he promptly had autographed and sold for as much as $5, a hefty sum for a teenager during the Depression.

One of the highlights of McBride's career as a batboy came in 1933, while the Century of Progress World's Fair was in full swing. It was the first-ever All-Star Game and the first time so many great players had been gathered together on the same field. Among the stars were Babe Ruth, Lou Gehrig, Gabby Hartnett, Al Simmons, and Jimmie Foxx.

On that summer day in July at Comiskey Park, McBride had a feeling something big was about to happen. Just as Ruth came to the plate, McBride positioned himself to greet him if he hit a home run. Ruth did so, with a drive into the right-field stands, and McBride was right there at home plate to shake his hand, with Gehrig standing at his side.

"Nice goin', Babe," McBride said.

"Thanks, kid," Ruth replied, as McBride recalled.

To cap off the moment for McBride, a *Tribune* photographer captured the handshake, and the picture ran in the next day's paper. Later, the photographer gave McBride the negative. The batboy then had Ruth and Gehrig sign it, and the enlarged photograph became his prized possession for years.

"We've had it forever, and he's given lots of copies to friends," said McBride's daughter Alana McBride-Piech.

McBride, a batboy for the Sox from 1929 to 1934, loved to share stories from his Sox days years later. He was featured in numerous newspaper articles and was interviewed by several radio and television stations.

He said the All-Star Game—which turned into a 4–2 American League victory—remained etched in his memory for years.

"The Babe was quite a guy," McBride once told the *Tribune*. "He was the originator of the standing ovation. Mr. Baseball. He had a very nice personality and was very obliging with autographs. When he hit that home run, it was the most electrifying thing I ever saw in my life."

After his batboy fame, McBride went on to a career as a painter and interior decorator. He spent many years working in the Field building on South LaSalle Street and later as a painter for Ford City Shopping Center. While raising five children in Evergreen Park, baseball remained his favorite pastime.

After he retired at sixty-five, McBride became locally famous in his Woodstock neighborhood for a most unusual talent: pie baking.

Each fall, he baked dozens of pies for friends and neighbors in Woodstock and then delivered them personally.

In 1987 McBride won first prize for his peach pie and second prize for his apple pie in a contest at the McHenry County Fair.

Although baseball and pie baking were always loves of McBride's, his daughter said he was most proud of his fifty-six-year marriage to his wife, Dorothy.

Other survivors include two other daughters, Laura Kubaszko and Maureen McBride; two sons, Timothy and John Terrence; seven grandchildren; and four great-grandchildren.

FRIDAY, OCTOBER 30, 1998

Dustin Nickel, Three and a Half; Unique Child
By Meg McSherry Breslin, *Tribune* Staff Reporter

Little Dustin Nickel's fight is over. The three-and-a-half-year-old boy with big brown eyes whose catastrophic birth defects prompted the city of Lockport to rally around him died Wednesday in his home. Family members said his bodily functions simply failed.

But as sad as Dustin's short life may seem, it provided some unforgettable lessons about the nature of love. Born missing the parts of his brain that control cognitive ability, motor skills, vision, hearing, and the digestive system, Dustin required constant attention and medical care from his mother and father, Karen and Michael Nickel.

For nearly two years, his parents took shifts sleeping because they didn't know when their son woke up or fell asleep simply by looking at him. Their home became a small medical office, complete with a wide assortment of machines and medications to serve their son.

Yet despite the enormous stress the couple faced in caring for him around the clock, the Nickels focused more on the blessings their special son provided.

"We were lucky to have him even for this long," his mother said. "He

Karen Nickel with her son Dustin in a 1997 *Tribune* file photograph.

taught us patience, and I think he made me strong . . . You just couldn't help but love that little boy."

"There's just so many little things you learn from him," his father said. "Unlimited patience is one. . . . Neither of us would ever trade a minute of it, the good and the bad."

Throughout his short life, Dustin never really developed a personality of his own, his parents said. Most of the time, he simply would lie on his parents' lap or a couch, looking up at the ceiling. He also required numerous medications for pain control and suffered from seizures and poor motor control, which sometimes made him difficult to hold.

There never was an explanation for the birth defects. The problem in Dustin's brain was unique, making the couple's struggle sometimes lonely and frustrating.

Community and family support helped boost the spirits of the couple. After his story first appeared in the *Tribune*, Lockport town officials held a fund-raiser for the family, and members of the couple's church cooked meals for the family a few days a week. In recent months, regular nursing care was provided so the couple could get a short break or a much-needed nap.

"It was an overwhelming feeling," Michael Nickel said of the community's response to their son's illness. "You just feel so much gratitude when you realize there are people out there to help."

And in the latter part of Dustin's life, the couple saw small signs of hope. Dustin seemed to recognize their voices better, and he especially enjoyed his nightly baths with his father. His mother insists he was a "daddy's boy."

"Every night he'd sit up on my lap and I'd just keep telling him over and over, lift your head up, and he'd struggle and strain to get halfway up," Michael Nickel said. "That was a high point."

Before Dustin was two, his mother sent letters to more than 200 people and organizations for the disabled in hopes of finding someone who could help explain his disability. The mystery was never solved, but the quest became less and less important.

For many people touched by Dustin's life, there were unexpected things to learn about life.

"This was a very, very devoted family with a very difficult child to take care of, and they did a wonderful job in caring for him," said Jerold Stirling, an assistant professor of pediatrics at Loyola University Medical Center and one of Dustin's doctors.

In addition to his parents, Dustin is survived by his brother, Jason Brula; four sisters, Patricia Gregory, Michelle Nickel, Cynthia Nickel, and Christine Nickel; grandparents Natalie Bradford, Dudley Burkland, and Richard and Elaine Nickel; and great-grandparents Leon and Nancy Zak.

SATURDAY, DECEMBER 19, 1998

Leonard Rieser, Seventy-Six; Keeper of Doomsday Clock
By Meg McSherry Breslin, *Tribune* Staff Reporter

Leonard M. Rieser, a physicist who took part in the Manhattan Project to create the atomic bomb and later became a leading voice on peaceful alternatives to nuclear war, died Tuesday of cancer in Dartmouth-Hitchcock Medical Center in New Hampshire. A resident of Norwich, Vermont, he was seventy-six.

Rieser became well known nationally as the chairman of the board of the *Bulletin of the Atomic Scientists*, a magazine founded in Chicago in 1945 to prevent nuclear war by providing valuable information to policy makers.

Since 1985 Rieser has been the keeper of the *Bulletin*'s symbolic Doomsday Clock, moving its minute hand closer or farther away from midnight based on the threat of nuclear annihilation.

He also earned a national reputation in scientific, academic, and policy circles for his role as past provost of Dartmouth University, as president and chairman of the board of the American Association for the Advancement of Science from 1972 through 1975, and as the chairman of the fellows selection committee for the John D. and Catherine T. MacArthur Foundation, responsible for overseeing the foundation's prestigious "genius" grants for exceptionally creative people.

Friends and colleagues said Rieser was an extraordinary leader who was extremely intellectual and socially conscious, but also quietly humorous and engaging. He became well known in his Vermont hometown for owning a pet donkey and amused elementary school students in his children's school with physics tricks and gimmicks, including his electrified tie.

"It was this global/local connection that he had. Whether it was in Norwich, Vermont, or Los Alamos or the boardroom of the MacArthur Foundation or the boardroom of the *Bulletin*, he found a way to do what was needed at the time," said George Lopez, who succeeded Rieser as the *Bulletin*'s chairman. "He had a way of drawing from many of us our better selves, and that's pretty unique."

Adele Simmons, the MacArthur Foundation's outgoing president, sought out Rieser for the fellows selection post because of his creativity, good judgment, and skill in working with a diverse group of people.

"There were a lot of people a generation younger who view him as a mentor and a wise uncle in a way," Simmons said. "Just when you thought you had everything figured out, he'd come up with a question you hadn't thought of."

After earning his bachelor's degree in physics from the University of Chicago, Rieser was assigned by the U.S. Army to the Manhattan Project, first at the Metallurgical Laboratory in Chicago and then at the Los Alamos Laboratory in New Mexico, where he witnessed the first atomic-bomb explosion.

After the war ended, he continued working at Los Alamos as a research assistant and later earned his doctorate in physics from Stanford University. He became an instructor at Dartmouth in 1952 and rose through the ranks rapidly. In 1964 he began eighteen years of administrative service at Dartmouth, alternating between the positions of faculty dean and provost.

He was credited with overseeing major changes at Dartmouth, guiding the university through the shift to coeducation and a more diverse student body as well as a greater focus on research.

Though Rieser didn't regret his involvement in the Manhattan Project, he felt a social responsibility to educate the public about the real threat of nuclear arms, said his son Leonard.

"It had a huge impact on his thinking about science and the responsibility of scientists to help people understand what the right uses of science were," his son said. "I think having seen a test run, he had a very acute sense of what the potential was and how easy a nuclear disaster could be created. He was very concerned about that for the rest of his life."

Rieser also became heavily involved in promoting science education in his local community. He helped develop a local science museum in Vermont and often visited local schools to interest more students in science. The lessons, of course, also came at home with his children. "Our house was full of stuff the physics department had decided to get rid of and yet he saw alternative uses for—all sorts of bells and magnets and wires, test tubes and telescopes," his son said. "He was just always a very curious person."

Rieser is survived by his wife, Rosemary; a daughter, Abigail Rieser; two other sons, Timothy Rieser and Kenneth Willis; two brothers, Lawrence and William; and three granddaughters.

SATURDAY, JANUARY 9, 1999

Walter R. Woodbury, Sixty-Nine; Dairy CEO
By Bechetta Jackson, *Tribune* Staff Reporter

During his tenure as vice president and general manager of the former Hawthorn Mellody company, one of the largest dairies in the Midwest, Walter R. Woodbury made a decision that affected thousands of lives.

During a business meeting in Iowa, he saw piles of milk cartons with pictures of children who had disappeared while delivering newspapers in Des Moines. After returning to the Chicago area, Woodbury approached police here about starting a similar effort.

"He met with [then mayor] Harold Washington and police officials, and the idea was well received," recalled his wife, Eileen. "I think he just thought of it as a way of giving back to the community."

Woodbury, sixty-nine, a former Palatine resident whose goodwill gesture later was joined by other dairy companies across the nation, died Monday at his home in Oldsmar, Florida.

In 1985, the same year his company debuted the cartons containing the photos of missing Chicago-area children, Woodbury received a citation from President Ronald Reagan.

Born in Corona, New York, Woodbury graduated from the Maritime College at Ft. Schuyler in the Bronx. He worked for a naval engineering firm and later for Columbia Presbyterian Hospital in New York City.

Woodbury became a vice president of the Borden dairy division in New York City. He moved to the Chicago area to take a position at Hawthorn Mellody in the 1980s and worked his way up to president and chief executive officer before retiring in 1990.

In addition to his wife, survivors include three sons, Tim, Joe, and Mark; three daughters, Stephanie Spoor, Kim Redmond, and Cyndie; two brothers, Andy and Robby; a sister, Barbara LaGarenne; and fourteen grandchildren.

FRIDAY, JULY 2, 1999

Amelia S. Curin, 106; Witnessed Sinking of the *Eastland* in 1915

By James Janega, *Tribune* Staff Reporter

Amelia S. Curin, anticipating a nice Lake Michigan cruise, avoided becoming a casualty in a famous Chicago disaster when she got off the steamship *Eastland* before it capsized in the Chicago River in 1915, killing more than 800 people, including many friends and neighbors. Curin got off the boat because she thought the *Eastland*'s sister ship, docked nearby, looked more luxurious.

A thirty-six-year resident of Brookfield, who lived in the Pilsen neighborhood for decades before that, Curin died Wednesday at age 106 at the Lexington Health Care Center, La Grange.

Curin was born near the beginning of Grover Cleveland's presidency and watched eighteen administrations pass in her lifetime. A homemaker, she had little interest in politics until she began volunteering in local Brookfield races in 1977.

An employee of Western Electric when the *Eastland* capsized, Curin never forgot the events of that day, said her son, John.

"She got off the *Eastland* and went onto the *Roosevelt*, because she thought it was a nicer ship. And she watched the *Eastland* capsize. All the neighbors on her block and the blocks all around perished on the *Eastland*," her son said. A few years later, Curin married John J. Curin Sr.

Curin was active with the St. Barbara Senior Citizens Club in Brookfield and the St. Barbara Catholic Council of Women. The oldest of five children, Curin outlived her siblings despite the fact that she enjoyed eating hearty ethnic foods.

Curin lived by herself until she was 100, when she broke her wrist in a fall while mowing the lawn. Two years later, she broke her hip and moved in with her son. In 1997 she moved to the Lexington Health Care Center.

In addition to her son, Curin is survived by five grandchildren and six great-grandchildren.

SUNDAY, AUGUST 15, 1999

Philip Klutznick, Ninety-Two; Statesman, Developer Shaped Suburbia, City Skyline

By John McCarron and Anthony Burke Boylan, *Tribune* Staff Reporters. *Tribune* Staff Reporters Jennifer Vigil and Anthony Colarossi contributed to this report.

Philip Klutznick was a major force in building suburbs for veterans after World War II.

He did not invent the atomic bomb, public housing, the modern suburb, or the State of Israel.

But Philip M. Klutznick, who died Saturday at age ninety-two after a battle with Alzheimer's disease, played an important role in the development of all those things, leaving an indelible imprint on Chicago, the nation, and, indeed, the world.

He was Chicago's man for all seasons: statesman, multimillionaire, adviser to five Democratic presidents,

and dean of real-estate developers in a city famous for big-name developers.

For all his achievements, though, "Phil" Klutznick was possessed of a low-key humanity that set him apart from the hard-chargers and corner-cutters who built so many of Chicago's skyscrapers and suburbs. From his late teens until the last years of his life, Klutznick devoted as much time to good works and philanthropy as to his worldly projects, which were legion.

"He is considered by many to be the

leading Jew in the United States," the director of the Holocaust Memorial in Washington told the *Tribune* in 1985. That was after two decades of leadership with the World Jewish Congress and the B'nai B'rith, but before he led a team appointed by the late mayor Harold Washington to straighten out the chronically troubled Chicago Housing Authority. At the time, he said the CHA job was the toughest he'd ever faced.

That may have been an overstatement.

This was the man who, during the Depression, helped develop the federal government's first efforts at slum clearance and public housing; who, during World War II, supervised construction of entire residential cities around defense plants; who, with his business partners after the war, built the suburb of Park Forest and later the Chicago region's first, and arguably best, shopping malls.

He was never apologetic about abetting "suburban sprawl" or the out-migration from cities, figuring that GI mortgages, superhighways, and cheap gasoline made that inevitable. Klutznick had a sharp eye, however, for changes in public taste, and when "back-to-the-city" chic caught on in the 1970s, he conceived a vertical shopping mall for North Michigan Avenue and dubbed it Water Tower Place. It was his crowning achievement in real estate—a seventy-four-story mall-hotel-condominium spectacular. He and his wife, Ethel, took a condo there so they could live, as he said, "over the store." He situated his office across the street, at Olympia Center, in such a way that Water Tower Place was outside the window like a picture on the wall.

And what walls they were, lined with photographs of presidents Franklin Delano Roosevelt, Harry Truman, John Kennedy, Lyndon Johnson, and Jimmy Carter. Klutznick worked for them all, at the highest levels, finishing his avocation as a federal troubleshooter with a stint as secretary of commerce in the early 1980s. His closest political ties, though, may have been to two-time Democratic presidential nominee Adlai Stevenson. As ambassador to the United Nations, Stevenson used Klutznick's political acumen and financial connections to energize Third World redevelopment efforts and, at one point, bail out the UN itself by organizing a $200 million bond issue.

Born in Kansas City, Missouri, to Eastern European Orthodox Jewish parents, Klutznick remembered making his first contribution to the Zionist cause when he was thirteen years old, when he dropped some pennies in a pushka, a collection box to fund, someday, a Jewish homeland. At the University of Kansas, the University of Nebraska, and later at Creighton University Law School, he was steadily active in Jewish causes and philanthropy.

A favorite professor at the latter school got him started in government with a job as assistant city attorney in Omaha, Nebraska. He evinced a gift for solving housing problems and was quickly put in charge of Omaha's fledgling office of urban renewal—a previously unheard-of science that was emanating from the first Franklin Roosevelt administration in Washington.

Klutznick wheedled so much federal money out of the new Works Progress Administration—enough to widen Omaha's main street and launch two housing projects—that he was summoned to D.C. and promptly made assistant U.S. attorney general for public lands.

The Japanese attack on Pearl Harbor changed that mission totally. Klutznick was put in charge of building temporary housing for defense workers across the eastern United States. His staff threw up thousands of apartments near the Hampton Roads shipyards, Detroit tank factories, and Iowa's Hawkeye ammunition complex. One of his biggest instant towns was Oak Ridge, Tennessee, where a small army of scientists and technicians developed the first nuclear bomb.

He once told the *Tribune*: "I don't know if the atomic bomb could have been built if it weren't for the expandable trailer."

After the war Klutznick served briefly as commissioner of the federal public housing authority before moving to Chicago, where he saw an opportunity to put his city-building skills to profitable use.

Cities and their close-in suburbs were overwhelmed by mortgageable veterans eager to start families but with no place to go. Klutznick and a partner, Nathan Manilow, formed a company called American Community Builders, bought up 2,400 acres of cornfields twenty-seven miles south of Chicago, and dubbed it "GI Town." Later named Park Forest, the community became America's first "new town," a vision of a now-familiar suburban future that had quiet, winding streets leading to high-capacity arterials and all converging on a central shopping mall.

"We were able to take a veteran with wife and child," Klutznick said, "and set him up in a three-bedroom house for $75 a month." To show that the modest ranches were good enough for a budding millionaire, Klutznick and his family moved in.

Author and urbanist William H. Whyte, in his best-selling study of the aborning postwar middle class, *The Organization Man*, derided the instant suburb as a hotbed of conformism. But Klutznick set about perfecting the most profitable element of the Park Forest mix—the regional shopping mall. There was Old Orchard in Skokie, Oakbrook Center in Oak Brook, and River Oaks in Calumet City. Mall-less suburbs complained that their old downtowns couldn't compete, but Klutznick saw that only as another problem to be overcome with good design, financing, and marketing.

"The automobile had changed everything," he later said. "But I didn't feel guilty about it. We were just keeping up with the needs of the people."

Meeting those needs was Klutznick's Urban Investment and Development Co. (UIDC), which had formed a mutually beneficial alliance with the Aetna Life and Casualty Co. Constantly improving on the Park Forest formula, the enterprise specialized in large, complete packages such as New Century Town in Lake County.

Never much of a golfer, card player, or vacationer, Klutznick spent much of his early retirement years on the phone, tweaking old friends to give more to his favorite causes (Israel and the Democratic Party being the leading two), preparing an occasional speech, answering his mail, and doting on his family. From retirement he also quarterbacked the residential counterpart to Water Tower Place—a new-town-in-town called Dearborn Park, built on fifty acres of derelict railyards south of the Loop.

"If there is anything I have learned at all," he once said, "it is that everything is temporary in this world, and there isn't much difference between peoples."

Said his son James, who along with his brother Thomas helped guide UIDC after his father's retirement, "He was a visionary in many ways. He led probably ten lives. The intelligence and energy was a very rare combination. Such men do not come along that often."

Klutznick is survived by his sons, Thomas, James, Robert, and Samuel; his daughter, Bettylu Saltzman; and numerous grandchildren and great-grandchildren.

THURSDAY, NOVEMBER 11, 1999

Louis Werhane, Eighty-Seven; Northbrook Farmer
By Meg McSherry Breslin, *Tribune* Staff Reporter

Louis J. Werhane, who held on to his family-owned farm in Northbrook for decades while the bustling suburb grew around him, died Monday in Highland Park Hospital. A lifelong resident of Northbrook, he was eighty-seven.

Werhane's Wayside Farm dated to 1848, when his great-grandfather bought the land. After Northbrook became a commercial and residential hot spot, Werhane held on to the property before finally selling it in 1986.

The picturesque white farmhouse and surrounding red buildings stood out as suburbia sprouted around the property, squeezed between Interstate Highway 294 and the Deerbrook Shopping Center. Farming on an isolated tract was a daily challenge, requiring drives as far as fifty miles for agricultural supplies. Werhane once told the *Tribune* that operating the farm was like "operating a gas station in the middle of the ocean."

Even after the site had shriveled from its maximum size of 240 acres to 7 acres, Werhane and his wife, Olive, never intended to sell it off. But after Werhane suffered a heart attack, he could no longer handle all the farm chores. He sold the farm to a motel chain and an office building developer. At the time, it was the last farm in Northfield Township.

Although the sale of the valuable land wedged between two affluent northern suburbs, Northbrook and Deerfield, helped make Werhane a millionaire, it was a trying time for him and his family. "This is the only place I've ever lived. I was born here," he said just before the sale. "We're going to miss it."

Werhane and his mother opened a farm stand that was a magnet for sixty years for nearby residents shopping for fresh eggs and vegetables, especially sweet corn, that had been handpicked that morning.

And customers could also count on a joke and a smile from the affable Werhane, who was known for his sense of humor and endless stream of stories, said his son John.

As a founding member of the Northbrook Historical Society, Werhane also contributed many historical items to the museum there and was an active member of the group. To keep his love for farming alive, he rented out a farm in Huntley, where he treated the people who ran the property like second sons, John Werhane said.

"He had trouble accepting it [the sale of the farm]," his son said, "but he moved on."

In addition to his wife of sixty-three years and his son, Werhane is survived by another son, Will; five grandchildren; and three great-grandchildren.

THURSDAY, JANUARY 6, 2000

Corydon Gates, Eighty-Two; United Pilot
By James Janega, *Tribune* Staff Reporter

The weather on July 5, 1964, was clear, but Corydon Gates, at the time a twenty-three-year veteran United Airlines pilot, was still a little nervous as he nosed the Boeing 727 steeply into a landing at Midway Airport.

It was the first-ever attempt to land a jet at compact Midway. And the cockpit, crammed full of officials from United and the Federal Aviation Administration, was crowded.

Still, Gates—who began his flying career in a biplane, barnstorming across the Midwest with a flying circus—landed without incident. He then did it sixteen more times over the next three hours to demonstrate how safe it was for the gathered officials. The feat ushered in a new chapter for Chicago's burgeoning aviation business.

After his retirement in 1977, Gates wrote a poem about the experience and others like it:

A big business it is
And I hope they don't forget
That the crux of the thing
Is the pilot and jet.

Gates, eighty-two, died in his sleep at his Oak Brook home on Tuesday, December 28.

"You had to be a pilot, I mean a real pilot," said Gates' son Larry, himself a longtime pilot for United Airlines.

During his thirty-six-year career with United Airlines, the elder Gates was given increasing responsibilities. In addition to being entrusted with the first jet aircraft landings at Midway, he trained other United pilots and helped test then groundbreaking inertial navigation systems as they were introduced on 747s. He also worked a stint as 747 flight manager for the airline, a position placing him in charge of thousands of United's pilots. He later negotiated a way to return to the cockpit, his son said.

"I think he loved the independence of it. And the challenge. He always wanted to be his own person," said his son. "Every time he told me about things he did, it wasn't the accolades, it wasn't the recognition, it was the thrill of the experiences."

The more harrowing experiences grew fewer and farther between after Gates gave up flying circus stunts like the one where he plucked handkerchiefs with the wings of his biplane from upheld broomsticks. But he never tired of flying—even the sober stuff required of airline pilots.

In addition to his son, Gates is survived by another son, Lance, and two granddaughters.

WEDNESDAY, JANUARY 26, 2000

Sam H. Kaplan, Eighty-Five; Improved Color TV
By James Janega, *Tribune* Staff Reporter

Sam H. Kaplan, eighty-five, who almost got credit for inventing color television, and who was said by colleagues to have certainly improved it, died of heart failure Saturday, January 22, at the Breakers of Edgewater.

"Sam Kaplan is best known—will forever be known—as the coinventor of one of the most successful inventions in the color TV business," said John Taylor, vice president of public affairs for Zenith Corp.

With Joseph Fiore, Kaplan invented the Chromacolor picture tube in 1969, which doubled the brightness of color television sets.

The invention made Zenith the top television brand in the 1970s, a major victory in a decade-long battle between Zenith and RCA for dominance of the color-television market.

Kaplan spent thirty years at Zenith, receiving credit for more than fifty patents, including the Chromacolor advancement.

Yet in the 1950s, he was almost credited for inventing the color-television picture tube itself.

But as family legend has it, two others filed for patents with similar methods to produce color television tubes: a German inventor and RCA. RCA came up with the idea two weeks earlier than Kaplan and received the patent in 1954.

"He wasn't bitter about it. He accepted life as it came," said his daughter Barbara Schwartz.

John Pederson, a retired patent counsel for Zenith, said he still recalls Kaplan, who worked for the post office at the time, coming to Zenith with the idea for color television, willing to share it with the company in exchange for help in fighting off RCA's patent challenge.

"He was only two or three weeks away from being the inventor of this, the inventor of the basic color-television picture tube," Pederson said. "It was absolutely astounding that one person could come up with this without having a laboratory and a whole bunch of contributing technicians.

"As a result of this, we employed him," Pederson added.

Kaplan retired in 1989 as Zenith's director of television research, a job he loved so much that he went to work early every morning and looked forward to returning from vacations, his daughter said.

A quiet, intellectual man with a bachelor's degree in chemical engineering from the Armour Institute of Technology, Kaplan enjoyed collecting books on engineering and technology, as well as voraciously reading technical journals. He frequently lounged in a living room chair with a pencil and pad of paper in hand, drafting rough technical drawings at home, his daughter said.

In his retirement, he and his wife stayed in a Florida condominium for six months each year, where Kaplan went to the local library in between shopping trips with his wife.

In the 1970s, Kaplan served as a trustee on a chemical technology advisory committee at Oakton Community College.

In addition to his daughter, Kaplan is survived by his wife, Ruth; another daughter, Janet Lapidos; three grandsons; and a granddaughter.

SATURDAY, MARCH 11, 2000

Melvin Miles, Fifty-Six; Writer, Raconteur, Ex-Quiz Kid

By James Janega, *Tribune* Staff Reporter

A parade of former newspapermen, barroom buddies, and colleagues from a handful of trades filed past the pictures of Melvin Miles last week.

The fifty-six-year-old freelance marketing writer and raconteur died Sunday, February 27, at Northwestern Memorial Hospital of kidney failure, but his March 1 memorial service quickly became as jocund as the person it was honoring.

There were pictures from Miles' days as one of TV's youngest Quiz Kids, a six-year-old boy smiling from beneath a mortarboard cap; a later picture showed him giving a speech on marketing communications; in another, he was holding court at a reporters' bar downtown.

The friends were a loyal sort, as was Miles, a former reporter for the old *Chicago Daily News* from a time when being an ink-stained wretch held a certain romantic allure. Idealism pulled a lot of coworkers into the trade, although many, like Miles, also left for the greater freedoms and bigger paychecks of freelance writing.

But even when he gave up writing for newspapers, Miles kept a love of storytelling, which he continued to do through lofty documentaries, business-related press releases, and humorous narratives in downtown taverns.

"He could sit down, and within half a day [he] had magic down on paper," said his second wife, Karen Brown, the marketing director at the Chicago Historical Society.

Her husband won three Emmy Awards for his documentaries, but he also had books of poetry that he never told anybody about. She said he always had an eye out for a good story.

More friends showed up for the memorial service, and the people at the funeral home had to open a second parlor and then a third.

Friend Bill Linden told the group about the time Miles stole a globe from the bar at a downtown hotel, was pulled over for speeding on his way home, and got out of the ticket because the police officer had a passion for globes. His wife told one about Miles vacationing in Florida and having a few drinks with a young entertainer; he later found out it was Frank Sinatra.

Miles outlined trade shows for companies such as Kellogg's, scripted the first cable-TV Ace Awards show, and did public relations work for pro wrestler Bob Luce. A letter from J. Edgar Hoover sat among Miles' photographs, thanking him for his interest in the FBI, something Miles professed on TV while still a Quiz Kid. He was once mistaken for actor Christopher Walken by a fan leaving a downtown talk show; Miles gracefully signed an autograph.

"Mel always had this larger-than-life experience," his wife said.

At his most serious, Miles enjoyed using his talents to help his friends, whether it be with a well-written press release or by helping a kid from his neighborhood start his own company. A lot of the people he touched, about 200 in all, showed up for his memorial service.

Before long, the memorial had turned into a party—which was all Miles had asked for, anyway—and made its way back to his Lincoln Park home. As the evening wound down, the sounds of jazz music were still coming from his apartment windows, mingling with the street noises outside.

It was Sinatra again, singing "My Way."

Besides his wife, Miles is survived by two sons, Mark and Jason; a stepson, Clayton Brown; his mother, Alice; and a brother, Larry.

TUESDAY, MARCH 21, 2000

Henry McGee, Ninety; City's First Black Postmaster
By James Janega, *Tribune* Staff Reporter

Henry W. McGee Sr., ninety, the first African American postmaster in Chicago history, died of cancer Saturday, March 18, in his Hyde Park home.

He took the reins of the Chicago postal region in 1966, at a time when racial intolerance in Chicago was perhaps at its worst and the postmaster position had generally been held by German Americans.

During McGee's appointment ceremony, Mayor Richard J. Daley praised him as a man who rose to the top through hard work, and McGee vowed before the crowd of almost one thousand people to allow others to do the same.

Although his appointment and confirmation as postmaster were racial milestones for the city, it marked the culmination of an aggressive career for McGee, who had joined the postal service in 1929 as a temporary substitute clerk.

From the time he became a full-time postal clerk in 1935 (he had dabbled with selling insurance in the meantime), McGee rose quickly through the ranks.

He took night classes at the Illinois Institute of Technology during the late 1940s and earned a master's degree in public administration from the University of Chicago in 1961. The title of his thesis was "The Negro in the

Henry McGee, Chicago's first black postmaster, also was president of the Chicago chapter of the NAACP in the 1960s.

Chicago Post Office," and it reported that things were improving.

At the same time, McGee supervised the city's postal employment office, then served as general foreman of finance at the old Loop post office, and later managed the personnel office for the region.

"I remember him with the light on at his desk, studying," said his daughter Sylvia Morrison. "When some job opened up, he would say, 'I can do it.' He would say, 'I can do anything.'"

The president in the 1960s of the

Chicago chapter of the National Association for the Advancement of Colored People, McGee also served on the Hyde Park–Kenwood Community Council and a handful of other neighborhood organizations and literacy groups. When McGee retired in 1973, Daley named him to the Chicago Board of Education.

"When I look back on it all, it seems like it must have been a rat race,"

McGee told the *Tribune* in an interview in the 1960s. "But it didn't seem so at the time because of the capacity of the human mind and body to extend itself when there is a vital interest involved."

In addition to his daughter, McGee is survived by a son, Henry W. McGee Jr.; another daughter, Marguerite "Penny" Porterfield; eight grandchildren; seven great-grandchildren; and a great-great-grandson.

SATURDAY, APRIL 22, 2000

Carl P. Miller, 100; Sold Produce, Lived Life His Way
By James Janega, *Tribune* Staff Reporter

Carl P. Miller Sr., 100, who joined the army at the end of World War I and spent most of a lifetime hawking vegetables, preparing food, and doing things the way he thought they should be done, died in his sleep on Thursday, April 6, at his home in Riverside.

"He died in his own house, in his own bed, in his own time," said his son Robert.

While many members of the centenarian club attribute their longevity to temperance and moderation, Miller ate and drank what he wanted: his mother was a good cook, he told his family, and he ate a lot of red meat and potatoes in 100 years. He also had a soft spot for Scotch old-fashioneds, which he drank without fail every Saturday until he died, according to his son.

Miller's father owned a grocery store in Green Bay, Wisconsin, and Miller's first job was running errands

for the shop. When the store was sold a few years later, he went to work in the kitchen of the residence hotel his grandmother owned across town.

"He could wield a knife like a pro," recalled his son, and Miller was apparently unequaled when it came to carving a Thanksgiving turkey.

In his twenties, Miller started helping out in his uncle's produce business, selling vegetables out of the back of a Model-T Ford in areas north of Green Bay. The North Woods roads back then were rutted and muddy, and if he ran out of spare tires (he kept two or three, just in case), then he knew how to fix a flat with rubber bands.

After a few years, both Miller and his produce-selling uncle moved to Chicago, where they bought and sold fruits and vegetables at the South Water Market, often for ten hours a day, sometimes seven days a week.

Miller moved to Riverside in 1925, and in 1929 he built the home in which he died. He retired in 1965, and from then on, he and his wife, Gladys, traveled around the United States on visits to relatives. Those were his first real vacations, his son said. She died in 1997.

In his lifetime, Miller watched the world move from kerosene to gas lighting to electricity, and he remembered the establishment of indoor running water and the invention of such items as radio and television.

He liked to read and grew prize roses in his retirement. He kept high standards and tried to instill them in his family, and he was a deacon and later an elder in his Presbyterian church.

He kept quiet unless he had something to say, his son said, and when he talked, people listened.

"He was a happy camper, and I think that's a good part of long life: minimize the stress," his son said, noting that while his father had plenty of stress in his life, "He rolled with things."

In addition to his son, he is survived by another son, Carl P. Jr.; four grandchildren; four great-grandchildren; and a great-great-grandson.

FEBRUARY 16, 2002

Daniel N. Sloan, Eighty-Four; Fruit and Vegetable Vendor Loved, Beloved on West Side
By James Janega, *Tribune* Staff Reporter

Two days after race riots left the West Side smoldering in 1968, Daniel N. Sloan unloaded his canvas-covered truck at the corner of Roosevelt Road and Spaulding Avenue; set out his crates of pecans, bananas, grapefruits, and apples; and sold produce just as he had done for the previous twenty years.

For the next eighteen years, Sloan did exactly the same thing in exactly the same place—often the only white man in a black neighborhood violently distrustful of whites.

Besides showing entrepreneurial stubbornness befitting Chicago, his decision to remain in the neighborhood was a positive and highly personal statement on race relations at a crucial time.

Sloan, eighty-four, who hawked his wares with good-natured banter on the same corner until 1986 and scoffed at the idea that people with different-colored skin couldn't get along, died of an aortic aneurysm Monday, February 11, in Northwestern Memorial Hospital.

"Let me tell you," he told the *Tribune* in 1969, "in this world you've got to be nice to people. I'm nice to them. I help them and they're nice to me."

Variously nicknamed "Uncle Dan," "Nunny," or simply the "Fruit Man," neighbors said Sloan by any name was a beloved community fixture, a living landmark in a neighborhood where the bricks-and-mortar kind had been burned to the ground.

Fruit vendor Daniel N. Sloan, who stayed on his street corner after race riots in 1968, scoffed at the idea that people of different skin colors couldn't get along.

"I'm fifty now, and he was here when I was a little girl," said Yvonne Riley, who has lived most of her life within blocks of Sloan's produce stand. "We would come from far and near to see the Fruit Man. He would joke with the grown-ups and be nice to the children."

Sloan once paid Riley's brother to unload his truck or bag fruit for customers, she said. Other times, he would make sure an extra pound of apples found its way into a family's grocery bag—no charge.

And, she said, "I believe he knew that for some of those kids, that was the only food they would eat that day. Sometimes he would grab an apple, take out his pocketknife, and peel that apple for you."

Sloan grew up on the West Side in a family with nine children and may have made it through the fourth grade, his son, Michael, said. After that, he helped his father sell produce from a pushcart until joining the army in 1940.

After being discharged from the army in 1945, Sloan opened a produce market downtown but moved his operation to Spaulding and Roosevelt the next year.

After retiring, he and his wife of fifty-six years lived in Skokie until moving to the Near North Side.

Besides his son, Sloan is survived by his wife, Evelyn (whom he had chased through their old neighborhood on a bicycle as a boy); a daughter, Arla Taksin; and five grandchildren.

SATURDAY, APRIL 20, 2002

Robert Stewart, Sixty-Four; Unfinished Castle His Legacy
By Stanley Ziemba and James Janega, *Tribune* Staff Reporters

Robert Stewart tried for ten years to build a 5,700-square-foot mansion in Worth. His unfinished castle ultimately had to be torn down.

Neighbors in Worth complained about the sprawling Italian villa Robert Stewart created at the corner of 110th Street and Oketo Avenue.

But it was a testament to his personality that during his quixotic ten-year effort to build the house, strangers brought him food and contractors lent him supplies and assistance on weekends.

As the 5,700-square-foot, $750,000 house took shape, then faltered, and finally was torn down by the village, it became symbolic to others with improbable dreams, a monument to the perseverance of a sunny iconoclast.

Stewart, sixty-four, a onetime monk who became an electrician, an artist, and an endearing eccentric, died Tuesday, April 16, in South Suburban Hospital in Hazel Crest.

He had suffered a massive stroke and heart attack on April 7 in the Oak Forest mobile home where he had been rebuilding his life. He often visited the vacant lot where his house once stood. Friends thought he hoped to rebuild the home.

More than forty people attended his short funeral in Oak Forest's St. Damian Catholic Church on Friday, where Stewart was lauded for—in most cases—triumphing over adversity.

His wife of more than thirty years, Carole, was at the service. Though the couple had separated because of his obsession with building a sweeping mansion in their quiet Worth neighborhood, Carole had been at his side during his numerous court appearances, struggles with lung cancer, and frequent bouts with bronchitis and pneumonia.

Rev. Francis Kaucky, assistant pastor at St. Damian, said Stewart had faced physical challenges and risen above them. "There is a Good Friday in everybody's life," Kaucky said in his homily. "Robert Stewart had a lot of Good Fridays."

Friends recalled a devout and philosophical man who spent a dozen years in a Kentucky Passionist monastery as a young man but who later left religious life to work as an electrician in the Chicago area.

Stewart and his wife were married in the late 1960s and moved to Worth in 1970, where they bought a three-bedroom ranch house on a corner lot surrounded by bungalows. In 1990, after retiring to a life of oil painting and wood sculpting, Stewart approached village officials with a plan to convert his garage into a two-story art studio.

In a fateful decision, the village refused the permit.

"If they just would have let me have my art studio," he later told a reporter, "I never would have started in on the house."

The house swelled to 3,300 square feet, then 5,700 as plans were drafted to make it still bigger. His wife moved out when only two of the house's original walls remained.

But Stewart, convinced he was in the midst of his greatest work of art ever, remained.

"I'm trying to beautify and raise up the village of Worth," he told a Cook County Circuit Court judge in 1995. "If . . . an individual can't do what he wants with his own money, there's something wrong."

Friends called him a perfectionist who only needed more time to complete what was already a local legend. Others wondered why the perpetually half-finished building wasn't condemned and torn down sooner.

"He can get on with his life," his wife told a reporter. But his friend Frank Soczek said Mr. Stewart—to his credit—never really did.

"I guess you need to express your-self in a way, and he did, in a grand way," Soczek said. "Unfortunately, I just feel he was never really adept at working the system."

Stewart is also survived by a sister.

SUNDAY, MAY 5, 2002

Eleanor Page Voysey, Eighty-Eight; Longtime *Tribune* Society Editor Set Standard for Covering Elite
By James Janega, *Tribune* Staff Reporter

Eleanor Page Voysey, veteran *Tribune* society editor, was as worldly and glamorous as those she covered.

Eleanor Page Voysey, eighty-eight, the longtime *Chicago Tribune* society editor who gracefully chronicled the city's elite for forty-six years, died in her sleep Wednesday, May 1, in the Desert Regional Medical Center in Palm Springs, California, where she was being treated for injuries from a fall in her home four days earlier.

From the time she joined the

Chicago Tribune's society staff in 1933 until her retirement as society editor in 1979, Voysey and her elegant descriptions of Chicago's upper crust remained a constant as American culture lurched through the Great Depression and World War II and into postwar prosperity, women's liberation, and a culture of fame that would eventually spell the doom of big-city society coverage.

"Every major charity wanted Eleanor at its fund-raiser. She interviewed royalty. She interviewed America's business elite," said Margaret Carroll, former editor of the society column at the old *Chicago Today* and later an assistant editor for the *Chicago Tribune Magazine*. "In the years that society coverage counted for something, she pretty much set the standard for coverage in Chicago."

At the height of American society reporting after World War II, Voysey, who always wrote under her maiden name Eleanor Page, helped establish the criteria that set members of Chicago's elite apart from those in other cities. She contended one could be admitted into New York society by having money; in the South, with an important family name. In Chicago, she later wrote, only charity work had the power to allow someone to know everyone and go everywhere.

"Society does not mean somebody in a leghorn hat holding a Pekingese," she told a Chicago cultural board in 1969. "To me, people have to be doers."

Among her professed favorites were Mrs. Howard Linn, "slim, chic, witty, urbane, and 'with it' in her interests and activities"; Mrs. Brooks McCormick of the Illinois National Republican Committee, "for daring not to have rock 'n' roll at her daughter's debut party"; and former Lyric Opera Women's Board leader Mrs. Edward Byron Smith, "a glamorous-looking blonde who speaks French as well as English, who travels the world over, who lives in a marvelous new home in Lake Forest, and who has a pied-à-terre in town."

Wealthy and cultured, Voysey was every bit as worldly and glamorous as those she covered, a woman proud of achieving what she had without a college degree but quick to mention she had spent "five winters" in Italy and France growing up, plus "one year at school in Paris."

Still, she was as intimidating to competitors as she could be to colleagues. She was known to lapse into Italian during interviews, and she once told a shorter assistant struggling to match her brisk, long-legged gait down North Michigan Avenue, "You'd better take a bus."

Voysey grew up in Highland Park but moved with her parents downtown to a fashionable home on Astor Street. She abandoned her plans for her own formal coming-out party in 1932 and a year later joined the *Tribune*'s society staff under the formidable eye of India Moffett, who nearly sent her home from a Lyric Opera opening night for being too jittery.

She was fired a few years later by the *Tribune*'s publisher, Col. Robert R. McCormick, after misidentifying then-Indiana governor Paul McNutt as being three sheets to the wind at a Chicago convention.

McNutt, a Democrat, convinced that the conservative McCormick had planted the story in the paper, sued him for libel. The former Miss Page was rehired after Moffett sent the beguiling nineteen-year-old to apologize personally to McNutt, who swiftly dropped the suit. Page eventually succeeded Moffett as society editor in 1947.

By the time the *New York Daily Express* ten years later called Voysey the "social arbiter of the Middle West," Voysey had seen the focus of Chicago society drift from its founding families in the 1930s to a more democratized base of civic volunteers during World War II, and then increasingly to an era defined by public relations.

"She just knew her business so well. She was so well informed and so gracious and so charming," said newspaper columnist and television interviewer Dorsey Connors Forbes. "The people she worked with, that she interviewed, became her friends for life. She was a real lady."

Voysey was married in 1936 to Norman W. C. MacDonald, with whom she had three children. After he died in 1968, she married Frank E. Voysey in 1972. Voysey's second husband died last year.

Voysey lived in Winnetka and Wilmette after her 1979 retirement but spent winters in Palm Springs, where she wrote a country-club newsletter.

She is survived by her son, Malcolm C. MacDonald; two stepsons, Peter and Rev. Stephen Voysey; and four grandchildren.

SUNDAY, JUNE 23, 2002

Eppie Lederer, Eighty-Three; Ann Landers Was a Friend to Millions; "She Really Wanted to Make Things Better"

By Jon Anderson, *Tribune* Staff Reporter. *Tribune* Staff Reporters Aamer Madhani and James Janega contributed to this report.

Frank, feisty, funny, with a voice as brash as her advice, Eppie Lederer— better known as Ann Landers, advice giver to the world—had a ready answer for people who wondered why strangers turned to her for help with their most intimate problems.

"Well, they don't consider me a stranger," she once explained, with sacks of letters to back her up on the matter. "I'm the lady next door, their best friend, the mother they couldn't communicate with before, but they can now. Most of all, I'm a good listener."

For more than forty years, Ann Landers wrote the world's best-read and most widely syndicated newspaper column, a fixture in 1,200 newspapers, offering a daily snapshot of a society in transition to an audience of some 90 million readers. Since 1987 her home base was the *Chicago Tribune.*

She died in her East Lake Shore Drive home Saturday afternoon, June 22. She was eighty-three, and the cause was multiple myeloma, a cancer of the

Eppie Lederer, better known as Ann Landers, was considered a friend by millions of Americans.

bone marrow, said her daughter, Margo Howard of Cambridge, Massachusetts.

Lederer is also survived by three grandchildren and four great-grandchildren, as well as her sister and competitor in the advice column business, Pauline Esther "PoPo" Phillips, also known as Abigail Van Buren, author of the "Dear Abby" column.

"She was like America's mother, and I'm not alone in my sadness," said Howard, who pens her own column, "Dear Prudence," for the online magazine *Slate*. "She was about fixing the world. She really wanted to make things better. She really cared about the people."

A *World Almanac* poll once named Ann Landers as the most influential woman in the United States. Millions of her newspaper readers bought copies of her six books, from *Since You Ask Me* in 1962 to *Wake Up and Smell the Coffee* in 1996.

"Her column had a finger on the popular pulse," noted David Grossvogel, a Cornell University professor who did a computer analysis of ten thousand of her columns for his 1986 book, *Dear Ann*

Landers: Our Intimate and Changing Dialogue with America's Best-Loved Confidante.

Using word searches, Grossvogel tracked topic changes, starting with "sex," a matter that was virtually nonexistent in the columns when she started in 1955. Later, he found it came to dominate her letters, along with frank advice about masturbation, penile implants, and homosexuality, topics editors would have axed if she'd mentioned them decades before.

Over the years, Grossvogel also reported, Landers' readers became much less concerned with matters of appearance and acceptance—how they looked, how popular they were—and began to run head-on into such tougher problems as smoking, drinking, drugs, and sexual diseases.

There was also much said by Ann Landers about the changing structure of the American family. On her watch, it shifted from the "Father Knows Best" paternalism of the 1950s to an often-chaotic linkage of people of differing ages, many of them writing to her for direction.

Over four decades, her readers shared everything from infidelity to incest, domestic violence, obnoxious children, panic attacks, animals stuck in toilets, and adult bed-wetting.

She once did a rare book plug, for *Fighting Cancer*, published by the Bloch Cancer Foundation of Kansas City, Missouri. In the first three days after her column appeared, some 876,000 people tried to reach the foundation's 800 number, swamping the phone lines.

A woman of tiny physique, Eppie Lederer added four inches or so with high heels, plus her bouffant hairstyle, which she never changed. With much panache, she tooled around Chicago in a navy blue limousine with license plates AL 1955 to mark her column's birth. She often dined at the International Club in the Drake Hotel, where a brass nameplate marked her regular table.

"I see myself as a listener," she once told a friend, when asked for the secret of her success. "Just getting people to write problems down is partway to solving them," she said. "They can think about the problem, then they cope with it in a more objective way."

Along with facing up to people she called "the gun nuts," she backed a woman's right to have an abortion, stood against the death penalty, discouraged adopted children from tracking down biological parents who did not wish to be found, and suggested that suicide, as a way out for incurably ill patients, was not an option to be universally condemned.

Over the years, she herself admitted: "I've changed my mind about a few things. Early on, I knew nothing about homosexuality. Later, I became sympathetic because I understood they were born 'that way.' I believe I helped them in their struggle for acceptance."

Another regret was a 1995 interview in *The New Yorker*, after which she used her Sunday column to apologize for offensive remarks she made about Pope John Paul II and others of Polish origin.

"I regret what I said and am deeply sorry for the hurt and offense I caused," she wrote. "Writing this column over the years has given me a much greater understanding of human weakness, and I have learned that each of us is capable of doing something completely irrational and totally out of character at some time during our lives. This doesn't mean we are intentionally trying to hurt others. It simply means we are human."

In recent years, "with people living longer," her mail brought "more letters from senior citizens, writing about illness, loneliness, estrangement from their kids," she said.

One piece of advice she frequently gave was simple—"Get a pet."

"I look for letters that teach something. Or that people can relate to. Or that are very offbeat," she explained, when asked how she picked from among the two thousand letters delivered daily to her office on the fifth floor of the Tribune building at 435 North Michigan Avenue.

The result was a telling and important body of work, said Rick Kogan, her editor for the last five years.

"I think that 200 years from now, if an anthropologist really wants to know what life in these United States—all of these United States—was like, all he or she might have to do is read every one of Ann Landers' columns," Kogan said.

To come up with good answers, she had to read her letters alone, she noted.

"It's just strictly instinct," she said. "It comes from my gut. Something catches my eye that says this is good material."

Often her replies were quite snappy.

"Midfifties is too young to settle for ashes if there's still fire in the furnace," she once advised "Cheated and Angry in Missouri."

"A father who diapers his daughter at the age of twelve has a geranium in his cranium," she once barked at another reader who seemed to be asking her permission.

On occasion, she shared her own sorrows with her audience, notably in 1975 when she announced the end of her marriage to her husband, Jules Lederer, the builder of the Budget Rent A Car empire, after thirty-six years. At her request, it ran with the bottom third of her daily space left blank, "in honor of a great marriage that never made it to the finish line."

The column drew fifty thousand supportive responses.

Lederer did not remarry, though she talked, in recent years, of "a serious flame, a prominent lawyer in Washington," whom she coyly declined to further identify.

Home was an eleven-room apartment on Lake Shore Drive, which she and her husband had bought after she saw a picture of it in a newspaper.

"It belonged to the French consul general. I called up to see if it was available. Eventually, it was," she said.

There, wandering, pondering, and gazing over Lake Michigan, she did most of her work. One favorite spot for reading and writing was a contoured bathtub with a rubber pillow where she soaked "until the water got cold," once staying in for an hour and fifteen minutes.

"Yes, I've dropped bundles of letters in the water," she once admitted. "I just shake 'em out and hope the ink doesn't run."

Later, she typed out her column on an IBM electric, never using a computer ("hate them") and eschewing email ("Migod, I get enough mail already").

The woman who became Ann Landers was born Esther Pauline Friedman in Sioux City, Iowa, on July 4, 1918. Her twin sister, Pauline Esther Friedman, later to be known as Abigail Van Buren ("Dear Abby"), arrived seventeen minutes later. There were two older sisters.

Lederer's parents, fleeing czarist pogroms in Russia, had emigrated from Vladivostok in 1908, speaking no English. Her father started out peddling chickens, then got into the movie business, owning theaters in Sioux City. One also booked burlesque acts.

"That's where we got our sex education, talking to the chorus girls," she said.

She also picked up smarts from her father who, she noted, "was one of the first theater owners to install popcorn machines. Those machines took in more money than the box office."

It was a lesson in spin-offs that Ann Landers put to good use, later using her column to sell myriad booklets on everything from alcoholism to *Necking and Petting and 10 Ways to Cool It*.

All of her books were best-sellers.

At fifteen, she made a firm decision to never use either alcohol or cigarettes. There was, she insisted, no horror story involved.

"I just thought these are things I don't have to get involved with. That decision has served me well," she said, on the eve of her eightieth birthday. "I look around at people my age and, well, they look a lot older."

Lederer attended Morningside College in Sioux City, "majoring in boys," as she put it. She dropped out in her senior year, along with her sister, when both found husbands. At age twenty-one, the twins were married, on the same day, in matching gowns, to two men who became best friends.

The Lederers moved to Wisconsin. Eppie Lederer's volunteer work got her elected head of the Eau Claire County Democratic Party. She also developed an index of important phone numbers, a communications aid that was to stand her in good stead in her career as a columnist.

In 1955 she arrived in Chicago with her husband and a teenage daughter, Margo. She had never held a paying job, but was intrigued by newspaper work after she met a *Sun-Times* executive on a train from Wisconsin and whiled away the hours talking about the business.

"I had absolutely no experience," she admitted, talking of the day she landed in the office of Larry Fanning, managing editor of the *Sun-Times*. It was a propitious moment. The previous writer of that paper's "Ann Landers" column had died.

"She was a nurse, Ruth Crowley. Did three columns a week, mostly problems facing young mothers," Lederer recalled. "I said, 'I'm no nurse. I wouldn't have any idea what I should write about.' Larry said, 'Well, expand it.'"

Fanning gave her five sample letters. One had to do with walnuts falling from a tree onto a neighbor's lawn. What, worried the neighbor, could he legally do with them?

Lederer rang up Supreme Court Justice William O. Douglas, an old friend.

"He chuckled, assigned a clerk to work up a quick opinion, then called me back," Lederer recalled. "The neighbor could do anything she wanted with the walnuts, except sell them."

The next day, Lederer, one of thirty candidates, came in with her answers, quoting everyone from Justice Douglas to a fabled specialist at the Mayo Clinic. Fanning was aghast.

"He told me, 'You can't just make up these quotes.' I said, 'I didn't.' And he said, 'Okay then, you're hired.'"

On the job, Lederer proved to be a quick study.

One editor told her how to avoid burnout in a field with considerable emotional drain.

"He told me, 'Baby, you gotta remember what they tell you is happening to them, not to you,'" Lederer said. "He told me, 'You have to learn how to separate yourself from the people who have the problem.'"

"These people depend on me," she later liked to say. "And it only costs 32¢ to get my attention."

And she kept on quoting experts. "I've always made it a point to be with people smarter than I am. That's how I learn. If you hang out with people not as smart as you are, you won't learn anything," she explained.

In 1987, after a change in ownership of her syndicate, Lederer left the *Sun-Times*, moving her home base to the *Tribune*, where she was greeted by then *Tribune* editor James D. Squires as "a longtime Chicagoan who built a magnificent career, making her the best-read columnist in Chicago and grande dame of Chicago journalism."

"I think she had more spirit than just about anyone I've ever dealt with in the editorial area. She was just unique in that respect, and loved what she did, loved the people that she worked with," said John Madigan, president and CEO of Tribune Co., the parent company that owns the *Chicago Tribune*. "She was unquestionably the best at her craft. In the end, everybody knew she was the best."

Even in later years, Lederer never slackened her pace in ministering to those described in a *New Yorker* magazine profile in 1995 as "the lorn, the afflicted, the battered, the disenchanted, the lonely, and the confused."

As she put it, in 1998: "I still enjoy it. It's never a bore. Every batch of mail contains surprises, excitement, fun, and some new sorrow."

Each day, at her office in the Tribune building, two clerks opened two thousand or more envelopes, sorting the letters into categories. Her four long-time staffers—Kathy Mitchell, Marcy Sugar, Barbara Olin, and Catherine Richardson—selected anywhere from 200 to 500 for her to read. A chauffeur took them to her home. If Lederer was on the road, as she frequently was, a box was delivered by express mail.

From the pile, she chose letters to print, editing them "to extract the guts," correcting grammar, cutting out profanity. She wrote all the answers herself.

She served as a board member, trustee, or committee member for many of the nation's most prestigious educational and medical institutions, among them the Harvard Medical School, where she served for more than twenty years on various visiting committees; the Yale Comprehensive Cancer Center; and the Rehabilitation Institute of Chicago, of which she was a life board member.

She received honorary degrees from, at last count, thirty-three colleges and universities. In 1985 she was the first journalist to receive the Albert Lasker Public Service Award, for pressuring Congress to approve millions of dollars for cancer research and referring her readers to a wide variety of health-care agencies.

"But awards are not what I'm proudest of," she said, referring to a deeper satisfaction, one that came from her job.

"I've been in a position to help people," she began, talking of relationships she forged with "people who have been writing to me for years."

One girl in Iowa, for example, "started writing in junior high school. Got engaged. Married. Had a baby. A second child. Now she's a grandmother. And still thinks of me as her surrogate mother."

One of the woman's problems, Lederer recalled, was "with her in-laws, who were of a different faith. And I just told her, 'Carry on—and ignore them.'"

As to Lederer's own faith, "I am very much aware of my Jewishness," she said. "My heritage is important to me. I was brought up to be proud of my Jewishness. I've always felt I've been blessed, and the Lord has been good to me. I'm not devout, but I do light Sabbath candles every Friday at sundown and say a Hebrew prayer. I haven't missed a Yom Kippur service since I was eighteen. I feel close to my God and feel that I am a religious person."

There will be no new Ann Landers, a point about which she felt quite strongly.

"That name is worth at least a million dollars. I've been offered that, but it's important to me that the name be connected to me—and nobody else," she said in a 1998 interview. On Saturday, her daughter agreed. It was unclear whether the columns Lederer had already penned would be published.

Among friends, Eppie Lederer wore her fame lightly, often turning conversations around to them—their triumphs and challenges. Nor is anyone likely to replace her on the Chicago social scene, where, she admitted, people often came forward to press their personal concerns.

"I am very recognizable. I expect it. It's okay," she said. "I say, 'Just write me a letter.' And they did. They'd say, 'You remember me? I was the person with the red dress and the curly hair. I met you at a party.'"

As for humanity as a whole, she also had her hopes.

"The world is getting better," Lederer said not long ago. "People are better educated. And their handwriting is easier to read."

TUESDAY, SEPTEMBER 17, 2002

J. Wayne Cole, Eighty-Eight;
Chemist Who Helped Open Door to Birth Control Pill

By James Janega, *Tribune* Staff Reporter

J. Wayne Cole, eighty-eight, of Deerfield, an organic chemist who helped establish a process to create estrogen in a laboratory, thus paving the way for the birth control pill and societal change, died Thursday, September 12, in Highland Park Hospital of lung cancer.

Before such work, the estrogen-related hormone equilinen could be found only in the urine of pregnant mares, which kept it in too short supply for convenient use.

In the late 1930s, Cole and others in a University of Michigan laboratory worked to artificially synthesize equilinen. He was one of three credited in a 1939 Michigan study with being the first to produce equilinen in the United States without horses.

"It opened the door, said that, yes, you could take this complicated, naturally occurring organic compound and synthesize it," said Gene Woroch, retired director of analytic and chemical services at Abbott Laboratories in North Chicago, where Cole later headed steroid research. "It was a landmark synthesis."

Cole worked alongside famed chemist Percy Lavon Julian at Glidden Co. in pursuit of artificially created steroids, and at Abbott he helped create chemical reactions that ultimately brought about cancer-fighting drugs.

Cole's son John suggested his father's career began in an Indianapolis alleyway, where Cole tinkered with car batteries and ham radios in a childhood so dirt-poor he would joke that the Depression hardly affected his family. High school teachers later campaigned to get him a college scholarship when he seemed satisfied with a career in painting.

Cole graduated with honors from DePauw University in 1935, received a master's and doctoral degree from the University of Illinois at Urbana-Champaign in 1938, and went to the University of Michigan in 1939 on a postdoctoral fellowship.

In World War II, Cole joined Glidden, where he and Julian extracted everything from durable paints to firefighting foam from soybean-based chemical compounds.

From 1958 to 1979, Cole headed steroid research for Abbott.

He was a former president in the Illinois chapter of the American Chemical Society, among other notable posts in a career that brought him scores of patents for chemical processes and pharmaceutical compounds.

In retirement, he worked as a consultant and remained intensely interested in anything scientific, no matter how macabre, said Woroch, who once found a dry hummingbird under glass in Cole's lab.

"He said, 'It's a hummingbird. I

wanted to find out how much a hummingbird weighed devoid of all the water,'" Woroch recounted. "How many people think of how much a hummingbird weighs dry? But that was Wayne. Anything related to science was of interest to him."

In addition to his son John, Cole is survived by a daughter, Christine Cunningham; two other sons, David and Forrest Cole; two brothers, Robert and George Cole; a sister, Joan Geocaris; eleven grandchildren; and four great-grandchildren.

SEPTEMBER 25, 2002

Roy M. Chappell, Eighty-One; Fought to Save Meigs Field; Ex–Tuskegee Airman Helped Found Program to Expose Inner-City Children to Aviation
By James Janega, *Tribune* Staff Reporter

From the air, Chicago's lakefront stretches out like a string of jewels and there's a perfect view of Meigs Field, one of the city's most contentious bits of real estate.

Some argue the field should be an extension of the city's showpiece museum campus; others see it as the fastest way to fly into Chicago. Roy M. Chappell looked at the airstrip against a backdrop of public-housing high-rises and saw a way out of the inner city.

The former Tuskegee Airman, who was a central figure in efforts to keep Meigs Field open to air traffic as well as a staunch supporter of using it to provide inner-city children with exposure to careers in aviation, died of cancer in his Burnside neighborhood home Sunday, September 22. He was eighty-one.

Chappell had been the longtime president of Chicago's Tuskegee Airmen chapter—one of the most active in the nation—and chairman for the last year of Friends of Meigs Field, the group that has fought to keep the airfield open.

Through both organizations, he also helped found a chapter of the Young Eagles program at Meigs in 1994. Through the program, volunteer pilots have taken more than six thousand children on free flights out of Meigs.

"He saw that it was a fantastic facility for letting people know about flight, that there was no other location in the country that is as accessible to inner-city kids," said Steve Whitney, past president of Friends of Meigs Field.

By profession, Chappell was an educator, not a pilot.

He was a native of Williamsburg, Kentucky, and grew up in Monroe, Michigan. He was the only African American in his high school graduation class and lettered in football and track before attending Kentucky State College.

At the height of World War II, he left college to join the army air forces because, as his wife, Lucy Lang-Chappell, said, "he didn't want to be dragging on the ground with rifles." He trained to fly in Tuskegee, Alabama, and became a navigator for the 477th Bombardier Group.

But as a member of the Tuskegee Airmen, the first African American aviator unit in World War II, Chappell saw more conflict in the officers club than in the sky. He was among more than 100 officers arrested in 1945 at Freeman Field, Indiana, for defying a general who forbade them to enter an officers' club on the base. They also refused to obey an order to sign a paper condoning discrimination.

Since it was wartime, their actions amounted to treason, and the airmen received disciplinary letters in their files. The highly publicized incident led President Harry Truman to end segregation in the military three years later; the letters weren't expunged until the 1990s.

Like other Tuskegee Airmen, Chappell met blatant racism in the airline industry after war, preventing a career as a commercial pilot. The bitter discovery prompted Chicago's Tuskegee Airmen's chapter to name itself Dodo—

after the extinct bird that was unable to fly.

Chappell finished his degree at Roosevelt College in Chicago and worked as a postal supervisor and as a grade-school special-education teacher for the next thirty years. In 1989 and again in 1991, he was elected to the local school council at Burnside Scholastic Academy on the South Side.

Yet he never lost his love of flying, or his view of it as a tool for inspiration—including for other Tuskegee Airmen chapters, said Brian Smith, national president of the Tuskegee Airmen Inc., who called Chappell "a real confidence builder" for the national organization.

In 2001 and 2002, he won the Humanitarian Award from the Experimental Aircraft Association for his involvement in the Young Eagles Program, the National Leadership Award from Phillips Petroleum Co., and the Merrill C. Meigs Spirit of Flight Award, among others.

Besides his wife, survivors include two daughters, Camille Chappell-Johnson and Kathy Chappell, and three grandchildren.

NOVEMBER 12, 2002

Guilia Mordini, 110; Highwood "Supercentenarian"
By James Janega, *Tribune* Staff Reporter

Neighbors said Guilia Mordini in a snowstorm was a remarkable sight. The small woman well beyond 100 years of age would emerge, with a broom to attack the flakes on the front walk of her Highwood home like some ancient, furious dervish.

"She was like the pride and joy of this town, being that old," said Irv Symonds of Seguin & Symonds Funeral

Home in Highwood, who had known Mordini long before he handled her funeral this week. She was 110 when she died of a stroke Tuesday, November 5, in the Highland Park Health Care Center in Highwood.

Born in a tiny village in northern Italy, she had lived long enough to become one of the oldest women in the world, a member of a closely studied and heavily documented demographic older than 110 years old that gerontologists call "supercentenarians."

Of that group, Kamato Hongo, 115, of Kagoshima, Japan, is currently the oldest, while the oldest living American of a proven age is 113-year-old Mary Christian of San Pablo, California. The oldest believed ever to have lived was Jeanne-Louise Calment, who died in southern France in 1997, 122 years and 164 days after she was born.

Thomas Perls, director of the New England Centenarian Study, a survey of New Englanders older than 100, believes there are "about sixty" people older than 110 in the United States right now. According to researcher Robert Young, the number may be more than double that, with 139 people in the United States claiming to be older than 110 and receiving Social Security.

Because the central evidence of Mordini's claim to longevity is a thin sheaf of paper written in Italian and dated 1892, not much is known with exactitude about her age, except for one thing, Perls said: "She certainly is among the oldest in the United States."

And how is it that a person manages to live past 110?

"It's primarily genetic," Perls said.

"And part of it is probably some luck, too. And maybe she did a few things right."

As unassuming as she was active, Mordini never talked about why she lived so long.

"I don't know if my mother ever thought about long life," said John Mordini, seventy-nine. "She just never quit thinking that she had something to do tomorrow."

The former Guilia Bertucci grew up in a big family in Pievepelago, Italy. Despite a hardscrabble existence, the Bertucci family was "pretty tough," her son said, and was full of old people. Mordini's parents lived into their eighties. Of her family members who immigrated to the United States, two of Mordini's uncles lived to be 100, and an aunt lived to be ninety-three.

Guilia Bertucci came to the United States in 1920, when she moved in with a brother living in Highwood. Within the year, she was engaged to Dominic Mordini, a friend of her brother's and an assistant golf course groundskeeper. They married in 1922, had a son, and eventually bought a house across from what is now the Highwood post office.

Mordini's single job lasted sixteen years, when she worked at a Highwood dry cleaner's starting in World War II.

But long after her husband's death in 1960, Mordini stayed in their house, mowing the lawn with a push mower, picking up leaves each autumn by hand, and keeping its front walk free of snow until moving to a retirement home in 1997.

"She was a lively little dickens," her son said, and "voiced her opinion, good, bad, and otherwise. She was an independent girl, and she became a legend in this town because of her age. And," he added, "because of her feistiness."

Besides her son and daughter-in-law, Netty, Mordini is survived by two grandchildren and a great-grandson.

TUESDAY, NOVEMBER 11, 2003

Irv Kupcinet, Ninety-One; Kup Brought City Along to Party: He Hung with Royalty and Swung with Big Stars, but the Westside Kid Never Forgot His Roots

By Rick Kogan, *Tribune* Staff Reporter. *Tribune* Staff Reporters Ron Grossman, Jon Yates, and Liam Ford contributed to this report.

Before Irv Kupcinet began writing his daily newspaper column on January 18, 1943, Chicago was a place celebrities stopped on their way to someplace else. They often came by train, pausing here for a few hours during which they always made time to see Kup in the hope of getting a bold-faced mention in print.

For a half century and more—in newspapers and books and on radio and television—Kupcinet, who came to be known simply as Kup, not only chronicled but helped define the world of celebrities and power brokers. He took us on a star-studded ride from the time of crooners to the era of rappers, from Bogart to Crowe, Sinatra to Madonna. In the process he became not only friends with most of the big stars of the past three generations but also one of this city's most influential and recognizable figures.

He wrote what is commonly referred to as a "gossip column," but it was actually the result of hard-nosed and tireless reporting and a vast network of sources, from the corner newsboy to the White House. Beset over the last decade by a variety of physical ailments and the inevitable infirmities of age, Kup died of pneumonia Monday after being rushed to Northwestern Memorial Hospital on Sunday. He was ninety-one.

"I've never wanted to do anything but be a newspaperman ever since I was thirteen," Kupcinet once said. And that's what he was doing up until his death, still writing his column for the *Sun-Times*.

News of his death saddened admirers from coast to coast.

"Like Herb Caen [in San Francisco] and Walter Winchell [in New York], Kup made us understand his city better," said comedian Mort Sahl from his home in California. "They took their cities and their jobs seriously, and in that way they became inseparable from the cities they covered."

In New York, former *Sun-Times* editor Jim Hoge recalled Kupcinet as a tireless chronicler of the comings and goings and ups and downs of celebrated, powerful, and ordinary people alike.

"Kup loved Chicago and showed it in every column he wrote," said Hoge, now the editor of *Foreign Affairs Quarterly.* "He treated readers to what was going on around them with a sense of enthusiasm and also with care and affection."

Mayor Richard Daley said Kupcinet's death would leave a void. "Irv Kupcinet was as closely identified with Chicago as the Picasso, the Hancock Building, and the Sears Tower," Daley said. "And he was an important part of this city long before they were."

Irving Kupcinet was a product of the West Side, born in 1912 and the last of the four children of Anna and Max Kupcinet. The family shared a small two-bedroom apartment above a grocery at Sixteenth Street and Kedzie Avenue. He attended Harrison High School, and it was there as a freshman that he got his first taste of what would be his life's calling. "I saw a journalism class where students were putting out a weekly newspaper," he later recalled. "It touched a responsive chord in me."

When he graduated in 1930, Kupcinet had become editor of the school paper, senior class president, and star of the football team. Northwestern University gave him a scholarship to play football, a sport he always referred to as "my alter ego."

But in those Depression years, he had to work for a year first before attending college. A relative got him a job cleaning Pullman Co. railroad cars. Everyone else on the work crew was black. The experience, Kupcinet said, was the genesis of the root-for-the-underdog liberalism that would become the resident politics of his column.

Change of Scenery

At Northwestern, Kupcinet cut his athletic career short by slugging the coach's younger brother, a football teammate, in a practice-field altercation. So he jumped at the chance to transfer to the University of North Dakota in Grand Forks, which sweetened its offer by making him director of athletic publicity, paying him $25 a month.

"During the week I typed up publicity releases on the team and sent them out to the papers, on Saturday I suited up to play quarterback, and in between I'd find a little time to study," Kupcinet said a decade ago. "I didn't know enough to think it a rough schedule. As a kid, I'd get up at 3:00 in the morning during school vacations to help my father on his bakery-truck route. He didn't get a vacation from that schedule."

Kupcinet handled the football part of his college chores well enough to go on to the Philadelphia Eagles of the National Football League in 1935. But, injured that same year, he returned to Chicago and got hired at the *Chicago Times* newspaper to cover the Bears. Unable to stay off a football field, he doubled as a head linesman for the NFL, a few times officiating and reporting the same games.

Promoted to sports columnist, Kupcinet took to ending his columns with a series of personality items. In 1943 the paper's editor suggested he expand upon that device by including notices of news makers from all walks of life.

And "Kup's Column" was born.

He was by then married to the former Esther Joan Solomon, whom he had met on the Northwestern campus and proposed to at a hockey game he was covering for the *Times*. Wed in 1938, they spent their honeymoon at spring training in Florida. His wife, who was known as Essee, would become his companion and inspiration (and even helped produce his television shows).

In his 1988 autobiography, *Kup: A Man, an Era, a City*, he wrote, "Through my work and Essee's multi-talents, we've had the opportunity to 'see it all,' as she puts it. And we've seen it together. As far as I'm concerned, the honeymoon isn't over." The couple had two children, a daughter, Karyn, born in 1941, and a son, Jerry, born in 1944.

Initially, "Kup's Column" appeared to some an imitation of Walter Winchell, then king of the gossip columnists based in New York. Their formulas seemed similar: short items about celebrities, separated by three dots to give the column a telegraphic sense of immediacy. Winchell was at first flattered to have a disciple in the Midwest, but he later complained that Kupcinet was lifting column items. He sent Kup a nasty note: "Send me back my three dots."

In fact, "Kup's Column" quickly developed its own style. Winchell played tough guy, using his column to settle scores in numerous personal feuds, while Kupcinet had a nice-guy newsprint personality. Admonishing a wayward celebrity, he would type a schoolteacher's we-both-know-you're-better-than-that reproach between the

three dots.

"Kup's Column" also gave voice to Chicago's wondrous parochialism, alternating items about visiting celebrities with notices of local personalities and creating a resident cast of characters.

Like Kupcinet himself, many were children and grandchildren of immigrants, who by sheer determination had escaped the city's blue-collar neighborhoods for Lake Shore Drive. Bestowing them with titles like "trucking tycoon" and "pharmacy mogul," Kupcinet became their Rush Street Boswell.

In 1958 he began a twenty-seven-year run as host of a late-night TV show, *At Random* (later called *Kup's Show*), interviewing a weekly crazy quilt of guests ranging from Nobel Prize winners to casting-couch starlets. One show matched the former king of Yugoslavia with fan dancer Sally Rand. Kupcinet was also doing radio broadcasts of Bears games during this TV stretch.

"*At Random* ran on Saturday nights for as long as the conversation was still lively," Kupcinet said. "Sometimes, I'd finish way after midnight, then hop a plane for whatever city I was working a football game that Sunday." For more than two decades, he was the color analyst on radio broadcasts of Bears games.

Pump Room Regular
Weeknights, Kupcinet and his wife would take their dinner at a celebrity-watching spot. Then they might move on to two or three nightclubs, looking for the tidbits of café-society gossip that gave readers a sense of having been

invited to the party too. The Kupcinets spent so much time at the Pump Room of the Ambassador East Hotel that they decided to mimic its decor for their rare meals at home, a large apartment on Lake Shore Drive.

"We built a replica of Booth No. 1 in our dining room," Kupcinet said. "The Pump Room management helped us carry out the theme by sending over place settings to match."

Kupcinet was not interested only in stars. His column was also filled with items about charity events, needy people, battles against disease, and, as he said, "anything that fell within the social realm." Donations, large and small, were always forthcoming.

In spring 1945 he founded and became host of the Purple Heart Cruise, a one-day cruise intended to honor hospitalized veterans, elderly veterans, and young men and women in training. The cruises would last for forty-eight years.

And during almost every one of those years, Kup got out-of-town job offers. "I told the *New York Mirror* I didn't care for New York's faster pace and didn't want to go through the battle of starting over. When the offer to replace movie columnist Hedda Hopper was made in 1963, I couldn't see myself going to Hollywood under any circumstances," he said.

One of the principal reasons was the death that year of his daughter, a young actress who was slain in her Hollywood apartment near Sunset Strip, a crime that devastated the Kupcinets and has never been solved.

"The last thing Essee and I wanted then was to move to Hollywood," Kupcinet said. "Besides, Hollywood is a one-industry town."

Chicago, he knew, was an ever-fascinating human carnival. Syndicate hoods and big-business men, university eggheads and machine politicos competed for a place in his column. So did the biggest of the big shots. Harry Truman, a longtime friend, used to call Kupcinet saying that his daughter Margaret was coming to Chicago and asking him to take her to the Pump Room. They would inevitably be seated at Booth 11, the second most prestigious spot in the room. Then she made a guest appearance on Jimmy Durante's TV show, and she and Kupcinet were escorted to Booth 1.

"I asked the maître d' how come we'd moved up in the world," Kupcinet said. "He replied: 'Before, she was just the president's daughter. Now, she's a big star.'"

On the Town

Kup never lost his zest for the nightlife and for "the lively art of conversation." There was not an opening night of a theatrical production or other event that did not find him and his wife sitting on the aisle, not a charity event that he would not chair or emcee. Inevitably, though, he had to cut back on the workload, signing off from his weekly television show in 1986.

Kupcinet's talk show, under various titles and at various stations, is regarded to be the longest-running consecutive program of its kind: 1,300 shows, with approximately seven thousand guests. It won seventeen local Emmys, as well as the 1967 Peabody Award for distinguished achievement. He would continue to do television specials and was for many years a contributor on various local newscasts.

And he kept prowling the night and working the phones, even as age and various ailments robbed him of his vigor.

Asked in the early 1990s why he didn't slow down, he said, "It just wouldn't be fair [to my readers]."

During the last decade he was in and out of the hospital. He had a history of heart problems and in 1995 underwent angioplasty to open a clogged artery. But he always bounced back. With the aid of longtime assistant and later collaborator Stella Foster, he continued to write a thrice-weekly column filled with scoops.

To Foster, Kupcinet was "a really great friend, almost a father figure."

In recent years, friends and colleagues increasingly worried about his well-being, especially after Essee's death in June 2001. But Kup kept at it. There he was on TV, being interviewed in his apartment by Bob Sirott for *Chicago Tonight* on WTTW. There he was making an appearance last month to watch his grandson David serve as emcee for a benefit at the North Shore Center for the Performing Arts.

Love for Life

"Every day was a great day to him," Foster said. "He never wanted to leave this planet. Trust me. We lost a great person who had a love for life that you wouldn't believe."

Kupcinet was brought to the emergency room Sunday morning after complaining of shortness of breath, according to Dr. Michael Zielinski, an internal medicine specialist.

Zielinski said Kupcinet was diagnosed with severe pneumonia and had trouble breathing. Although Kupcinet was conscious when he was brought in, Zielinski said he later fell unconscious. He was admitted directly into the intensive care unit and given intensive therapy, including antibiotics. He died at 3:13 PM Monday.

"He was absolutely comfortable," Zielinski said.

When Kupcinet died, there were three people in the room: his son, grandson, and granddaughter, Kari Kupcinet Kriser.

"I was holding his hand, I kissed his head, and I whispered in his ear that I loved him and that for the first time he didn't have to fight anymore, that it was okay and that he could let himself relax, and within a few minutes . . ." David Kupcinet said.

Both David Kupcinet and Kriser said their grandfather was active until the end. Kriser said her grandfather even had his weekly Saturday lunch at the Drake Hotel with friends, as he had been doing for roughly forty years.

One of those friends was Erwin R. "Red" Weiner, a former general superintendent of the Chicago Park District, who met Kupcinet in high school and spoke to him every day. "I'm brokenhearted. I'll miss him," said Weiner, ninety-one.

When Kupcinet turned ninety last year, hundreds of well-wishers, friends, and colleagues hailed him at a birthday bash at the Palmer House Hilton. He heard singer Tony Bennett belt out a jazzy version of "Happy Birthday" on video and laughed at broadcaster Mike Wallace's video tribute. He heard that other legendary Chicago ninety-year-old, author Studs Terkel, tell the gathering that Kup had "the right stuff." Radio personality Wally Phillips said, "Kup isn't a piece of Chicago. He is Chicago and always will be."

Finally, Kup spoke and in his self-deprecating style said that he had stayed in Chicago all these years "because nobody else wanted me."

It was a decision that paid off for the city and for Kup. Some years ago, he told a reporter, "There is nothing in my career that I would change. I've achieved everything I ever tried to. I never get up in the morning thinking, 'Oh, I've got to go to work.' Instead I look forward to the new people I'll meet, the new stories I'll get, the new discussions I'll have, the new challenges. They keep me going, and who knows where they'll lead."

In addition to his son and grand-children, Kupcinet is survived by two great-grandchildren.

TUESDAY, SEPTEMBER 7, 2004

Ethel Bernstein, Eighty-Nine;
Outlook on Life Was "So Beautiful" Despite Share of Heartaches
By Antonio Olivo, *Tribune* Staff Reporter

Ethel Bernstein's dying words, "So beautiful," seemed to sum up her eighty-nine years of life for the loved ones gathered around the Chicago woman who, after retiring, studied music in Italy, formed a seniors band, wrote an aerobics book, and, for laughs, was an extra in three movies.

Bernstein died of age-related complications Wednesday, September 1, in Highland Park Hospital after a few last jokes that filled the room with laughter, her family said.

"She had such a spirit," her daughter, Lesley Shapiro, said. "People gravitated toward her because she was always smiling and always upbeat and always fun."

In her twenties, Bernstein read aloud to injured World War II soldiers as a volunteer with the American Red Cross's Gray Ladies corps. She then married Harry Dahlin and, with him, had two children, Lesley and Bob.

By 1949 Dahlin had multiple sclerosis and was unable to work, her son, Bob, said. Bernstein rejected suggestions from friends that she place her husband in a nursing home and instead found work with the R.H. Donnelly Corp., becoming one of the company's first female advertising agents.

She supported her husband and children by selling advertising space in the Yellow Pages. During the 1970s, Bernstein also appeared in a few television commercials—one for Budweiser—and worked as a film extra in *Damien: Omen II, A Wedding,* and *Mahogany,* said her son, an assistant director on those projects.

Bernstein retired from R.H. Donnelly in 1980. Harry Dahlin died five years later.

"Up until then, her life was raising her family," her son said. After that, she met and married Nathan Bernstein, and "that's when she started her life again," Dahlin said.

Bernstein began teaching aerobics to seniors and in 1985 wrote an unpublished book circulated among area nursing homes called *Body Fix: The Fun Way to Fitness after 60.*

During the late 1980s Bernstein began studying music, earning associate degrees in the subject from Harold Washington College in Chicago and the University of Sienna in Italy, her family said.

At seventy-nine, Bernstein started her own band: Ethel's Songfest, a quartet that featured her on piano, a drummer, a bass player, and a flutist playing hits from the 1920s, 1930s, and 1940s.

Bernstein's second husband died from heart complications after surviving two occurrences of cancer, her son said.

Through it all, "she kept her sense of humor," he said. "She had this ability to laugh at herself."

It was Bernstein's humor that lightened the mood during her final hours in the hospital, after she had experienced lung complications and other ailments. Going in and out of consciousness, she awoke one moment to a nurse's question: would she like to hear some live harp music?

"That would be nice, but I think it would send the wrong message," Bernstein joked.

When her family played a recorded version of Richard Strauss' "Moonlight Music from Capriccio," Bernstein awoke again and uttered her last words.

"So beautiful," she told her family.

Besides her two children, Bernstein is survived by four grandchildren and three great-grandchildren.